THE REFUNDING OF INTERNATIONAL DEBT

Henry J. Bittermann

DUKE UNIVERSITY PRESS   Durham, N. C.   1973

© 1973, Duke University Press
L.C.C. card no. 72-93542
I.S.B.N. 0-8223-0280-2

Printed in the United States of America

PREFACE

Some countries whose external debts have been refunded in the past will need refunding again in coming years. Others, which have not, will. Conditions may change rapidly, but some of the basic problems are perennial. This study is intended to clarify some of the issues and to summarize past experience. It is my hope that it will prove useful to the officials in creditor and debtor countries who will be responsible for action, as well as to international economists. Members of congresses and parliaments may find some matters of general policy interest.

The varied audience to whom the book is directed has determined the selection of material. Some aspects of the problem have been treated in greater detail for the benefit of some readers, who may not be as familiar with developments in particular countries, or in the less developed world generally as are the specialists in finance and development. Debt refunding cannot be considered in isolation from economic and political circumstances. In several places arguments have been developed because discussion with interested individuals, here and abroad, indicated that more explanation was needed, or as the consequence of criticisms of earlier drafts of this essay. For practical people, precedents may seem more important than theoretical analysis, particularly when fairly prompt action must be taken in a situation which is often emotionally charged or politically difficult (see chapter 4). There are some policy suggestions in the concluding chapter, but this should not be considered a "how-to" book. A good "how-to" book should give clear and simple directions. The complexities of the debt situations of the less developed countries, however, do not admit of uniform, ready, or simple prescription.

Published sources have generally been cited. References to *International Financial Statistics,* the U.S. Treasury's *Foreign Credits by the United States Government,* Moody's *Municipal and Government Manual* and the reports of the financial institutions have not always been given. In some cases they have been cited specifically when there were contrary data in other places. I have relied heavily on U.S. materials and the statistical work of the IBRD. These data are more readily available and probably more consistent than some others. The IBRD debt statistics have been invaluable. They are as full as possible in an area where information is scattered and not always reliable. Some governments are rather chary about publishing data on their debts, or the loans they have made or guaranteed. Some unpublished materials prepared by the staffs of the International Monetary Fund and the World Bank have been used with their permission. In a rapidly changing situation it is practically impossible to present data on a completely current basis. To the extent feasible, information has been carried to the end of 1971. The editor of the University of Oregon Books has kindly given permission to reproduce two charts in the text.

This study started as a by-product of my work in the U.S. Treasury, which since 1943 was in good part concerned with international loans and lending policy. The research could scarcely have been done without use of the Department's facilities and suggestions of members of the staff. This monograph should not, however, be regarded as representing the Treasury's views or having its approval. It has not been reviewed by the Department. Staff members of the Export-Import Bank and AID as well as of the IBRD, IDB, and IMF have supplied data. Neither they nor their agencies are responsible for the use made, or the inferences drawn from, the facts supplied.

The study owes much to discussions with friends in the U.S. government, in other governments and in the international agencies. I had many fruitful conversations as early as 1950 with the late Sir Ernest Rowe-Dutton, the U.K. Executive Director of the IBRD, on such topics as debt-servicing capacity, debt service ratios, balances of payments and related problems of international finance. Some residuum of these discussions may remain here. Among the many friends who were especially helpful in supplying data, giving me expert opinions on particular points, or who read and criticized parts of the manuscript relating to their areas of interest, I am happy to mention Ernest F. Chase, Michael F. Cross, Allan J. Fisher, Edgar T. Gordon, Walther Lederer, Robert A. McPheeters, Jr., Charles L. Merwin, Raymond F. Mikesell, Eugene E. Oakes, Helen W. Paulson, R. H. Rowntree, Ernest Sturc, Arthur E. Tiemann, Robert S. Watson, James W. Westcott, John Westley, Alfred D. White, and Richard C. Williams. I have not always accepted their criticisms, and they may not agree with my views—nor necessarily with each other. Chapter 2 and the appendix had the invaluable help of Cedric W. Kroll, the U.S. government Actuary.

The librarians of the Treasury and of the Joint IMF-IBRD library helped find many items. Mrs. Alice H. Benson, who prepared the earlier typescripts and the tables, eliminated errors in the process. Mr. W. N. Hicks ably edited the text despite numerous emendations required by events occurring while the work was in press.

Kathleen Studdart Bittermann gave many useful leads to sources of information, explained matters in her special area and discussed many moot points. She has endured my preoccupation with the problem of debt during the long period when this work was being written.

Henry J. Bittermann

Washington, D.C.
July 22, 1972

CONTENTS

ABBREVIATIONS

ADB, AsDB Asian Development Bank

AfDB African Development Bank

AID Agency for International Development (U.S.A.)

Berne Union Union d'assureurs des crédits internationaux

CCC Commodity Credit Corporation (U.S. Department of Agriculture)

CMEA Council for Mutual Economic Assistance—Comecon. (Eastern bloc)

COFACE Compagnie française d'assurance pour le commerce extérieur

D Dinar

DAC Development Assistance Committee of OECD

DLF Development Loan Fund—the corporate aid agency of the United States, (1955–61)

DM Deutsche Mark

E Estimated

ECA Economic Cooperation Administration (U.S.A.)

EEC European Economic Community

EMA European Monetary Authority

EPU European Payments Union

Ex-Im Export-Import Bank of the United States (Washington)

FSO Fund for Special Operations (IDB)

FY Fiscal Year

IBRD International Bank for Reconstruction and Development

IDA International Development Association (affiliate of IBRD)

IDB Inter-American Development Bank

IFC International Finance Corporation (affiliate of IBRD)

IFNS *International Financial News Survey* (IMF Weekly)

IMF International Monetary Fund

IFS *International Financial Statistics* (Monthly publication of IMF)

K.f.W. Kreditanstalt für Wiederaufbau (Reconstruction Credit Corporation—Germany)

LDCs Less-developed countries

MFN Most favored nation

MOV Maintenance of value of payments in local currency in terms of a foreign currency (usually dollars)

MSA Mutual Security Agency (U.S.A.)

M$N Argentine pesos

n.a. Not available—not published

NAC National Advisory Council on International Monetary and Financial Policies (Problems)

OAS Organization of American States

OECD Organization for Economic Cooperation and Development (Paris)

OEEC Organization for European Economic Cooperation

p Preliminary data

P Pesos

P.L. 480 Agricultural Trade Development and Assistance Act of 1954, as amended. (Public Law 83–480)

TIAS *Treaties and International Agreements Series* (U.S. State Department)

U.A.R. United Arab Republic (Egypt)

UNCTAD United Nations Conference on Trade and Development

World Bank International Bank for Reconstruction and Development

THE REFUNDING OF INTERNATIONAL DEBT

1. THE PROBLEM

INTRODUCTION

Economic development in the low-income countries has been financed by external borrowing, direct investment, receipts of grants and the investment of local savings. External public debt is now almost $60 billion and annual payment of interest and amortization is about $6 billion. Both amounts may be expected to increase over the coming years as more resources are transferred on loan terms from the industrial to the less-developed countries,[1] in the hope of raising their standards of living. The end is nowhere in sight except for a relatively few countries which are emerging from the underdeveloped group, and whose balances of payments have improved to the extent that they could begin net repayment. Individual debts to institutions, governments and private investors have been paid off, but the aggregate external debt has been increasing for most. To an important degree old debts have been paid off by new borrowing. With additional debt arising from borrowing for new purposes, principal and contractual annual debt service (interest and amortization) have been mounting at compound rates of 13.47 and 10 percent respectively (1961–69). In the face of persistent balance of payments deficits, the strain has been increasing to the extent that the situation has sometimes been decribed as the "debt explosion." The decisions on debt to be taken over the next decade or two will be crucial to the development process and may have significant social and political consequences.

This study of debt refunding[2] is confined to the forms of debt relief given to less developed countries. The debt problems related to the liquidity issue and capital movements of industrialized countries with heavy foreign obligations, such as the U.K., Japan and Canada, will be regarded as a separable issue.

1. In current usage, the terms "underdeveloped," "less developed" (LDC), and "developing" countries are used interchangeably. There is no satisfactory line of demarcation between "advanced" and "developing" countries. The DAC classification, based on historical accidents, includes Portugal with the advanced and Spain and Argentina with the developing, though the per capita incomes of these countries are considerably higher than Portugal's and they are as industrialized. IBRD and DAC statistics are generally according to this definition. These figures have been used frequently below.

2. "Refunding" here does not include the practice of replacing a maturing bond issue or other debt instrument by a similar debt instrument as a mere market mechanism, as the U.S. Treasury and other governments regularly do. Solvent corporations, such as public utilities and railways with a large debt in proportion to equity, frequently "roll over" their obligations. Similarly, the IBRD regularly rolls over its short-term debt issues. These are generally mere matters

The term "refunding" is used here as the most general term applying to the debt relief operations. The specific arrangements made may take a variety of forms, discussed below. This study deals with both the actual refundings which have taken place in recent times, and with some general problems which have resulted in refundings, since these conditions are applicable in part to the countries which have thus far not sought debt relief, though probably to a lesser degree than to the countries which have.

The refundings discussed here are arrangements which have been made either after default [3] in the payment of interest or amortization of outstanding international debts, or by agreements between creditors and debtors to avert default in the light of the severe balance of payments problem of the debtor country, or agreed as part of over-all programs of economic development financed on favorable terms by the various creditor countries.

This study is directed primarily to the refunding operations affecting the less developed countries since World War II. The refunding of international debts, however, is not a phenomenon of recent years. In the nineteenth century there were many defaults and refundings of bonds issued by less developed countries in the markets of the capital exporters, and many of the countries which have been in debt difficulties in recent years have had a long and checkered debt history. These earlier refundings are noted incidentally, particularly in chapter 4 below, since they shed some light on the problems now existing. Many of the factors responsible for default in the last century have been present in the recent period, particularly inflation, balance of payments deficit, and overborrowing.

Prior to the Great Depression, external long-term debt consisted primarily of bond issues floated abroad. Only rarely could a refunding be arranged prior to actual default. Then some agreement had to be reached by the debtor and the bondholders, often represented by committees, which could not bind the bondholders but could merely recommend acceptance of the proposal. In some instances the debtor

of financial convenience rather than arrangements necessary because of the inability of the debtor to meet service requirements.

3. The term "default" is used here to apply to the failure of payment of contractual interest or amortization so that the term is used more narrowly than the term "default" as defined in loan contracts, which frequently specify that a default occurs, not only with the failure to pay interest or amortization, but to perform a great number of other acts specified. There can, of course, be dispute as to what should properly be regarded as default. Some governments, for example, have claimed that they had not defaulted when they had made an offer for refunding outstanding debt, even though this offer had not been accepted by the creditors. Mere short delays in the payment of charges, though technically defaults, are not considered here as such.

made a unilateral offer to the private creditors, which they could accept as the alternative to not being repaid at all. The governments of the creditors were not parties to the agreements, though they could use diplomatic means to protect their nationals.[4]

The depression and earlier defaults dried up the market for portfolio investment except for a few countries, notably Canada, which had maintained their debt service. Only in the last few years has there been a significant issue of bonds on world markets, a movement in part facilitated by the Euro-dollar market. Relatively small amounts of the bonds refunding earlier issues by the developing countries are still outstanding.

Even ordinary exports in the postwar period would not be financed by exporters and their banks without governmental guarantees in view of all of the political and commercial risks in a period when currencies were inconvertible, trade subject to restrictions, and even the governments of the importing countries uncertain. To restore their export trade, the countries of Europe particularly created or expanded governmental or quasi-public corporations to guarantee both short- and medium-term transactions. National (e.g., The Export-Import Bank of the United States, the Commonwealth Development Corporation) and international institutions were established to finance investment in, exports to, and development of the LDCs. Hence, when debt difficulties have arisen, governments have had to play a larger role in the debt relief measures, either as direct creditors or as the representatives of the export guarantee organizations. One of the consequences has been that in recent years debt refunding has been arranged to forestall default, rather than, as in the earlier period, to settle debt after default had occurred.

In the course of the last ten years it has been necessary to make one or more multilateral refunding arrangements of the external debts of the largest less developed countries, Argentina, Brazil, Chile, India, Indonesia. There have also been multilateral agreements for Turkey, Ghana, and Liberia. These countries account for more than one-third of the total outstanding public debt of the LDCs to governments, private creditors, and international institutions. In addition to the multilateral refundings, there have been bilateral refundings of part of the

4. In an earlier period, they also occasionally intervened militarily. Customs receiverships are no longer acceptable procedure. See e.g., Herbert Feis, *Europe the World's Banker, 1870–1914* (New Haven, Conn.: Yale University Press, 1930), and *Diplomacy of the Dollar, First Era 1919–1932* (Baltimore: Johns Hopkins Press, 1950); Dana G. Monroe, *Intervention and Dollar Diplomacy in the Caribbean, 1900–1921* (Princeton, N.J.: Princeton University Press, 1934).

debt of Peru, Yugoslavia, U.A.R. and other countries. That is, developing countries whose debt is more than half of the total have had to have refundings.

Certain conditions appear to be characteristic of the countries obtaining debt relief. Almost all have heavy debt service in proportion to their earnings of foreign exchange. There has generally been an inflationary situation over a period of years. They have had prolonged balance of payments deficits and overvalued exchange rates. Crises have been precipitated by political events and by the cessation or diminution of the rate of capital inflow as a consequence of political events or shifts in policy, or the refusal of the creditors to continue extending additional credit.

Inflation, deficit, overvaluation and heavy debt are characteristic, however, of many other LDCs. As a broad generalization, it is probably fair to say that most of the developing world has suffered from inflation to a greater degree than the creditor countries, and again, as a broad generalization which might require qualification in some cases, that their exchange rates have been overvalued. This is probably a fair assumption for any country which needs general balance of payments assistance over a period of years, except when this aid is provided for a few years to support a stabilization effort at a new and realistic exchange rate.

With the increasing amount of debt service and the slower increase in exchange receipts, it may be anticipated that other countries, which have thus far been able to meet the contractual requirements of interest and amortization on their borrowings, will find themselves in the course of the next few years in a situation in which they, too, will be seeking relief from their creditors. In the period since World War II, refunding has been an arrangement reluctantly agreed to by the creditors and proposed by the debtors only in extreme circumstances. Myrdal has called it a "more considerate way of managing a bankruptcy."[5] Unlike bankruptcy proceedings under municipal law, the governmental debtor's debt is not discharged through international action. The debtor generally has to pay back the same principal, but over a stretched-out period.

As more adjustments are made, the debtors may have fewer compunctions of conscience and less fear of destroying their image of "credit-worthiness" if they have to refund, and, on the other hand, the

5. Gunnar Myrdal, *The Challenge of World Poverty*, (New York: Pantheon Books, 1970), pp. 291–92.

creditor countries and lending institutions will be perhaps less reluctant than they have been to face the realities of the situation. In the quite recent period debt refunding has become an alternative to additional concessional aid, and in fact, a precondition to such aid, as the countries offering the easiest terms have been reluctant to see their aid indirectly used to pay off debt to creditors on harder terms.

Moreover, three important studies, which may be expected to exert considerable influence on the thinking and policies in the creditor and aid-giving countries, have proposed extended debt rescheduling as part of the program of aid to the less developed countries. The Pearson report [6] recommends that "debt relief should be recognized as a legitimate form of aid. If future debt crises are to be forestalled, sound financial policies must be pursued and the terms of aid must be lenient. The cooperation of aid givers in consortia and consultative groups also calls for greater uniformity of terms."

The Rockefeller report [7] recommends that "the United States policy for the Western Hemisphere should recognize the multiple advantages of a *generous rescheduling of debt service requirements* for countries facing balance-of-payments problems."

The Peterson report not only states the problem of the debt burden of the developing countries, but also has a concrete recommendation for a general procedure to deal with the debt refunding problem.

The debt burden of many developing countries is now an urgent problem. It was foreseen, but not faced, a decade ago. It stems from a combination of causes: excessive export credits on terms that the developing countries cannot meet; insufficient attention to exports; and in some cases, excessive military purchases or financial mismanagement. Whatever the causes, future export earnings of some countries are so heavily mortgaged as to endanger continuing imports, investment, and development. All countries will have to address this problem together. [8]

The Peterson task force proposed a "comprehensive strategy" for dealing with the problem of the 5 to 10 countries with the most severe problems, including (1) debt rescheduling proposals by the IBRD and IMF on the basis of the future debt service and export potential of the

6. Lester B. Pearson, Chairman, *Partners in Development, Report of the Commission on International Development* (New York: Praeger, 1969), pp. 18–19. Hereafter cited as *Pearson Report*.

7. Nelson A. Rockefeller, "Quality of Life in the Americas: Report of a U.S. Presidential Mission for the Western Hemisphere," (mimeographed, 1969), p. 78. Hereafter cited as "Rockefeller Report."

8. Rudolph A. Peterson, chairman, "Report to the President from the Task Force on International Development: U.S. Foreign Assistance in the 1970s: A New Approach" (March 4, 1970), pp. 10, 33–34. Hereafter cited as "Peterson Report."

debtors; (2) rescheduling of bilateral and government guaranteed loans, but not international agency loans; (3) internationally agreed ceilings and minimum maturities of commercial credits; (4) IMF stand-by credits; (5) undertakings on development and financial policies by the debtors; and (6) provision of new loans to the debtors on the "most concessional terms."

David M. Kennedy, former Secretary of the Treasury, also pointed to the need for dealing with the problem and suggested that governments and lending institutions address themselves to the subject of "amortization assistance." He said:

> Many of us feel that in the years ahead the burden of debt amortization may not only seriously impede economic growth, it could also lead to casualties in the development process. We already have examples of past and prospects of future situations of debt rescheduling when the coming maturities could not be met.
>
> Forward looking financial planning requires creditor nations and institutions to address themselves to this subject of "amortization assistance."[9]

With these distinguished policy recommendations, it may be expected that additional countries sooner or later may request debt relief. The situation could well be precipitated on a fairly generous scale by the reestablishment of equilibrium in the U.S. balance of payments, which would have the effect of reducing earnings of dollars by the LDCs either directly, or through the intermediate step of a reduction of the dollar receipts of other creditor countries. (A large part of trade and debt transactions is denominated in dollars even when no American finance is involved.)

DEBT SITUATION OF DEVELOPING COUNTRIES

The less developed countries of the world have external public debt of about $60 billion, requiring debt service in 1970 of about $6 billion annually. Outstanding debt has been increasing by about $4 billion to $5 billion annually and debt service by several hundred millions. There are no complete or entirely accurate figures for the growth of this debt, nor even of the amount now outstanding. In fact, it is difficult to establish in many cases the extent of the indebtedness of particular countries, and this happens to be true, incidentally, of some of the

9. David M. Kennedy, "Remarks at the Cincinnati Council on World Affairs, February 20, 1970" (U.S. Treasury, press release, Feb. 20, 1970).

Table 1. External Public Debt Outstanding and Debt Service Payments of Developing Countries, December 31, 1955 to 1969 (Millions of Dollars).

	Outstanding debt including undisbursed	Service payments
1955	9,689	
1956	10,473	795
1957	12,116	986
1958	14,091	1,374
1959	16,430	1,746
1960	18,654	2,223
1961	21,587	2,314
1962	25,942	2,585
1963	29,713	2,749
1964	33,175	3,177
1965	37,532	3,415
1966	42,727	3,787
1967	48,441	3,978
1968	54,258	4,528
1969	59,331	4,968

Source: IBRD, see *Annual Report,* 1969, p. 48, 71; 1971, pp. 63, 68. Data for 1961 to 1968 include 80 or 81 countries, which probably account for 90–95 percent of the debt. Data for the earlier years were based on reports from 92 countries, but are probably less reliable.

countries whose external debt has been adjusted in recent years. [10] The reports of the debtor countries made to the IBRD are not always consistent. Involved are matters of coverage, currency valuations and terms. The creditor countries, other than the United States, [11] do not generally publish detailed reports of their credits extended to other countries. The IBRD may eventually be able to reconcile apparent inconsistencies in the data, [12] but has not been thus far wholly successful. Its estimates are, however, the best available. The IBRD believes that there may be some understatement of amounts. [13] Tables 1, 2, and 3 show the growth of the debt and debt service and a breakdown by classes of debt.

The IBRD data cover only external public debt, that of governments, their subdivisions and governmentally guaranteed private

10. See chapter 4 below.

11. The Department of the Treasury issues a report to Congress, *Foreign Credits of the United States Government,* as of June 30 and December 31 of each year.

12. The need for adequate and consistent data on debt transactions is the raison d'être for the "Expanded Reporting System" under IBRD-DAC auspices. The principal creditor countries are submitting reports on their transactions to the Bank and DAC. When the system is fully operative, reliable data will be available though the restrictions on the use of the data, necessary to get agreement on submission, will still leave some gaps. See H. J. Bittermann, "Treasury Reporting on Foreign Grants, Loans, and Credits," *Statistical Reporter,* April 1968, pp. 161–66.

13. IBRD, *Annual Report,* 1971, p. 50. The Bank's estimates have been revised from time to time. Apparently some countries have excluded in recent reports items formerly reported as public debt. Some credits for military purposes are probably not reported, as being "classified."

Table 2. Outstanding[a] External Public Debt of Developing Countries, by Area, December 31, 1969 (Millions of Dollars).

	Outstanding debt including undisbursed	Disbursed outstanding
Africa	9,183.5	7,010.3
Southern Europe	6,228.3	4,619.9
East Asia	7,609.2	5,548.6
Middle East	4,883.2	3,882.7
South Asia	13,809.0	11,112.6
Western Hemisphere	17,618.3	13,566.9
Total	59,331.4	45,741.0

Source: IBRD, *Annual Report*, 1971, p. 63.

a. Included are debts with an original maturity of more than one year, payable in foreign exchange.

Table 3. External Public Debt, Including Undisbursed, of Selected Developing Countries as of December 31, 1969 (Millions of Dollars).

Total (81 countries)	59,331.4		
Africa total	9,183.5	Middle East total	4,883.2
Ghana	637.9	Iran	2,520.5
Morocco	787.8	Israel[c]	1,715.0
Nigeria	633.9	South Asia total	13,809.0
Tunisia	732.6	Ceylon	469.6
U.A.R.[a]	1,721.7	India	8,910.5
Europe total	6,228.2	Pakistan	3,779.5
Spain	1,483.7	Western Hemisphere total	17,618.3
Turkey	2,181.3	Argentina	2,323.5
Yugoslavia[b]	1,718.3	Brazil	3,522.2
East Asia total	7,609.2	Chile	2,227.0
Indonesia	2,984.8	Colombia	1,515.9
Korea	2,124.8	Mexico	3,511.3
		Peru	1,117.1

Source: IBRD, *Annual Report*, 1971, pp. 64–65.

a. As of 1968. Figures for 1969 are not published.

b. Figure does not include nonguaranteed debt of the "social sector," contracted after March 31, 1966, amounting to $960 million.

c. Outstanding disbursed only.

obligations when payable in foreign exchange. Excluded are private obligations not guaranteed by the debtor countries' governments[14] and loans repayable in the debtors' currencies, e.g., the loans of the (U.S.) corporate Development Loan Fund (1955–61) and other agencies when repayable in local currency, Cooley loans,[15] and other loans made from P.L. 480[16] currencies.

14. These credits often have "exchange assurances," i.e., the central bank agrees that it will provide exchange against local currency to enable the debtor to meet his obligation.

15. Loans to private enterprises, repayable in local currencies, made from local currency proceeds under P.L. 480 (Sec. 104e).

16. Agricultural Trade Development and Assistance Act of 1954, as amended.

As of January 1, 1970 (see Table 2), $13.6 billion (22.9 percent) of the credits previously committed remained unspent. The amount was small in the category of "other private credits" which includes bond issues and credits from nonbank, nonsupplier sources. Supplier credits are expended more rapidly than governmental or international institution loans. While some of the undisbursed amounts may never be utilized because of the limitations imposed by the loan agreements, such as the commodities which may be purchased, it may generally be assumed that the bulk will eventually be used. There is always a lag in disbursement of funds on projects. Credits for imports generally are spent more rapidly, though it may take time to select goods and place orders. A country receiving balance of payments credits may also, as a matter of prudence, maintain a "pipeline." Accordingly, projections of principal repayments are best taken at committed amounts and contractual amortization schedules, since project loans usually have a grace period on principal repayment corresponding to the construction time. There may, of course, be grace periods which are set for longer periods to reduce the strain on the debtor's balance of payments. Projections of interest are made on the basis of amounts actually disbursed, since this is the usual payment method. On the basis of debt in existence on January 1, 1970, the IBRD has projected debt service of $6 billion in 1970, $6.1 billion in 1971, and decreasing amounts thereafter to $2.9 billion in 1980.[17] As new indebtedness is incurred, net of repayments, the total service will increase, though it cannot be projected statistically without having the amounts, interest rates, and amortization schedules.

In addition to servicing their public debts developing countries must pay on nonguaranteed private obligations to foreigners. The amount of this debt is unknown in the aggregate. The long-term claims of U.S. banks and nonbanking concerns, mostly loans, on developing countries were about $3 billion at the end of 1969. The proportion of these claims included in the public debt figure is not known, since American entities have loaned to governments, or have received guarantees. The Treasury data also exclude loans from American corporations to their subsidiaries abroad. In other industrial countries private loans to private firms abroad are often guaranteed in the creditor country, but such figures as are available do not admit of a breakdown in the overlap with public credits. A guess based on the known unguaranteed

17. This projection excludes about $800 million of loans whose terms are not known, but also includes some nonguaranteed supplier credits in Brazil and India. It also excludes service on $960 million of the debt of the "social sector" in Yugoslavia, which is not guaranteed by the state.

credits of a few countries would be that the private credits which the LDC economies must service exceed $5 billion.

COMPOSITION AND TERMS OF DEBT

The breakdown of debt by creditor class in Table 4 is analytically useful in that the interest rates and maturities vary as among classes of creditor, though there is also considerable variation within any category. International organizations and governments lend from several "windows" at quite different terms. Suppliers' credits and private bank credits are more homogeneous. The distinctions are particularly important in the analysis of balance of payments strains leading to refunding, and the problems of arranging debt relief differ with the classes.

Table 4 shows some of the broad differences. The projected debt service in 1970 on supplier credits is about 20 percent of the principal (including undisbursed). The corresponding percentages for international organizations and DAC governments are 6.6 percent and 7.1 percent respectively. Banking credits require service of 23.6 percent of principal, but this ratio may be misleading in that banks by renewing credits reduce actual amortization to a smaller figure. CMEA credits have special conditions applicable.

The prospective borrower may have a degree of choice in obtaining

Table 4. Outstanding Public Debt of 80 Developing Countries, January 1, 1970, and Projected Debt Service, 1970, by Creditor Class (Millions of Dollars).

	Outstanding including undisbursed	Outstanding disbursed	Percent	Debt service 1970	Percent
Suppliers' credits	7,708.0	6,334.0	13.9	1,537.2	25.7
Private bank credits	3,574.7	2,879.5	6.3	845.1	14.1
Other private credits	4,528.8	4,370.2	9.6	502.7	8.4
International organizations	11,333.3	7,265.9	15.9	744.6	12.5
DAC-member governments	24,814.1	19,803.9	43.4	1,763.3	29.5
CMEA governments	5,083.0	3,915.6	8.6	436.9	7.3
Other governments	1,486.3	1,013.0	2.2	146.8	2.5
Total	58,528.2	45,582.2	100.0	5,976.5	100.0

Source: IBRD. The total differs from the preceding table by the amount of credits whose terms were not known and by certain adjustments in the figures for particular countries, for which comparable data could not be derived. Data differ slightly from the IBRD *Annual Report*, 1971, p. 67.

development funds, depending on the purpose, the conditions of procurement, the policies of the lenders, and the availability of funds at a particular time for a particular place. National and international organizations both finance development projects. National agencies, which have been export oriented, generally limit procurement to their own country, while international agencies for the most part use international competitive bidding. National agencies for political or traditional reasons have geographic preferences, as of course, do the regional multilateral banks. Terms and maturities vary. As an alternative, the governmental borrower may secure supplier credits or obtain a loan from a commercial bank abroad to finance procurement. Smaller private projects have probably been financed mostly by supplier credits. Many larger projects have been financed by obtaining loans from international and national institutions as well as supplier credits. While bond issues give national governments and their subordinate agencies the greatest latitude in the use of the funds, only a few of the underdeveloped countries have recently been able to use this form of finance.

Accordingly, the debt profile[18] and the amount of debt service in relation to the borrower's capacity to repay vary from country to country, depending on the sources from which it has borrowed and particular loan terms. In practically all developing countries, the debt profile shows increasing amounts for the first few years after the given date, with slowly diminishing amounts as credits are paid off. The larger the proportion of bank and supplier credits in total debt, the larger will be the "hump" in the schedule.[19] The profile shifts as new indebtedness is incurred, and the shape of the curve varies with the terms of the new debt. This "hump" problem has precipitated debt refundings in the past, which have generally smoothed out the curve for a few years, and in others, pushed the "hump" forward a few years.

Commercial Credits[20]

From the standpoint of debt refunding, commercial credits, particularly suppliers' credits, have been most important since their rela-

18. The "debt profile" is the projected future contractual service (interest and amortization) on loans outstanding on a given date. It does not include service on indebtedness not yet incurred.

19. The IBRD does not publish the debt profile projections for individual countries. Its projection for all countries has been mentioned above. The "hump" is sometimes more formal than real. Bank loans often have a formal maturity of one or two years, but are frequently renewed at maturity. The debt profile may well exaggerate the actual amount due in the given period for countries using this form of credit.

20. For description and analysis, see IMF, "The Use of Commercial Credits by Developing Countries for Financing Imports of Capital Goods," in IMF, *Staff Papers,* 17 (March 1970):

tively short terms have frequently resulted in acute debt problems for the borrowing countries. Moreover, until relatively recent years, countries other than the United States, and the U.K. and France in special areas, have supplied development finance principally in the form of supplier credits though, as noted below, these credits have been importantly supplemented by governmental credits.

Commercial credits may take several forms. In the broadest sense they include the short-term credits, bank loans and acceptance credit for financing trade, which have not generally been a part of debt relief exercises except when short-term credits have been refunded at longer terms. In 1970 suppliers' credits (over one year) to the developing countries were estimated by IBRD at $7.9 billion equivalent and bank credits at $3.6 billion. Other privately held debt was $4.6 billion, and this sum included publicly and privately issued bonds and notes amounting to about $4.4 billion.

Supplier credits generally are used to finance exports of capital equipment and have maturities from one to ten years. While terms of under five years were most common, since 1961 credits of more than five years have been growing faster than those of one to five years.[21] Amortization in 1970 of $1,233.2 million (16 percent of principal) would indicate an average term of 6.66 years. The exporter generally makes the sale conditional upon securing credit, then obtains the guarantee of the export credit agency, and finally discounts the paper with a commercial bank or a medium-term credit institution, particularly when the commercial banks are reluctant to finance longer-term credit transactions. Sometimes these steps are arranged simultaneously. The importer may also have to obtain and pay for the guarantee of his obligation by a commercial bank, central bank or other public authority. Typically, the exporter credit is relatively small, say, under $3 million per transaction. But exporter credits have been used to finance ship sales, the construction of steel mills, textile mills, metal refineries, cement plants, chemical plants, manufacturing plants of a considerable variety and even hydroelectric installations.[22] The borrowers have been both public and private entities.

Many of the projects are on a "turnkey" basis, with the exporter of

29–109; U.N., *Export Credits and Development Financing* (1967), pp. 122; IBRD, *Suppliers' Credits from Industrialized to Developing Countries* (1967). (The IMF and IBRD studies were prepared for UNCTAD.)

21. OECD, *Development Assistance Efforts and Policies, 1967 Review*, p. 72; IMF, "Use of Commercial Credit," pp. 100–01.

22. For some illustrations, see U.N., *Export Credits*, pp. 36–38.

the equipment assuming responsibility for installation and often the associated civil works construction. Borrowers have frequently preferred this arrangement not only for the technical efficiency of the operation, but for the financing of local currency expenditures. Construction of highways, port facilities and other projects has also been financed on supplier credit terms and the contractors have sometimes been paid in serial notes due over a short period of time (e.g., Liberia, Ghana). It seems fairly obvious that ten years is too short a period for amortization for many of these projects.

From the standpoint of the borrower, the exporter credit has certain distinct advantages in comparison with borrowing from an international agency, or even a national agency such as Ex-Im and its counterparts in other countries. The first is avoidance of the delay inherent in institutional lending, since investigation of plans, credit-worthiness, legalities, etc. take time. The firm offering supplier credits is anxious to make the sale; the institution has to consider priorities, and is limited by its ability to borrow, legally or practically. Secondly, the borrower may establish a continuing relation with the supplier (as he would generally not with competitive bidding) in terms of technical assistance, ready availability of replacement parts and sometimes trade connections. In some instances, a private borrower may acquire rights to use the patents and brand names of the supplier. Sales have sometimes been said to involve bribery or "shakedowns" when made to public entities.

Exporter credits also have substantial benefits to the economy of the importing country. Institutional lending has generally been concentrated on larger infrastructure projects which yield returns over a longer period, while the exporter credit may finance the equipment needs of a going concern and so add to production in a short time and often earn foreign exchange. Even when new smaller enterprises are so financed, benefits may be realized over the short run. These advantages have been recognized by the institutional lenders (IBRD, IFC, IDB, and Ex-Im) in loans to private development companies or banks, which can finance the equipment import requirements of the private sector more readily. Loans by these companies are an alternative to borrowing on exporter credit terms. They may be cheaper and they generally allow greater flexibility in choosing suppliers than when supply and finance are joint.

A second form of commercial credit, sometimes called buyer's credit or financial credits, consists of loans from commercial banks or intermediate credit institutions, such as Edge Act Corporations, made directly to the borrower who then pays cash or obtains very short-term credits from the actual supplier. Commercial banks in making these loans may also obtain guarantees from the export credit insurance agency, though probably the largest portion, especially in the U.S., is uninsured and unguaranteed. Commercial banks sometimes are reluctant to lend abroad at terms of more than a year. Often this is a nominal requirement since the loan to the foreign borrower, particularly a foreign government, may be in the form of a line of credit or, at the maturity of the individual note, the bank extends a new loan of an appropriate amount. Commercial banks in the United States, Canada and the U.K. have frequently extended such credits, and Latin American countries have frequently had debts of a year or two maturity which could readily be rolled over. Of course it is precarious credit, since the commercial banks may not renew or may reduce their exposure, partly in response to credit regulations. The rate of interest, and sometimes additional commissions vary with market conditions, and may not be subsidized by governments as are the rates on exporter credits. On the other hand, financial credits have sometimes been used to reduce the cost to the borrower. Sometimes the credits, particularly in the recent period of rising interest rates, have had a variable interest applied to the outstanding amount, depending on such factors as an agreed differential over the central bank rate (e.g., U.K.), or the prime rate in the market, e.g., credits from New York banks, or the rate on Euro-dollars. The borrower in this case may find the cost of the loan considerably higher than expected, and may find this form of finance more costly than supplier credits, while the debt service may mount for reasons entirely beyond the borrower's control.

Exporters and banks would normally not be willing to take the risk of medium-term loans in a developing country since exchange controls are unpredictable and the prospective debt burdens of the borrowing country may be such as to inhibit private risk-taking. To push exports for balance of payments or other reasons, most of the industrial countries have established public or quasi-public corporations to insure foreign credits. The organization and structure of these concerns and the policies which they follow vary considerably from country to country. In general, it may be said that the guarantee agency charges a fee for its guarantee, which is passed on to the ultimate borrower. The fees are generally held in revolving funds though sooner or later losses fall upon the government, even in the case of the quasi-public guar-

antee agencies.[23] Countries in their export drives have also often
provided some form of subsidized interest rate on these transactions
through such devices as rediscounting of the paper with the central
bank at a favorable rate, budgetary allocations to the export credit
institutions or rediscounting of the paper with special financing institutions created to provide longer-term credit than would the commercial banks.

To harmonize the terms for export financing the principal European
agencies established the Berne Union (1934), which the American,
Canadian and other agencies subsequently joined. While the Berne
understandings required a minimum downpayment on the part of the
importer and originally tried to limit the maturity of supplier credits to
5 years, the developing competition among the capital exporters has
greatly loosened these terms, though the members are obligated to
inform the union ex post of guarantees over 5 years and on request to
supply information on proposed credit terms to other members so as
to allow the possibility of matching. It had been argued in Europe that
the tied-project credits of the Ex-Im gave American exporters an
undue advantage, since maturities were longer and interest rates
lower. The result has been the loosening of the Berne Union understandings and the provision of governmental funds to provide financial credits parallel to the exporter credits at lower interest rates or
longer maturities.

In face of the export drives by the industrial countries, the importers
were in a position to bargain for longer maturities or lower interest
rates and to put further pressure on the exporting countries. With
governments of LDCs as recipients of both export and buyer credits
as well as long-term development loans and concessional loans and
grants, the line between development finance and export financing has
become increasingly blurred. There are probably few credits, except
some bank credits, which in some way or other are not financially
assisted by the governments of the industrial counties, if only to the
extent of assuming the risk of nonpayment. In any event, the net cost
to the recipients is less than would obtain under "pure competition."

There are continuing efforts being made by the principal industrial
countries to restrain competition in credit terms. Berne Union terms
did not apply to private financial credits or to government loans, so
that governments rather than credit insurance agencies became di-

23. For a recent description of the structure and operations of the guarantee agencies, see
U.N.. *Export Credits*, pp. 47, 49–122.

rectly involved. In 1960 the European Economic Community established a "Co-ordinating Group for Policies of Credit Insurance, Guarantees and Financial Credits" to suggest means of harmonization of terms and policies with regard to these credits. The member countries have agreed to an exchange of information and consultation procedure and in 1962 the Council of EEC agreed on limiting insurance to 90 percent of the credit, a six-month period for settling claims and a common premium system for medium-term transactions. Policies adopted by the EEC could not control actions by nonmembers so that the discussion moved in 1958 and 1962 to the OECD, with its broader membership of industrial countries. The OECD Group on Export Credits and Credit Guaranties was established in 1963. While there has been further analysis and discussion of the problems, agreement has been reached thus far only on the terms applicable to ships, propeller aircraft, satellite communication stations, and nuclear power plants.[24]

There is a degree of contrariety in the objectives of the OECD credit group trying to limit "unfair" exporter competition by securing agreement on maximum maturities and standardized interest rates and the work of DAC emphasizing longer terms and lower rates of interest. There would be no problem if exporter credits were extended only to purchasers in advanced countries, but in practice they are made to many developing countries as alternative to project credits. For a few industrial countries they are the principal form of assistance provided. Moreover, some supplier credits have been used in conjunction with institutional project credits, though mainly in more advanced developing countries, e.g., IBRD loans for Mexican and Brazilian electric power.

The Netherlands in 1964 suggested a sharp distinction between commercial credits with a maximum term of 10 years and aid credits of at least 15 years and a prohibition of mixing the two, but this proposal was not accepted. DAC, on the other hand, in 1965 and 1969 recommended terms for aid or concessional finance which would exclude supplier credits from aid statistics but would include them along with private capital in the flow of resources data. The practical problem has not been solved and some heavily indebted countries continue to borrow on commercial terms even when it has been necessary to refund earlier obligations.

The IBRD has estimated that, at the end of 1969, supplier credits of

24. IMF, "Use of Commercial Credit," pp. 60–65; U.N., *Export Credits*, pp. 26–30.

$7.9 billion were 13.4 percent of the total public debt, and bank credits of $3.6 billion were 6.1 percent. "Other private credits," including bond issues, were $4.6 billion, 7.8 percent of the total. Concentration of private credits of all sorts was heaviest in Latin America. These countries had $6.7 billion of the total of $16.2 billion of such credits (41.2 percent), which constituted 37.9 percent of their debt. For developing countries as a whole, the percentage was 29.4. Argentina's debt was 55.3 percent to private entities; Chile's, 36.3 percent; Mexico's, 54.2 percent; and Peru's, 62.5 percent. In other areas, heavy debtors to private creditors were Ghana (47.5 percent), Iran (41.7 percent) and Greece (58.3 percent).

The relatively high proportions of commercial debt in these countries, and in others, point to some of their difficulties in debt management. Supplier credits generally cannot be renewed though as one supplier is paid, another may lend. Bank credits, if they can be obtained, may refinance supplier credits. Bond issues (e.g., Mexico and Argentina) may stretch out the debt to longer terms. Aid from governments may help in paying off commercial debt. If the volume of aid is reduced, however, there may be more resort to supplier credits.

Supplier credits have been charged with responsibility for debt crises, since they are relatively short in term and may involve higher interest rates than other credits. Precise data on the interest and amortization rates are, however, lacking. In fact, the credit-insuring agencies, which report on the data to IBRD, do not often have a satisfactory breakdown. Nominal interest rates at the end of 1968 ranged from 5 to 8.5 percent, disregarding concealed interest through padding of prices. Considering the rates applied in the largest creditor countries, the average was about 6 to 7.5 percent, so that the amortization was about 12 or 13 percent per annum, indicating an average term of around 8 years. The projections on the basis of debt in 1970 indicate a reported interest rate of 4.8 percent and amortization over an average of 6.66 years. It seems probable that in many cases contractual interest was reported as payments of principal. Interest rates probably were higher and maturities shorter than indicated. The total annual cost to the borrowers appears to be about 20 percent of principal.

What is clear from the data is that the annual service on supplier credits is considerably heavier than on credits from the national and international bodies.

The IMF study, based on slightly different definitions, estimated $8,691 million of commercial credits at the end of 1967, representing

20.3 percent of the total debt ($43,018 million) of the countries included. Debt service in 1968 was estimated as $7,713 million or 19.7 percent of principal. For all public sector debt, the ratio was 7.1 percent. The rate of debt service was 2.8 times as heavy on commercial debt as on total. In terms of the usual debt service ratios (debt service over exchange receipts), commercial debt required 3.9 percent of receipts compared with 9.4 percent for all debt. It should be noted, however, in using these comparisons, that the debt service is exaggerated on the portion of the total constituted by bank loans whose principal is renewed on expiry.

A profitable private enterprise may well be able to cover the cost of borrowing on supplier credit terms through depreciation and interest costs. Unless it is directly earning foreign exchange, it covers these costs in local currency. The publicly-owned industrial or public utility authority, for various reasons, may not be able to cover such costs even in local currency. When the supplier credit is used for items such as highways, forts, or military hardware, returns are not likely to cover costs. In any case, the country's balance of payments must provide the necessary foreign exchange for service. Herein lies the difficulty since service increases rapidly as debts pile up. The debt difficulties of several countries have resulted from this process. Unfortunately, the creditor countries, in their drives for exports, have guaranteed their exporters, and in some cases have, or should have, realized that the governments would eventually have to refinance.

The Managing Director of the International Monetary Fund (Pierre-Paul Schweitzer) has well said: "In themselves export credits serve a useful and indeed a necessary function. However, we are finding that increasing difficulties have arisen, because of excessive resort to borrowing in this form by some developing countries whose balance of payments positions have become increasingly burdened by debt-servicing obligations. . . ."[25]

Government Loans and Credits

Governments through various agencies have loaned to the developing countries (1) as means of expanding exports, in part as supplements to commercial credits, (2) as deliberate development assistance, (3) as balance of payments assistance, and (4) as means of refunding

25. "Address to National Foreign Trade Convention, November 16, 1964," *International Financial News Survey*, no. 161, pp. 442–43. The role of the Fund in debt refunding is discussed below, chapter 3.

debts due to their nationals or agencies. For these purposes they have established a variety of credit institutions and, particularly in recent years, have provided budgetary allocations. Terms and conditions have varied with the purpose of the loan and the source, since each creditor provides loan funds on a variety of terms, and the outstanding debt of each developing country consists of loans from various sources and on a variety of terms.

Of the IBRD estimated $28.4 billion outstanding (December 31, 1968) from member countries and Switzerland, U.S. credits account for about 56 percent. The U.S. has provided more than half of the official flow of financial resources in recent years and at an earlier period its ratio was higher,[26] though grants and local-currency repayable loans do not create indebtedness to be serviced in foreign exchange.

In terms of outstanding credits (December 31, 1968), Germany was second (12.5 percent), followed by the U.K. (7.4 percent), France (5.3 percent), Japan (4.8 percent), and Italy (2.4 percent). Other countries (including Canada, the Netherlands and Sweden) made up the balance. Outstanding credits do not measure assistance to development, since grants are excluded.

1. U.S. credits. As of June 30, 1970, U.S. agency credits to developing countries amounted to $18.3 billion (commitments less repayments) and the outstanding, disbursed credits to $14.1 billion, geographically distributed in Table 5. Of the disbursed outstanding debt, $2.9 billion was owed to Ex-Im, $8.1 billion to AID, $1.7 billion in P.L. 480 dollar repayable credits, and the balance in other programs. These figures are not comparable, however, to the IBRD estimate above, since Ex-Im credits include a large amount of unguaranteed credits to private entities (though they may have exchange assurances from central banks) and AID loans are sometimes "two-step"[27] arrangements in which the government is not a full guarantor.

AID dollar repayable credits are now usually for a term of 40 years including a grace period of 10, with interest at 2 percent during the grace period and 3 percent in the repayment period. Earlier loans had lower interest rates. Ex-Im loans have had an average maturity of 10

26. Cf. DAC, *Development Assistance, 1968 Review*, p. 255; *1970 Review*, p. 199.

27. In these loans the government may (and almost invariably does) elect to collect repayment from the private borrower in local currency and to repay the U.S. in dollars on AID terms. The obligation of the primary obligor is generally at a higher interest rate and shorter maturity than payments to AID.

Table 5. U.S. Government Dollar-Repayable Loans and Credits to Developing Countries, by Area, June 30, 1970 (Millions of Dollars).

	Gross commitment	Amount repaid	Net commitments	Amounts outstanding
Western Hemisphere	8,129.3	1,757.8	6,371.5	4,779.6
South Asia	5,150.0	236.2	4,913.8	4,199.3
East Asia	2,405.1	313.1	2,092.0	1,470.9
Near East	2,946.1	494.2	2,451.9	1,895.8
Africa	1,375.2	106.2	1,269.0	896.4
Europe (LDC)	1,237.4	297.5	939.9	667.8
Unspecified[a]	279.6	58.1	221.5	167.2
Total LDC	21,522.7	3,263.1	18,259.6	14,077.0
Total Loans	33,229.0	6,901.6	26,327.4	20,865.7

Source: U.S. Treasury, *Foreign Credits*, June 30, 1970.

a. "Unspecified" consists of classified credits for military purposes. Known credits to developed countries have been eliminated, but the indebtedness of LDCs may be overstated to the extent that classified credits to developed countries may be included.

Table 6. U.S. Government Dollar-Repayable Loans and Credits to Developing Countries, by Type, June 30, 1970 (Millions of Dollars).

	Net commitment	Outstanding
AID	10,257.0	8,082.6
P.L. 480	2,436.3	1,726.7
CCC	186.6	186.6
Ex-Im[a]	3,710.6	2,859.2
Military[b]	955.9	534.8
Other	713.2	687.1
Total	18,259.6	14,077.0

Source: *Foreign Credits*, June 30, 1970.

a. Estimated loans to developing countries less military credits guaranteed by the Department of Defense.

b. Includes military credits sold to Ex-Im. Military credits to LDCs may be overstated and Ex-Im economic credits understated by the amount of classified military credits to developed countries included in "worldwide unspecified."

years, with the rate of amortization depending on the project, generally with a longer term for government projects than for private loans. Interest rates are now generally 6 percent, though there are many loans outstanding at lower rates and a few at higher. P.L. 480 dollar credits have varied in interest rates and term. They may now be made in appropriate cases at AID terms. Outstanding credits are mainly of 20-year maturities. CCC credits are generally from one to three years at rates based on the cost of money to the Treasury.

Ex-Im loans to developing countries have always had a heavy Latin-American concentration, both for projects and export and balance of payments credits. AID and its predecessors have provided assistance to a wider geographic area with a heavy concentration on Asia (India and Pakistan).

2. *France*. France is the second largest supplier of official development assistance (grants and soft loans) and has been second (or third in 1969) of the DAC members in terms of the net flow of public and private resources to the LDCs. [28] French official finance is highly concentrated in former possessions in which there is a continuing commercial and political interest. In 1969 grants to these areas were $623.8 million and to other areas $102.2 million. Official loans to the franc area were $189.4 million gross ($111.6 million net) compared with $51.3 million ($43.8 million net) to other areas. In contrast, 65.7 percent (average 1966–69) of private investment was in non-franc countries, and almost half of this was in guaranteed exporter credits. [29] Official loans have been concentrated in a few countries of the non-franc area, Mexico, Spain, Greece and small amounts in other Latin American countries. The low-interest, long-term loans supplement commercial credits at varying percentages (20–55) of the private credit. The French government has had to refinance guaranteed private credits in other countries as part of general or bilateral arrangements (U.A.R., 1967). Refunding credits from 1966 to 1969 were $116.1 million compared with other loans to non-franc countries of $133.7 million. There were apparently no refunding credits in the franc-zone countries.

3. *Germany*. Germany has in recent years supplemented its system of exporter credits with concessional loans under the Ministry of Economic Cooperation. Export credit insurance while administered by private companies has been at government risk. Medium-term commercial credits have also been financed privately. The Kreditanstalt für Wiederaufbau (Reconstruction Credit Corporation), a public corporation financed by borrowing as well as public capital, has financed supplier credits of more than 5-year maturities and long-term buyer credits to supplement other credits at its own risk. As agent (trust fund) of the government, the K.f.W. administers the bilateral aid loans of the Ministry of Economic Cooperation on terms set by an Interministerial Committee on Development Policy. These aid loans have had a concessional character and terms have been adjusted to

28. DAC, *Development Assistance, 1970 Review*, pp. 170–71.
29. France, Ministry of Finance, "Mémorandum de la France au Comité d'Aide au Développement," *Statisques et Etudes Financières*, no. 264 (Dec. 1970), pp. 41–43, 56–59.

circumstances, since they are financed by appropriations.[30] The effect has been to reduce the average of German interest rates and to lengthen the terms of credits to developing countries.

4. United Kingdom. In Great Britain the Commonwealth Development Corporation has for many years made long-term loans to Commonwealth countries, generally at rates which cover borrowing costs. The Ministry of Overseas Development, financed by appropriations, also concentrates largely on Commonwealth countries and makes loans at from zero to seven percent with long maturities and grace periods. Its softest loans apparently have been made in debt refundings and in countries facing serious debt problems.

5. Japan. The Japanese Export-Import Bank makes loans to Japanese exporters along with credits by commercial banks. It may finance as much as 70 percent of the credit extended by the exporter to the foreign purchasers at rates of 5 to 8 percent. The Export-Import Bank also has extended loans directly to governments for general imports or specific projects almost entirely in Asia. A Small Business Finance Corporation assists export lending by smaller firms. The budget also finances the Overseas Economic Cooperation Fund which makes loans on a more flexible basis. While Japanese aid concentrates on Asian countries, Japan has financed projects in, as well as exports to, Latin America and, to a small degree, Africa.[31]

6. Canada. Canada in 1969 established an Export Development Corporation, financed by borrowing and appropriations to replace the Export Credits Insurance Corporation. The former corporation, in addition to insuring suppliers' and buyers' credits, made long-term loans, when authorized by the Cabinet, for promoting exports. The new agency will have more extended powers, greater flexibility in financing to include development projects and, inter alia, "the consolidation and rescheduling of debts owed to Canadian exporters."[32] The Canadian International Development Agency (formerly External Aid Office) within its appropriation may make loans up to 50 years and has provided some interest free and others at low interest. The outstanding amount increased from C$44.1 million in 1968 to C$92.6

30. Cf. K.f.W., *Annual Report,* 1968, pp. 93–106; 1966, pp. 68–85; U.N., *Export Credits,* pp. 69–72.

31. Cf. Japan, Ministry of Finance, *The Budget in Brief,* 1969, pp. 36–37; Export-Import Bank of Japan, *Export-Import Bank of Japan Law* (1964); *Export-Import Bank of Japan: Its Object and Functions* (1964).

32. Canada, Export Credits Insurance Corporation, *1968 Annual Report,* pp. 9, 15; *Commons Debates,* April 14, 1969, pp. 7473–78.

million on March 31, 1969, and about C$178.6 million in 1970.[33]

7. *Other*. The smaller DAC member countries have agencies which have subsidized exporter credits and to a limited degree given aid on highly concessional terms. Refunding arrangements have been made largely on an ad hoc basis.

Most of the DAC member countries have got into the business of making intergovernmental loans as an adjunct to financing their export business on more favorable terms than could be obtained in the market, even with guarantees of suppliers' and buyers' credits. Circumstances have moved them increasingly to providing financial assistance as concessional aid so that outstanding debts of the LDCs on official credits represent a variety of terms, including the loans used in some cases to refinance credits given at an earlier date on harder terms.

The DAC has estimated that the weighted average interest rate on official credits by DAC members was 3.5 percent in 1962, 3.6 percent in 1965, 3.1 percent in 1966, 3.8 in 1967 and 3.6 in 1968. In 1964 these average rates[34] represented a considerable dispersion from 5.8 percent for Japan, 4 percent for Germany, 2.5 for the U.S. and 2 percent for Sweden. In recent years Denmark has given interest-free loans, the U.K. some interest-free and some low interest to reduce its average to about one percent. The Japanese average has come down to 3.7 in 1968. The average maturity of loans made from 1962 to 1968 has varied between 22 and 28 years with 26 years as the average in 1968. The U.S. average has ranged between 22.3 and 30 years; the U.K., between 21 and 24; Germany, 15 to 21. Austria, Italy and Japan have had the shortest terms,[35] and the lengthening of their terms in recent years has probably been affected by the relatively long term of refunding loans. The rather large variation in some countries from year to year probably results from the timing of transactions and the sources of funds available and disbursed in the given period.

8. *Soviet and CMEA credits*.[36] Information about credits from the

33. Canada, Receiver General, *Public Accounts of Canada*, 1969, 2: 7, 53; *Budget Papers, 1970–71*, p. 210.

34. The DAC average is heavily weighted by the terms of U.S. official flows, which are more than half of the total.

35. OECD, *Development Assistance Efforts and Policies, 1967 Review*, p. 76; *1969 Review*, p. 77; cf. Clive S. Gray, *Resource Flows to Less Developed Countries* (New York: Praeger.1969). pp. 48–55.

36. See U.N., *External Financing of Economic Development, 1962–66* (1968), pp. 15–18; "Financing and Invisibles," *Proceedings of the United Nations Conference on Trade and Development* (1964), 5: 44–52; Marshall I. Goldman, *Soviet Foreign Aid* (New York: Praeger, 1967).

U.S.S.R. and other CMEA countries is less readily available than for the West. The IBRD estimate (Table 4, above) indicates about $3.9 billion of such credits outstanding in 1970. U.N. estimates show $7,783 million equivalent in loan commitments through 1966 for economic assistance, of which $4,867 million (62.5 percent) was from the Soviet Union. These credits were concentrated in a relatively few countries, India, Indonesia, Afghanistan, Pakistan, and U.A.R., with smaller amounts to Ceylon, Ghana, Guinea, Ethiopia, and some credits to Argentina and Brazil. There is even less information about credits for military purposes, though they have been important in Cuba, North Vietnam, India, Indonesia, the U.A.R. and other countries.[37]

Some of these economic credits were general lines against which individual projects could be financed. Others took the form of Soviet exports of complete plants and installations, with incidental expenses for planning, technical assistance, and training of the nationals of recipient countries.

The usual terms appear to be repayment in about 12 years beginning a year after completion of the installation with interest at 2.5 or 3 percent, though in the Brazilian 1966 loan, the term was 8 years at 4 percent. Payment is generally made through bilateral trade agreements under which the recipient exports its usual products to the creditor country, though in the Afghanistan gas well and pipeline payment is made in natural gas. The terms are roughly comparable to hard credits from Western nations and international agencies with the low interest rate offsetting the shorter maturity.[38] Depending on the relative importance of the loans in the recipient economy, some portion of its usual exports has to be earmarked for debt service at prices

37. A newspaper story from Moscow (*New York Times*, Nov. 13, 1971, p. 8) estimates Soviet military and economic aid at about $2.2 billion equivalent annually. Aid to Cuba is estimated at $750 million (66 percent economic) and North Vietnam at $500 million (50 percent economic). Total credits since 1954 were estimated at $8 billion, with $3 billion undisbursed. These unofficial figures are not directly comparable with the IBRD data given in Table 4, which include only member countries and do not report details for the U.A.R.

A U.S. State Department study (Bureau of Intelligence and Research, *Communist States and Developing Countries: Aid and Trade in 1970*, RECS–15, Sept. 22, 1971, mimeographed), estimates, from Russian sources, a total of $11.6 billion equivalent of economic credits and grants between 1954 and 1970, of which $7 billion was from the U.S.S.R. These data are on a gross commitment basis and are not broken down between credits and grants, and there are no figures for outstanding accounts. Soviet cumulative military aid, 1955–70, is estimated at $6.8 billion. Aid to Cuba is not included in the totals. The modalities of CMEA credits, often in the form of frame agreements rather than specific loans, preclude precise comparison with other debt data.

38. The 1970 projection indicates an average rate of 2.1 percent interest and 9 percent amortization. This average is based on the data from countries reporting to the IBRD. It is possible that these countries do not report all credits, e.g., military.

mutually agreed upon in connection with other imports from the creditor country. When payment is made in long-staple cotton by the U.A.R., bauxite by Guinea, jute, tea, and nuts by India, commodities are earmarked which could be sold on world markets, perhaps at better prices. In short, the system has the disadvantages of bilateral trade agreements and may unduly restrict the recipient's foreign exchange income. On the other hand, it may facilitate trade in what could not otherwise be sold, a mutual exchange of shoddy products. The trade agreements with maintenance-of-value clauses in terms of dollars or sterling result in debit or credit balances with the creditor, but apparently the U.S.S.R. has been fairly lenient in permitting balances to accumulate without requiring settlement in hard currency.

9. *Cost of loans from governments.* Loans to LDCs from other governments have had interest rates from zero to seven percent and perhaps higher. Maturities have ranged from 3 years to 50, including different grace periods. Outstanding loans have been made at different times and rates. An average for all countries has, therefore, a limited significance.

The IBRD projections for 1970 indicate interest payments of $633.5 million on $20.8 billion disbursed and outstanding in loans by non-CMEA countries, or 3.04 percent. Amortization payments of $1,286.9 million on principal, including undisbursed, of $26 billion (4.94 percent) indicate average amortization, after grace periods, of 20.2 years. Borrowers as a whole pay about 8 percent of principal annually as debt service. For DAC members the apparent interest rate is 3 percent and the terms 21.4 years. For CMEA countries the average interest appears to be 2.12 percent and the average term, after grace, 11.6 years. These results correspond roughly with the analysis above.

International Organizations

Loans and credits of international agencies to developing countries at the end of 1969 were about $11.3 billion on a net committed basis and about $7.3 billion on a disbursed basis. Of this total, about $7.3 billion ($4.4 billion disbursed) consisted of IBRD loans, $2.3 billion ($1.7 billion) of IDA credits, $1.1 billion ($575 million) of IDB ordinary capital loans and the balance, loans from the Asian Development Bank and European and other regional organizations. As of June 30, 1970 the net committed amount was about $13 billion and the disbursed about $7.4 billion.[39] About four-fifths of the loans were on "conventional terms," practically all except IDA credits.

IBRD loans have been made at interest rates of from 4 percent (1950) to 7 percent (1969–70), and 7.25 in 1970–71 with an average on outstanding of 5.61 percent in 1968–69, 5.65 percent in 1969–70, and 5.35 in 1970–71.[40] The term of loans has ranged between 7 and 31 years, with an average of 21 to 22 years for loans made recently. The term depends mainly on the type of project financed, though apparently some weight has been given to the economic situation of the borrower. The grace period has generally been related to the time for construction of the project, though in some cases account has been taken of the debt profile of the borrowing country, that is, the grace period has been made longer than the construction time when there has been a "hump" in the future debt service of the borrower. World Bank loans are generally repayable, after the grace period, on the basis of a rounded annuity, so that interest plus amortization are roughly equal in any year after repayment of principal starts.

IDA credits are uniformly at a "service charge" of 0.75 percent of the outstanding amount to cover administrative costs. There is a grace period of 10 years, amortization of 1 percent per annum for the next 10 years, and 3 percent annually for 30 years.

Accordingly, the debt service on IBRD-IDA credits varies with the proportion borrowed from the two sources respectively.[41]

The Inter-American Development Bank, like the IBRD, finances its loans from ordinary capital, which are repayable in foreign exchange, mostly from funds borrowed in the U.S. and European markets, so that the interest rates reflect the cost of money. Rates of interest, including the 1 percent commission charge, have ranged between 5.75 percent and 8 percent (1969–71), with an average of about 5.7 on the amount outstanding in 1968 and 5.8 in 1969. Final maturities are from 5 to 25 years with an average of about 16 years. Loans made in 1970 and 1971 averaged 18.2 and 18.6 years.

The IDB has two soft-loan windows, the Fund for Special Opera-

39. These figures are estimates from IBRD data and the U.S. Treasury, *Foreign Credits*, Dec. 31, 1969 and June 30, 1970.

40. Calculated on interest and commission in the fiscal years over the average disbursed and outstanding during the year.

41. IFC investments on loan and equity bases are omitted here since they are made in private companies without government guarantee, and IFC loans are not included in calculations of public debt. Like other credits to private entities, they must be serviced through the balance of payments of the recipient country. Interest rates vary between 6 and 8.5 percent with an average of about 7.5 percent.

tions and the Social Progress Trust Fund financed by the United States, and some special funds provided by nonmember countries. These loans are mostly repayable in the borrower currencies so that they do not require foreign exchange for service except certain charges. When these sources are used in conjunction with ordinary capital loans, the exchange burden of debt service is in many cases considerably reduced.

The Asian Development Bank initially made its ordinary capital loans at 6.87 percent with an average maturity of 14 years, including 3 years grace. Its loans in 1970 were made at 7.5 percent with an average maturity of 19.2 years, including grace of 4.5 years.

The African Development Bank has had an average interest rate of 6.21 percent. Maturities have averaged about 20 years, including 4.5 years grace.

The cost to the borrowers is somewhat higher than indicated by interest and commission rates, since they also pay commitment fees on undisbursed amounts of loans. The interest rates on these "hard" loans are quite concessional in terms of the current cost of money to the multilateral institutions. Both the IBRD and the IDB in 1970 issued bonds with a coupon of 8.62 percent. Their older issues were at lower rates and, of course, they pay no interest on subscribed capital funds which are also at loan.

In 1969, total debt service of developing countries on hard and soft loans from international agencies was $677 million (excluding payments in borrower currencies) or 6.9 percent of principal at the end of 1968. This amount is projected (IBRD) to rise to $745 million in 1970, a maximum of about $900 million in 1973 to 1975, on the basis of loans now outstanding. As of 1970, the average interest rate on international organization loans and credits is about 4.6 percent and average amortization after grace of about 3.6 percent of committed principal, indicating roughly an average maturity after grace of about 28 years.

Bonds

Bond issues outstanding of the LDCs at the beginning of 1970 were about $4.4 billion, and there were public issues and privately-placed securities in 1970 of $377 million. Up to quite recent years, few developing countries could successfully borrow in financial markets. A large portion of the issues outstanding before 1966 consisted of old and refunding issues, many with low coupon rates as agreed in debt settlements with bondholders. From 1966 to 1970, $2.2 billion of new issues were sold. Some of the cash received was used to pay off maturing obligations. The largest borrowers (1966–70) were Israel ($837.2 million), Mexico ($423.9 million), Argentina[42] ($280.3 million) and Spain ($168 million). These four countries accounted for four-fifths of the total placed. The balance was made up of smaller amounts by other countries. The more recent issues had higher rates generally than the old, few lower than 6.5 percent, some as high as 9.5 percent, and many of the issues had rates floating with the Euro-dollar or other market rate.[43] (Israeli Bonds are not sold on the basis of market considerations.)

Bond and note issues have not been involved in the refunding exercises described below, except to the extent that they have been used to finance payments falling due under some of the refunding arrangements.

Summary

There is no unimpeachable, or even moderately satisfactory, way of comparing terms of loans from various sources, and the effects on the balance of payments and debt service of the borrowers. Debt service currently includes payments on obligations contracted previously, some at harder, some at easier terms than are now available. The proportion borrowed from the several sources has varied in the past and will continue to vary with changes in the policies of the donor-creditor countries and multilateral institutions as well as market conditions.

Strictly speaking, only interest, commissions, commitment fees, and incidental charges are *costs*. Amortization is a repayment of capital. Both must be covered by the balance of payments, unless amortization is deferred by refunding or market rolling-over of principal. Differences in the amortization terms of loans, particularly, make inter-source comparisons difficult.

Even contractual (or nominal) interest is not of itself conclusive. The apparently low average interest rate on suppliers' credits may be deceptive, aside from inaccuracy of the data, by padding of principal to show a low rate. This is sometimes charged, but as with payments for graft or shakedown, hard to establish in particular cases or to quantify in the aggregate. Tying of loans may have the same effect if

42. IBRD, *Annual Report, 1971*, pp. 76–77.
43. In view of the high yields at issue of bonds sold in recent years, the projected interest payments seem quite low (see Table 10. below).

the price of goods financed is higher than it would be if they could be more cheaply obtained elsewhere. A 5 percent loan is effectively a loan at 5.5 percent (with heavier amortization as well) if costs are 10 percent above the lowest price available for the same products.[44] The effective rate of interest is increased slightly by the use of commitment fees and other charges.[45]

There has been some variation in loan terms over the last 10 years with changes in interest rates, grace periods and final maturities (Table 7). The average terms over the years have been harder for Latin American and Middle-Eastern countries, which have obtained larger proportions of their borrowings from commercial sources and the "conventional loan" windows of governmental and international institutions, than for Africa and South Asia, which have had greater shares of the concessional loan money. On the basis of loans in 1969, developing countries on the average will pay 5.2 percent interest and 7.1 percent amortization in the first year after grace, and a total of about 9.5 percent of the principal in the middle year after grace. Global averages, however, are not representative of the situation of any one country and of the particular loans making up the total.

In 1968 the World Bank made a calculation of relative interest rates, grace periods and maturities for credits from various sources in 1966. To make a comparison of relative magnitudes of payment, two additional columns have been added to Table 8 to show the total payments of interest and principal in the first and the middle year after grace. Payments in the middle year of the total life of the loan would be slightly higher than in the middle year after grace, since less than half would be repaid. The difference would be greater the higher the interest rate and the longer the grace period in proportion to final maturity. It should be noted also that the composite averages for loans from international organizations and governments may be somewhat misleading since payments on average rates would not correspond to the payments on the components when the components have the dispersion of terms, as indicated in the table.[46]

44. One of the problems in trying to evaluate the cost of tying is that, with the exception of some standardized raw materials and semi-finished products, the items supplied are not identical. The higher-priced item may be more efficient, have a lower maintenance cost, or longer life than the cheaper. The purpose of a specific project may be served by a variety of specifications, at different costs. Even international competitive bidding may be frustrated by the specifications writer. These caveats are not intended to imply that there is no fire below the smoke.

45. In 1970–71 IBRD commitment fees were under 0.26 percent of the average amount outstanding during the year.

46. Cf. IBRD, *Possible Improvements in Techniques of Lending* (April 1970), p. 27.

Table 7. Average Terms of Loans Received by Developing Countries, 1960–1969.

	Interest rate (percent)	Grace period (years)	Maturity (years)
1960	5.7	3.1	13.3
1964	4.2	5.1	22.8
1965	4.3	4.4	18.8
1966	4.0	4.9	21.9
1967	4.6	4.0	17.2
1968	4.8	4.6	19.0
1969	5.2	4.7	18.7

Source: IBRD, *Annual Report,* 1966, p. 35; 1971, p. 69. Data for 1960 and 1964 were based on data from 34 countries. Data for later years, though not complete, covered 80 countries.

Since 1966, however, loan terms have changed with the rise of interest costs to the lending institutions. In 1970–71 the IBRD interest rate went to 7.25 percent and the IDB rate to 8 percent. U.S. government loan interest rates have not changed, but other governments have increased the amount of their concessional aid and have modified terms to some extent. Table 9 attempts to compare roughly the loan terms of various agencies in 1970–71, by showing (1) standard or average terms, (2) the payments which the borrower would have to make in the first year after grace, and (3) the payments to be made in the middle year.

Table 9 should not be construed as a price list for potential borrowers shopping around. Each of the averages is based on a heterogeneous collection of loans, most conspicuously in the case of Ex-Im. Its loans included small supplies and trucks, airplanes, petrochemical plants and a nuclear power plant. Its loans were generally made in conjunction with loans by commercial banks or other private companies, some guaranteed, others not, most commonly on a 50–50 basis, with Ex-Im taking the later maturities. The private portion also has interest rates based on market rates.

A second comparison of service payments is afforded by IBRD calculations of estimated service in 1970 of loans on the books at the beginning of the year for those loans whose terms were known (80 countries). The form of the data in Table 10 does not admit of direct comparison with Table 9.

The broad groupings of Table 10 indicate the harder terms of supplier and bank credits in comparison with loans subsidized by governments individually or collectively. Bank loans are frequently renewed so that the heavy amortization is more apparent than real. Suppliers'

Table 8. Weighted Average Terms of External Public Debt Contracted in 1966, by Sources of Funds.

	Interest (percent)	Grace period (years)	Maturity (years)	Average annual amorti- zation[a] (percent)	Total payments first pay- ment year[b]	Total payments middle year[c]
Publicly issued bonds	7.06	0.8	14.1	7.52	14.58	11.05
Privately placed debt	5.77	2.5	10.2	12.98	18.76	15.87
Suppliers credits	5.60	2.7	10.5	12.82	18.42	15.60
Other private	6.75	1.4	8.5	14.08	20.83	17.46
Loans from international organizations	3.21	7.7	36.8	3.44	6.65	5.05
IBRD	6.00	4.5	22.1	5.68	9.32[d]	9.32[d]
IDA	0.75	10.5	49.7	2.55	1.75[e]	3.45[e]
IDB	6.00	3.8	16.8	7.69	13.69	10.69
Other	4.96	6.1	28.8	4.41	9.38	6.89
Bilateral government loans	2.62	7.6	28.6	4.76	7.38	6.57
Canada	1.40	8.3	40.8	3.08	4.48	3.15
France	3.72	3.5	19.4	6.29	10.01	8.15
Germany	3.36	5.9	21.0	6.62	9.98	8.30
Japan	5.05	5.4	15.3	10.10	15.15	12.13
U.K.	0.44	8.9	25.2	6.13	6.57	6.35
U.S.A.	2.59	8.4	33.9	3.92	6.51	5.21
All sources	3.39	6.4	26.3	5.03	8.42	6.73

Source: IBRD, *Annual Report,* 1968, p. 60.

a. Average annual amortization is computed as a percent on maturity less grace period.

b. Total payment equals computed average annual amortization plus the rate of interest on full principal except in the case of IDA and IBRD. The assumption is that loans are amortized in equal annual installments of principal. Terms of loans differ, but equal payments are most usual. They often are semiannual, but this would affect the computed rates only by a small fraction. The rate for the U.S. is overstated since AID credits (half of total) are on an annuity basis.

c. Average annual amortization plus one-half of interest rate, assuming that half has been repaid.

d. An annuity at 6 percent for the repayment period of 17.6 years.

e. The rates are in terms of the IDA amortization schedule.

credits require service of about 20 percent of principal annually. The low interest and amortization of international institution loans includes conventional loans (IBRD, IDB, ADB) as well as IDA credits and other soft loans. The loans of the Western governments also include conventional loans and loans with low interest rates, sometimes zero interest, and long maturities. Taken as a whole, however, the developing countries must pay annually over 13 percent of the principal of loans disbursed and outstanding. The debt burden for any one country depends on the sources from which it has borrowed. But even if all loans were at the averages of Western government, CMEA,

Table 9. Approximate Relative Debt Service on Loans to Developing Countries by Creditor Class, 1970–71 (in Percentages of Original Principal).

	Standard terms			Payment in first year after grace			Payment in middle year after grace		
	Interest	Average grace (years)	Average maturity (years)	Interest	Amorti-zation	Total	Interest	Amorti-zation	Total
IBRD	7.25	4.75	20.83	—	—	10.76	—	—	10.76
IDA	.75	10.00	50.00	.75	1.00	1.75	.45	3.00	3.45
IDB	8.00	4.00	18.60	8.00	6.85	14.85	4.00	6.85	10.85
AsDB	7.50	4.51	19.18	7.50	6.81	14.31	3.75	6.81	10.56
AfDB	6.21	4.51	19.94	6.21	6.48	12.69	3.11	6.48	9.59
Ex-Im (a)	6.00	5.50	9.90	6.00	22.73	28.73	3.00	22.73	25.73
Ex-Im and private (b)	6.75	3.35	10.00	6.75	15.00	21.75	3.38	15.00	18.38
AID	2.00–3.00	10.00	40.00	—	—	5.03	—	—	5.03

Source: Data on grace, maturities and interest rates supplied by the institutions or computed from annual reports. Ex-Im (a) relates to the average terms applicable to the Ex-Im portion from its own funds. (Maturities and grace period calculated for 1970 by E. S. Kerber of the Department of Commerce.) Ex-Im (b) is a rough calculation of the payments of combined Ex-Im and private loans. Interest rates on the private portion have been arbitrarily assumed at 7.5 percent. These loans contractually bear interest at fixed rates, differentials above the prime or Euro-dollar rate and several other arrangements. Maturities and grace periods have been calculated on the basis of loans made in the second half of 1970. Grace has been taken as the time between Ex-Im board action and the first payment of principal to the private lender (excluding down payments) and maturity to the last payment to Ex-Im. The averages are affected by the large loan for the nuclear power plant. If this were excluded, the average amortization period would be 7.2 years, so that first year payments would be 20.63 percent of principal and middle year, 17.26 percent. Calculation of grace from commitment rather than contract date overstates the grace period and the final maturity. On a contract date basis, annual payments might be as much as one percent lower. (Data on these loans were kindly provided by R. H. Rowntree of Ex-Im from Bank records. He is not responsible for the calculation based on the data.)

Table 10. Projected Debt Service in 1970, by Creditor Class.

	Amount disbursed ($million)	Net commit-ment ($million)	Amorti-zation in 1970 ($million)	Interest in 1970 ($million)	Interest as percent of disbursed	Amorti-zation as per-cent of disbursed	Amorti-zation as per-cent of commit-ments	Total debt service as percent of commit-ments
Suppliers	6,334.0	7,708.0	1,233.2	304.0	4.80	19.47	16.00	19.95
Banks	2,879.5	3,574.7	664.9	180.2	6.26	23.09	18.60	23.64
Other private	4,370.2	4,528.8	340.7	162.0	3.70	7.80	7.52	11.10
Intn'l org.	7,265.9	11,333.3	407.0	337.6	4.65	5.60	3.59	6.57
CMEA	3,915.6	5,083.0	353.7	83.1	2.12	9.03	6.96	8.60
Other gov'ts	20,816.9	26,029.5	1,286.9	633.5	3.04	6.18	4.94	7.38
All debt	45,582.2	58,528.2	4,276.0	1,700.5	3.73	9.38	7.31	10.21

Source: IBRD.

or combined international agency credits, the borrowers would still have to pay almost 10 percent annually of the principal of loans that they have utilized. Table 10 is calculated on loans outstanding at the beginning of 1970, many of which had lower interest rates than loans made in more recent years. Hence, in future years, annual debt service is likely to be heavier as a proportion to principal.

Another method of reducing the heterogeneity of loan terms is to compute the present value, at a uniform rate of compound interest, of future payments of interest and amortization under various loan terms. In recent periods, largely under DAC stimulation, calculations of the "grant element" in loans have been made with the grant element equal to the difference between the original principal of the loan and the discounted value of service payments, usually stated as a percentage of principal.[47] The choice of the discount rate is crucial. If the discount rate chosen is equal to the coupon or nominal rate, the grant element is zero; if higher than the nominal rate for all loan terms compared, all loans will have a grant element, and vice versa. Thus, on loans in 1966, with a 10 percent discount rate, the concessionary element of supplier credits averaged 17.9 percent; of publicly issued bonds, 17.6 percent; IBRD loans, 27 percent; IDA, 84.9 percent; IDB, 10.1 percent.[48]

For bilateral assistance to LCDs, loans and grants were combined to yield a grant element of 78.9 percent on the average, with a range of 100 percent for Australia, which made only grants, to 49.8 percent for Japan, whose loans were relatively hard.

Calculations of the grant or concessionary element in loans may be used as an index of hardness with any given rate of discount, but comparisons must be used with due caution. The higher the rate of discount used, the greater is the grant element calculated, and the relative hardness calculated at two different rates will vary with the maturity, grace period, and interest rate. For 1966 data discounted at 8 percent, IBRD loans have a concessionary element of 15.9 percent compared with 27 percent at a discount rate of 10 percent. Publicly issued bonds appear more concessionary, compared with other private credits, including supplier credits, at 10 percent discount but less concessionary at 8 percent. In general, the index of hardness varies in the same direction as interest rates and in the opposite direction with

47. The IBRD study cited (*Possible Improvements*) discussed the problems, gives the necessary equations, and compares typical loan terms. It has a good bibliography.
    48. IBRD, *Annual Report*, 1968, p. 60.

maturities and grace periods, though not proportionately since the discount is at a compound interest rate.

The concessionary element in loans also does not indicate relative debt service, since two loans with the same concessionary element may have quite different service requirements in a given year depending on maturities and grace periods, and two loans with the same service as a proportion of principal may have different concessionary elements. Nor may the index be used satisfactorily to measure the cost of the concessionary element to the lender unless its cost of money equals the discount rate.

The results of using the present value calculations as well as the tabular comparisons (Tables 8–10) presented above quantify to a degree what is apparent from the simple comparison of loan terms familiar to those concerned with borrowing and lending. Private credits as a whole require heavier debt service than do the hard loans of national or international agencies. The latter, in turn, require more onerous service than the deliberately concessional loans (and grants) made by governments bilaterally or by the soft windows of the international bodies.

The developing countries have been borrowing at an increasing rate over the last few decades at commercial and concessional terms. Patterns vary. Some face more difficult debt situations than others because of the amounts involved and the terms secured. Adjustments of some debts have been made and there will probably be others in the next few years. The problem is more general, however, and involves other countries which are, for the present at least, in the clear.

2. SOME GENERAL CONSIDERATIONS

BALANCE OF PAYMENTS QUESTIONS

It is axiomatic that international debts can be serviced through the balance of payments of the debtor country only by (1) an increase in exports of goods and services, (2) a reduction of imports of goods and services, excluding payments on debt service, (3) net inflows of capital through direct investment, (4) use of reserves, or (5) additional borrowing. When exchange resources are actually or prospectively not adequate to pay interest and amortization in addition to normal import requirements, serious debt problems may arise unless the borrowing country elects to cut imports, through devaluation or exchange and trade restrictions, and accepts a lowering of its standard of living and curtailment of its development program at least until the debt problem is resolved.

For most less developed countries exchange receipts depend primarily on commodity exports. They are generally net debtors on shipping account as well as other invisibles, e.g., insurance, banking services. Some, however, have important net tourist receipts, such as Mexico, whose net travel receipts were 39.8 percent of commodity exports in 1968 and 34.7 percent in 1969, or Greece, 16.6 percent in 1968 and 18.3 in 1969. By 1970 Mexico's net travel receipts had increased to 54.2 percent, but Greece had a travel deficit. Some, like Turkey, have important receipts from remitted earnings of migrant labor, 23.8 percent of exports in 1969. The Greek balance of payments includes large receipts for shipping services and emigrant remittances, which in 1967 were 40.6 percent and 51.3 percent respectively and in 1970, 18.7 and 28.3 percent of amounts received for commodity exports. Increased commodity exports partly explain the change. By and large, for most developing countries commodity exports are the main source from which they can service their debt. Less developed countries as a whole had an average net deficit on services account of $5.4 billion annually (1964–66) compared with $28.9 billion of merchandise exports in these years, though this deficit included net current payments on investments by others of $3.9 billion, interest and dividends and the like, but not repayments of principal.[1]

1. John S. Smith, "World Summary of International Transactions, 1961–66," in IMF, *Staff Papers*, 16 (March 1969): 88–93. The data refer only to the countries for which adequate balance of payments figures were available. Total reported exports were higher for all developing countries as reported in IFS. The IMF classification of less developed countries excludes Spain and

Most of the low-income countries have had deficits on merchandise account in recent years, as would be expected in countries receiving grants or borrowing abroad. The relation of borrowing and the commodity balance may be illustrated by a hypothetical case. Assume that a country in a given year has a balance of payments in equilibrium, and for simplicity, assume that its imports of goods and services equal its exports at the level of $1 billion, and that it has no external debt. With the same level of exports, its imports will be increased when it borrows, by the amount of goods moving into the economy. If, let us say, the country borrows to finance an electric light plant costing $100 million, its imports may be expected to increase over several years by $100 million, depending upon the rate of disbursement and construction. Consequently, for a period of, say, 2 or 3 years it would have a commodity deficit aggregating the amount of the loan. If the loan is a one-shot affair, it must amortize the loan, say in 20 years, and pay interest at 6 percent, so that its trade balance will have to rise by an average of $8 million per annum.[2] The shorter the term and the higher the rate of interest, the more it would have to earn additionally, unless it borrows to pay the service.

The investment resulting from the loan may, or may not, depending on conditions, provide for its service. If it is amortized internally from electricity charges or taxes, in other types of investment in highway or other facilities, income which otherwise might have been spent on imports may be directed to loan service. If, as a result of borrowing, the productivity of the population increases, larger exports may follow. One could not expect this result from a single investment financed by borrowing; it is more likely to come from a series of productive investments. There are relatively few cases in which one may attribute directly to the investment financed by borrowing a net increment in the exchange receipts or exchange savings of the borrower. If oil is struck, or an iron mine is opened in Liberia or Mauritania, the export of the oil or ore, after a time lag, may result in a direct increase in exchange earnings. On the other hand, if the loan finances a power plant, a railroad, or a highway system, exchange receipts may increase as the result of more efficient utilization of the existing factors of production or as the result of production ancillary to the investment. There may not be a perceptible immediate improvement in exchange earnings, though of course the infrastructure may facilitate the production of exportable

Yugoslavia, which are usually included in data from IBRD and OECD-DAC sources.
    2. Assuming equal payments of principal and no grace.

goods. By contributing to the borrower's GNP, savings and exports, the loan may finance itself over time.

A loan may also be used to save exchange. The plant constructed may produce commodities previously imported, so that, assuming no change in exports, it may in time provide the resources for servicing the loan. If the new plant can in time produce at costs comparable to the cost of the displaced imports, there is not only a balance of payments saving, but also an increase in GNP. If on the other hand, the new plant is high cost, it may save exchange, but at a cost in terms of real income, if local capital and labor are diverted from activities in which the country has greater natural advantages. If the new plant employs otherwise unemployed labor, there may be some gain even in GNP. The problem here is the entire issue of the infant industries argument for protectionism, and its relation to the external economies of scale and the purported cultural and social advantages of industrialization.[3]

In contrast, if a country has a balance of payments deficit on current account not related to borrowing for capital works, the situation may be worsened. Returning to the illustration of a country with a billion dollars in imports, if for some reason, e.g., a crop failure, its exports drop to $900 million, and it finances its import requirements by borrowing, there is not likely to be an increase in production over previous levels. The balance of payments credit may enable the borrower to maintain its usual standard of consumption of imports or maintain its level of production insofar as the deficit finance provides materials and equipment, without which the economy would decline further. The borrowing may be essential and justifiable. Unless, however, as the result of borrowing there is more exchange available in the future, or imports curtailed, the borrower cannot meet debt service requirements. In the illustration, to maintain imports, exports would have to increase by $8 million to service the debt.

The illustration may seem needlessly belabored, but it points to a problem which has been realized for many years. This was essentially the reason for the stress given in the IBRD Articles to development *projects,* though the Articles did not define precisely what a project is, and in fact the borderline between productive projects and mere balance of payments assistance is sometimes hard to define. It was assumed by the drafters of the Articles that IBRD lending would be

3. This raises the entire question of development strategy, which is far broader than the debt servicing issue.

more productive than much of the borrowing in the period preceding the Great Depression and in the nineteenth century had been, much of which had been to cover budgetary deficits or to meet normal balance of payments requirements in periods of falling exchange receipts. It must be remembered, however, that the crisis in the servicing of the older debts (1930–34) was importantly related to the rapid decline in the imports of the creditor countries, mainly the United States, under conditions of economic depression.[4] Simultaneously, of course, the volume of foreign loans by the U.S. market dropped to a fraction, so that countries which were borrowing additionally to pay their debt service could not pay.

For the present purpose it may be assumed that the economies of the creditor countries will continue to grow and that they will pursue appropriate policies in their foreign trade, though assumptions of this sort may need considerable qualification. The problem for the near future is the potential growth of exports by the countries whose debt and debt service have been rapidly increasing.

The trade performance of individual countries depends on the commodities they produce and world prices and consumption of these commodities, their development policies, whether they are directed to export or production for domestic consumption, their fiscal and monetary policies, the degree of inflation and their exchange policies as they affect their competitive position and the direction of their production. To a considerable extent also the prospects depend upon economic conditions in, and the trade policies of, the industrial countries which provide their markets. To review the extensive literature, with the variations and complexities of method, would be a far more extensive study, so that only a few points will be noted as they may affect future debt servicing capacity.

Many, or most, of the developing countries will for the near future depend upon agricultural or mineral commodities for the expansion of their exports. Agricultural staples are characterized by relatively inelastic demand in world markets and low positive income elasticities in the consuming countries.[5] The consumption of, say, coffee or cotton will increase with population and income over time, but in the short run, changes in the amount sold in world markets will have more

4. See Hal B. Lary, *United States in the World Economy* (Department of Commerce, economic series, no. 23, 1943), pp. 99–110, 161–83.
5. The proposition on elasticity is stated dogmatically here without attempting an econometric solution. The problem of deriving statistical demand curves, both with respect to price and income, is fraught with many pitfalls which are beyond the scope of this study.

than proportional opposite effects on unit price. The exchange earnings of the principal supplying countries may fluctuate widely (e.g., Brazil and Colombia) as a result, and if they restrict sales, other countries can enter the market with considerable gain. While total demand may be price inelastic, there may be considerable elasticity for the product of any one small supplier. The problem is obviously related to commodity agreements and compensatory finance of export fluctuations, as well as price-support programs. In other instances, there may be a secular decline in demand, e.g., wool, silk, natural rubber.

Exports of metals, minerals and other raw materials depend, in good part, on cyclical and price and production conditions in the industrial countries. Exports of copper to the U.S. and Europe depend on demand and domestic production. Over the last 10 years copper prices have fluctuated between 28.9 cents and 77.1 cents equivalent on the London market.

Partly in response to these factors—prestige is also important—the lower income countries have directed a good part of their development programs to industrialization and diversification, with varied results. Some of these programs have aimed at import substitution. Some plants have been high cost and required "excessive" protection to keep them going. Others to be efficient require a scale for which the local market is too small (automobiles, steel mills in small countries) unless they can produce competitively for export.[6] Varying degrees of inflation and over-valuation have been a further factor in exchange receipts.

A careful study by B. A. deVries on the basis of the export performance of 29 countries reached a number of tentative conclusions. Countries which have diversifiied production oriented to the domestic market have had less than average performance in exports and have also had more inflation; countries whose exports formed a small part of the world total for particular commodities did better than those which were major suppliers; price inflation affected receipts from minor exports more than for major exports (i.e., where world conditions determined the receipts); countries concentrating on light industries in their development fared better than those developing heavy industry; and, policies fostering agricultural production have had good results both in terms of major and minor exports.[7]

6. Cf. Robert S. McNamara, *Address to the Board of Governors* [of the IBRD-IMF], Sept. 27, 1971, pp. 19–23.

7. See B. A. deVries, *The Export Experience of Developing Countries* (IBRD Staff Occasional Paper, no. 3, 1967); summarized in *Finance and Development*, March 1968, pp. 2–8.

A recent article, R. J. Irvine, Y. Maroni and H. F. Lee, "How to Borrow Successfully,"

The increase in exports of developing countries has been uneven, even in the last few years. China (Taiwan) has moved from $164 million in 1960 to $1,428 million in 1970; Israel, from $217 to $781 million; Korea, from $33 million to $835 million. These are countries which have received massive U.S. aid per capita, but have also directed their economies to exports. Hong Kong, without aid, raised exports from $688 million in 1961 to $2,514 million in 1970. The oil producers, Saudi Arabia, Iran, Kuwait, Libya, have generally fared better than other LDCs. Exports of a few countries have declined over the last 8 years, e.g., Burma, Haiti, South Vietnam, Ceylon, and the Dominican Republic (with considerable recovery 1968 to 1970). Increases have been shown by some of the countries with significant debt problems, though not proportionally to debt service. Indian exports have increased from $1.3 billion in 1960 to $2 billion in 1970; Colombia's from $466 million to $732 million in 1970.

In connection with UNCTAD, projections have been made of the growth of exports from the developing countries and for some individual countries. Without entering into the methodological problems of these projections, it may be noted that the Secretariat concluded that for foodstuffs, agricultural raw materials and nonfuel minerals and metals, the annual rate of growth, 1960–75, was between 2.8 and 3.5 percent, with, however, projected rates of 4.3 to 4.8 percent for the minerals and metals category. For fuels, the rates were 7.5 to 8 percent, and for manufactures (textiles, plywood and leather goods) between 8.3 and 9.3 percent. For all commodities, the projection was between 5 and 5.6 percent.[8] Projections of import requirements necessarily involve more complicated assumptions and technique. Within the framework of its assumptions, the trade gap in 1975 was estimated as between $3.4 billion and $10 billion measured in 1960 prices. Substantial gaps were estimated for most LDCs except the oil producers.[9] These projections are noted here for their interest. They are at least not contradictory to the less involved evidence from simple quantitative data for the last 8 years. Obviously, if aid or conventional borrowing do not fill projected gaps, the import figures would be lower, as presumably development would be slower or consumption reduced. If the

Columbia Journal of World Business, Jan.–Feb. 1970, pp. 41–46, forcefully states the argument on export policies, encouragement of private investment, monetary stability and debt problems, by comparison of the experience of Japan, Mexico, Thailand, Argentina and India.

8. UNCTAD, *Trade Prospects and Capital Needs of Developing Countries* (U.N., 1968), p. 19.

9. Ibid. pp. 41–43. For an earlier estimate and an analysis of the problems of estimation and projection see Bela Balassa, *Trade Prospects for Developing Countries* (Homewood, Ill.: Richard D. Irwin, 1964).

gap is filled, the debt will increase, though the burden may not be proportionally as heavy in the future if aid is provided on highly concessional terms.

From the point of view of the debt problem, it is a race between the increasing rate of debt service and the rate of growth of exports in the future, though debt difficulties may result from internal economic or political factors. So far, the developing countries have been, as a whole, losing out in this race. Only a few have decreased their outstanding debt. With some exceptions, they have continued in payments deficit and have increased their borrowings. Though increasing portions of the debt have been at concessional terms, even AID or IDA terms eventually impose a real burden.

REPETITIVE BORROWING

Pay-as-you-Go versus Repetitive Borrowing

The cheapest way for a country to finance its economic development is the pay-as-you-go method,[10] which would require a current balance of payments surplus equal to new investments. This would be possible for some countries which have had an export surplus. Pay-as-you-go would also avoid the political entanglements more or less inevitably involved in borrowing, or at least the pressure from the lenders on matters of economic policy. Borrowing from the Soviets for military or economic purposes presents an obvious case. The borrower becomes involved (or further involved) in bilateral trade arrangements which may not be advantageous and increase their dependence on the CMEA countries for their exports. If they have a deficit financed by a debit position in the trade accounts, their economies are tied up for the future. At the same time other lenders become more cautious, either for economic or political reasons.

If the country borrows from Western sources, either bilaterally or from multilateral institutions, the lenders wish to see appropriate policies pursued so that their assistance is not wasted and that conditions are conducive to repayment. The lenders may insist upon halting inflation—or a promise to slow down—which may involve tax policy,

10. Theoretically, the economy of a country could gain more by borrowing than by paying cash if it could lend abroad at a higher rate of return than the cost of borrowing. Certainly many individuals in LDCs find it profitable to export capital rather than invest at home, but this perverse movement of capital may be for safety rather than earnings since interest rates are at least nominally higher in LDCs than in industrial countries.

credit policy, exchange rates and policy, and administrative reform. In the case of project loans by the IBRD and IDB, reorganization of particular entities or assurances of adequate utility rates have been prerequisite to some loans. No doubt these have all been salutary measures, in the long-run interest of the borrowing economy as well as the safety of the loan, but they may be resented by the governments as undue meddling in their affairs. They would prefer to borrow without strings.

Despite these limitations, most developing countries have preferred to borrow. Iran, for instance, which has had a quite sizable commodity surplus for the last 10 years, has borrowed increasingly and has earmarked part of the oil receipts to service debt. The countries not producing oil have, on the other hand, generally had commodity deficits, certainly in part representing the inflow of goods financed by borrowing, though in part deficits arising from trade-related factors, including inflation and overvalued exchange rates. Development based on trade surpluses would be much slower than is necessary to keep up with the growth of population and the aspirations of people, sometimes called the "revolution of expectations."

From a theoretical point of view, borrowing has a net benefit to the debtor country whenever the marginal efficiency of capital is greater than the cost of the loan. That is, if the investment of the borrowed capital produces a stream of income over time greater than interest and amortization, there is a gain to the borrower. For some capital projects, e.g., a power plant, cost-benefit studies can be fairly precise, at least on stated assumptions. For others, e.g., highways and public works, it is more difficult to measure benefits in money terms. The benefits are largely in the area of imponderables, as they are, of course, for education, health, population control, sanitation and military purposes. They may be immeasurable though unmeasurable. Borrowing for balance of payments deficits, including debt service, may prevent economic collapse or default.

It follows that the gain is greater the larger the benefits compared with interest and amortization. This argument applies to domestic as well as foreign borrowing. The special characteristic of external debt is that it must be serviced through the balance of payments, and benefits realized in local currency may not be transferable in exchange. International borrowing and lending has scarcely been based on precise calculations except in some project lending. The developing countries have sought loans for projects and balance of payments purposes. If they cannot get capital on concessional terms, they will contract conventional loans or supplier credits. The creditor countries have provided funds because it seemed profitable, e.g., commercial loans, to push exports for neo-mercantilistic reasons, for political and humanitarian reasons. Whatever the motivation, the result has been the piling up of debt, in part to pay service on previously contracted debt.

Loan Terms and Repetitive Borrowing

It has long been recognized that if a country borrows abroad over a considerable period to finance its development or to meet its balance of payments deficits, the principal sum of its debt increases at some compound rate. It may pay off some loans and maintain interest payments on the outstanding, but has to borrow additional amounts to cover payments, borrowing from Peter to pay Paul. Debt service will also increase; whether at a higher compound rate than principal or at a slower rate depends on loan terms. If it refinances supplier credits by concessional borrowing at lower interest and longer maturity, debt service will increase less rapidly than principal.

This may be an entirely justifiable procedure for a developing country. As its production increases, so may its export potential, so that after some years it may be able to service its debt without additional borrowing and even become a net capital exporter. The case has been illustrated by the United States (with the help of two world wars) and some European countries which in time moved from net debtor to net creditor positions. This analogy may be applied to the present-day low-income under-developed developing countries, at least as a hope. Indeed, this assumption must be the rationale of long-term finance of development through loans, "hard," "soft," or "blended."

If exports increase at some faster rate than imports, starting from an initial deficit position, at some point of time a trade surplus will appear. If the deficit is financed by external borrowing, the annual amount needed will decrease over time, though debt service will increase, and eventually there will be a point at which the trade surplus will enable the debtor country to begin net amortization of debt, in increasing amounts until the entire cumulative principal is liquidated. The precise point in time for the appearance of the trade surplus will depend on the relative rates of increase of exports and imports, and the point of beginning net amortization will depend on loan terms. In the models which can be constructed, numerical results will depend on the assumptions made.[11] To the extent that reality conforms to the models, the borrower is economically justified in incurring debt and the lenders can make "sound" loans. The lenders, private or public, may become concerned if the debt service ratio becomes "excessive," a matter of judgment. Institutional lenders might continue to lend even when private sources are hesitant.[12]

The debt of practically all LDCs has been growing over the years. In some years, a few countries have reduced their outstanding debt but have borrowed again in succeeding years. Some have met interest from exchange earnings but have rolled over principal (e.g., Argentina and to a large extent Mexico). For the group as a whole, new borrowings each year have exceeded the total paid in interest and principal. Only a few have reduced the amount owed.[13]

As debt increases, a given amount of borrowing adds less and less to resources, so that sooner or later, depending on loan terms, debt service equals or exceeds new borrowing,[14] or conversely, to provide a country with a constant annual amount of resources, the annual amount of aid or new borrowing must increase at some rate which is a compound interest function, the "net aid concept." Debt difficulties have occurred for other reasons and refunding has occurred before the "break-even" point has been reached. In fact, aside from regular annual aid programs, borrowing has been intermittent and exchange receipts have fluctuated more than can be predicated on some export function of GNP.

Mikesell has illustrated the problem of the break-even point in

11. A recent model of this sort is in R. F. Mikesell, "External Borrowing and Debt Service" (Organization of American States, UP/G 29/3, Oct. 24, 1969). On the assumption of an initial deficit equal to a 10th of imports, an export growth rate of 5 percent, an import rate of 4 percent, and loans at 5 percent with linear amortization over 20 years, the trade balance would become favorable in the 12th year and net indebtedness would start declining in the 14th year. He illustrates with various other terms, grace periods and trade rates.

12. Mikesell, "External Borrowing," p. 2, says, "Therefore, external lending agencies generally insist that the debt service ratio does not exceed 20 percent." While there have been no announcements of this critical ratio, the banks have loaned to countries with ratios well above 10 percent. In the Indian case, the amount of debt relief was calculated to reduce the ratio to about 20 percent. Somewhat similar considerations seem to be involved in "blending" formulas.

13. From the available data, only Liberia and Rhodesia appear to have reduced the net outstanding (including undisbursed) debt. The apparent reduction of Brazilian public debt from $4.3 billion at December 31, 1968 to $3.5 billion a year later appears to result from a recalculation of data. The two figures, involving some private debt and excluding some undisbursed items in 1969, are not comparable. Details of debt operations for 1965 to 1969 are not available. The outstanding debt of Brazil to the United States, public and private on a disbursed basis, increased by $53.5 million, but including undisbursed was reduced by $50.4 million.

14. E.g., Raymond F. Mikesell, "The Capacity to Service Foreign Investment," in Mikesell, ed., *U. S. Private and Government Investment Abroad* (Eugene: University of Oregon Books, 1962), pp. 377–406; idem, *Economics of Foreign Aid* (Chicago: Aldine Publishing Co., 1968), chap. 4; Goran Ohlin, *Aid and Indebtedness* (Development Center of OECD, 1966).

borrowing and the increasing rate of gross capital imports to sustain a net flow of imports in a model based on 5 percent interest and 20-year amortization in equal annual payments. Debt service would equal gross capital imports in the 12th year and at the end of 20 years amortization and interest would be 153 percent of the annual borrowing rate (see Figure 1). On the assumption of a steady capital inflow, the annual rate of capital imports would have to increase indefinitely, and at the end of 20 years it would take 550 percent to maintain this flow (see Figure 2).[15]

Closely related concepts and calculations have been made by those concerned with the problem of economic aid and the terms on which it is given. An AID study[16] in 1965 made several interesting computations on the basis of aid and loan terms then in use. To maintain a net flow of resources by successsive borrowings and service of prior debt, a country would have to borrow 4.32 times as much in the 15th year as in the first if the loans were at Ex-Im terms, 3.15 times as much if on IBRD terms, 1.42 on AID terms, and 1.15 on IDA terms.[17] These percentages, of course, represent not only the lower interest rates but longer grace periods on AID and IDA credits as opposed to "conventional" loan terms by Ex-Im and IBRD (Figure 3). At present interest rates, the percentages would be higher for all except IDA credits.

Governments, international institutions and private lenders have provided the funds for development and balance of payments assistance at a considerable variety of terms.[18] The persistence of the deficits and the inability of most of the developing countries to shift their balances of payments have resulted in the accumulation of debts which partly represent borrowing for new purposes and partly borrowing to pay service on older debt. Almost inevitably they are caught in the compound interest problem.

To illustrate the nature of these problems, some relatively simple schemata have been constructed. The analysis may appear oversimplified to deal with the concrete debt problem of particular countries which represent composites of the various sets of lending terms described. To the mathematician the analysis may seem obvious. Never-

15. *U.S. Private and Government Investment Abroad,* pp. 392–95.
16. AID, "A Study on Loan Terms, Debt Burden, and Development" (mimeograph, April 1965).
17. There are similar computations in Dragoslav Avromovic et al., *Economic Growth and External Debt* (Baltimore: Johns Hopkins Press, 1964), p. 164.
18. See chapter 1, Tables 7 and 9. Calculations of borrowing, service and outstanding debt for a selected group of specific loan terms are in Avromovic et al., *Economic Growth and External Debt,* p. 164. These calculations are similar to those in Figure 3.

Figure 1. Annual Capital Imports and Debt Service, with Constant Annual Borrowing.

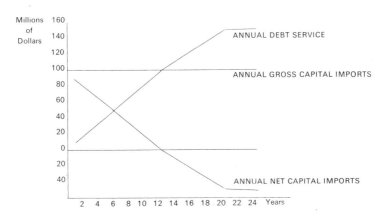

Assumptions: A country borrows $100 million per year for an indefinite period. The rate of interest is 5 percent per year and the rate of amortization of the amount borrowed each year is also 5 percent per year.

Figure 2. Gross Capital Imports and Annual Debt Service, with Constant Annual Net Borrowing.

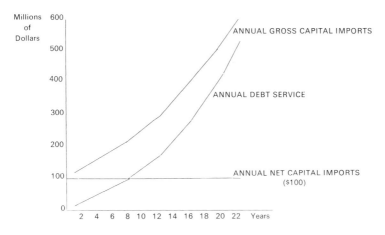

Assumptions: Net receipts from capital imports after allowance for all amortization and interest payments are $100 million annually for an indefinite period. Interest is 5 percent per year on the net debt, and the amortization payments are 5 percent on the amount borrowed each year. All interest and amortization payments are covered by new loans so that net receipts from capital imports remain at $100 million each year for an indefinite period.

Figure 3. Rise in Gross Lending Per Year Required to Maintain a Given Net Inflow of Resources.

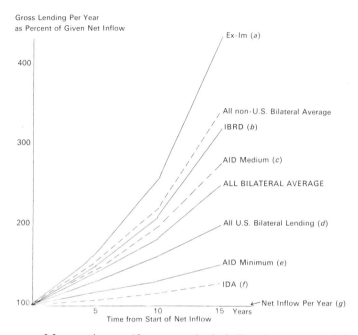

a. 5.5 percent interest, 13 years maturity, including a 3-year grace period.
b. 5.5 percent, 20 years, including 5-year grace.
c. 3.5 percent, 20 years, including 3-year grace.
d. Ex-Im and AID.
e. 2.5 percent, 40 years, including 10-year grace at 1 percent.
f. 0.75 percent, 50 years, including 10-year grace.
g. Includes all terms shown.

theless, the confusion even in the minds of lending and borrowing officers about various loan policies is such that an exposition of some fundamentals is indicated. The necessary algebra is relegated to the appendix.

At any given interest rate a short-term loan is cheaper than a long-term loan. A 6 percent loan paid off in 5 years (assuming equal annual payments of principal) has a total interest cost of 15 percent of the loan, but annual service will average 23 percent of original principal. On a 10-year basis interest cost is 30 percent, but annual service only 13 percent. Secondly, a grace period increases the interest cost, and the longer the grace period, the higher the interest cost for a given terminal maturity. A loan with amortization in 10 years after 2 years grace on principal has a total interest cost of 42 percent. A 20-year loan at 3 percent has the same interest cost as a 10-year loan at 6 percent, but the annual service is only 6.5 as opposed to 13 percent. Obviously, lower annual service costs are more likely to be met eventually from increased export earnings than are higher annual costs.

Case 1: Borrower pays interest but refinances amortization. On a single loan if the borrower pays interest from current exchange earnings, but borrows additionally to pay amortization, the annual cost is merely interest cost. Assume that a country borrows $100 with amortization in equal annual installments over 20 years with interest at 6 percent. At the end of the first year it pays back $5 in amortization, but borrows an additional $5 to cover it. Its debt continues at $100 indefinitely, and it would have an annual charge merely to cover interest.

If, however, it borrows for new purposes, say, $100 a year, it would have to refinance the principal payments at an increasing amount each year and, of course, its interest cost would go up annually but would still be simple interest on the amount outstanding during each year. The case is noted here because this may in practice be a solution to the cumulative debt problem of the LDCs on the assumption that the creditors are willing to roll over principal payment due to them through refunding in one way or another.

Case 2: Borrowing to cover interest and amortization. Again, assuming a single loan of $100 and 20-year, 6 percent terms, the borrower would have to borrow an additional $11 in the second year to meet service requirements; in the third year $5.50 for amortization plus $6.60 for interest and so on. On this assumption, the amount outstanding would grow at a compound interest formula of 11 percent. At the end of 10 years the debt would be $283.92 for each $100 originally borrowed, and at the end of 20 years, $886.85.

Even if the loan were made on very easy terms, say 2.5 percent and 40 years without a grace period—terms roughly comparable to AID loans—the outstanding amount would be $162.89 at the end of 10 years and $704 at the end of 40.

Case 3 (a): Repetitive borrowing, linear amortization. While certain project loans are one shot affairs, most of the developing countries have been borrowing annually for the purposes of their programs, which may be a succession of projects. To illustrate the effect of successive borrowings, assume that a country borrows $100 million each year for 10 years with amortization over 10 years and interest at 6 percent on outstanding balances. These terms correspond roughly to the average terms of Ex-Im loans extended in previous years, including some longer-term project loans and shorter-term export type of credit. The 10-year term is probably longer than the amortization rate provided in most supplier credits, though as noted above, the term of supplier credits has been increasing.

The relation of annual interest and amortization under these assumptions is given in Table 11. After the end of the 7th year, total debt service would equal the amount of borrowing. After the 10th year amortization would equal new loans, so that the total outstanding would continue indefinitely at $550 million with an annual interest cost of $33 million or 6 percent. At the end of the 10-year cycle, the case becomes analagous to Case 1, payment of interest with no reduction in principal.

Similar relations obtain for shorter or longer terms and various rates of interest. The year in which amortization equals new borrowings would be 5 years on a 5-year loan and 20 years on a 20-year loan. The shorter the term and the higher the interest rate, the sooner would be the year in which debt service equaled new borrowing. In the appendix there is a general formula applicable and calculations for various interest rates and maturities.

Case 3 (b): Linear amortization with grace and without grace on principal. With repeated annual borrowing of a constant amount, the allowance of a grace period on principal postpones the break-even point, but consistently less than the grace period. While a grace period

Table 11. Interest Cost and Amortization of a Succession of Loans of $100 Million Annually and Amortization in 10 Years, No Grace Period (Millions of Dollars).

Year	Loans outstanding in January	Interest payments	Amortization	Loans outstanding at end of year
1	100	6.0	10	90
2	190	11.4	20	170
3	270	16.2	30	240
4	340	20.4	40	300
5	400	24.0	50	350
6	450	27.0	60	390
7	490	29.4	70	420
8	520	31.2	80	440
9	540	32.4	90	450
10	550	33.0	100	450
11	550	33.0	100	450
12	550	33.0	100	450

on an individual loan may be quite important to permit the construction and start-up of a particular project, the advantage to the borrowing country in terms of its balance of payments is somewhat less if it borrows for a series of projects, or payments deficits. With a grace period the total interest cost is higher. For example, a succession of loans at 6 percent with a 20-year maturity and no grace period reaches the break-even point in 10.4 years. With a 23-year loan, including 3 years grace, the point is 11.3 years.[19] In the 20th year (no grace) amortization on a series of annual loans of $100 million would take $100 million and interest would be $63.6 million.

In general, the higher the rate of interest, the shorter the period before debt service exceeds new borrowing, and, of course, the longer the maturity of the loan at a given interest rate, the later this point is reached. With relatively long terms, say, 15 to 20 years, the date of the break-even point varies only about 1 to 2 years in the range of 5 to 7 percent interest. On the other hand, with short-term loans, say 5 years, the break-even point varies only by a few months with differences in interest rates in the likely ranges.[20]

Case 4: Level payments of interest and principal. A loan repaid by equal annual (or semiannual) payments of principal plus interest is an annuity of the specified term and interest rate. Compared with a loan with payment of interest on the outstanding balance and amortization in equal installments of principal, it has the advantage to the borrowers of reducing the debt service in the early years, but the payments are larger in the later years. The advantage to the borrower is considerably reduced, however, if there is a series of loans, since after a period it is making larger payments on old loans than it would under linear amortization.

In terms of the break-even point, the level payment loan is generally more advantageous to the borrower (assuming no grace period) than linear amortization, though the difference is slight, except for long terms and higher interest rates. For 5- and 10-year loans, there is no significant difference even at 7 percent interest. At 6 percent and 20 years, the break-even point is reached at 10.43 years on linear amortization and a year later on level payment. At 2.5 percent, the difference is a matter of 6 months.[21]

In short, if a country borrows year after year for a long period it

19. Cf. Tables IA and IB in the appendix.
20. Cf. Table IA, appendix.
21. Cf. appendix, Tables IA and IIA.

makes relatively little difference which amortization schedule is used. For a single loan or several loans with years between them, the level payment system is easier for the borrower, and so may make repayment more likely.

Case 5: Level payments after grace period. In a series of equal repetitive borrowings, with level payments, the allowance of a grace period on principal postpones the date at which debt service equals new borrowings, but always by a period that is smaller than the grace period. The postponement depends on the period of grace in relation to the repayment period and the interest rate. The higher the interest rate, the shorter the period until the break-even point is reached with a given grace period, and the less the advantage of grace periods as opposed to no grace. Obviously, the longer the grace period compared with the repayment period in a succession of borrowings, the greater the postponement of the date at which the borrower receives no net inflow of resources.

The appendix contains formulae and tables illustrating the point made. For example, a country borrowing on the basis of 20-year loans at 6 percent reaches the break-even point in 11.5 years; with payment in 20 years after 3 years grace, the point is reached in 12.4 years. There is also approximately one year's difference on a loan with payments in 10 years. The break-even point on loans of 40 years, including a 9-year grace period at 5 percent is 17.58 years, while 40-year loans without grace reach the point in 17.16 years. Level payments after a grace period are characteristic of IBRD and AID loans. At 1971 terms the annual payment after grace has expired is about 10.76 percent of principal. If a country borrowed an equal sum annually from the IBRD at present terms, debt service would equal new borrowing in about 10.8 years, about a year sooner than at 1966 terms.

On AID loans of 40 years with 10 grace, at 2 percent during grace and 3 percent during the repayment period, there would be no net inflow in about 25 years.

Summary. The preceding discussion and the generalized formulae and tables in the appendix have assumed a constant annual rate of borrowing for simplicity's sake. In practice the level of borrowing in any year is more variable, even with consortia and consultative groups, with a generally rising trend though with fluctuations about the trend.

On the simplifying assumption of a constant incremental amount of borrowing, the net addition to resources to the borrower decreases over time until a point is reached where debt service equals new loans. Thereafter debt service is greater until the point is reached where amortization payments equal the amount of borrowing. From this point on, borrowing at the given rate could continue and the debtor would merely be paying simple interest on the very large debt outstanding. It will have ceased to be a gross capital importer.

The break-even point comes earlier with higher rates of interest and shorter maturities. It can be postponed by longer grace periods and lower interest rates. Moreover, the time lag between the point of no net increase of resources from constant borrowing and zero gross capital imports varies with the maturity of loans and grace periods. On long-term loans the borrower would have to pay for a long time after it ceases to receive net resources.

With variable inflows of capital the break-even point will come sooner if borrowing is reduced, either by choice of the borrower or changes in policy or availability of resources to the lender as the result of market conditions or appropriations. If the level of lending or borrowing increases, the break-even point is postponed since new loans in greater amounts will provide more resources than will be required in payment of old loans. This could go on theoretically as long as funds are available.

Viewed trendwise, the latter condition has been characteristic more generally than the former. The advanced donor-creditor countries have been providing assistance on grant and loan terms to the developing countries, which generally have been content to take resources at the terms offered so that their debt has rather steadily increased. Probably both creditors and debtors have underestimated future problems. Additional loans have been made even in cases of known difficulty in servicing existing debt. Export guaranteeing entities have underwritten new credits as well. When given on concessional terms, additional loans under these circumstances are often a means of indirectly relieving the debtor's burden, as advocated by DAC.

On the other hand, the creditors may "crack down" and refuse additional loans unless there is some regularization of payments on existing credit. A reduction in the flow of resources to a given debtor by a reallocation of aid or a mere cut resulting from reduced availabilities may precipitate a crisis or at least entail some readjustment. In particular cases, as illustrated in chapter 4, several of these factors may be operative.

Finally, some of the debtors whose earnings have increased could start net repayment of their debts by voluntarily limiting new borrowing to an amount less than debt service, though the case is theoretical rather than actual.

The borrowings of almost all of the developing countries have, in fact, increased so that there is a compounding of interest and principal under any of the usual loan terms, though the net effect has been considerably offset by obtaining the newer loans at concessional terms.

Depending on loan terms, it is probably fair to say that under present conditions the break-even point is in the range of 10 to 20 years of borrowing, including the amount of concessional aid that has been given or is likely to be provided in the future, although the situation will vary from country to country with the terms of its borrowing and the proportion of concessional to harder loans.

Some Empirical Evidence

That the preceding discussion is not a purely algebraic construct appears to be borne out by IBRD-OECD calculations of reported debt service payments for 1965 to 1969 and loan and grant disbursements to the developing countries (80) for which adequate data are available.

Since loan disbursements and grant receipts are not regular for a given country, year by year, the figures have been combined in Table 12 for the 5-year period. Through this period, debt service and disbursements of loans have increased for practically all countries. Grants and grant-like contributions (P.L. 480 and IDB loans repayable in borrower currencies) have declined in the aggregate, with increases, however, in Latin America but decreases in South Asia, and elsewhere, as P.L. 480 was shifted to long-term dollar repayable loans.

Taking the low-income countries as a whole, debt service was about 58 percent of disbursements on loans and 44 percent of loan and grant disbursements. The averages are heavily weighted by Western Hemisphere countries. Their debt service was almost half of the total and the disbursement of loans and grants received by them about a third. In terms of the "net-aid" (grant and loan) concept discussed above, less than 60 percent was "net" and the rest was service on old debts.

The ratio of debt payments to receipts was heaviest in Latin America. These countries have borrowed over a longer time than others and at harder terms. They have also received less in grants. African countries (except oil and mineral producers) have little debt-servicing capacity. They obtained almost half of their external resources from grants.

Table 12. Debt Service Payments by, and Disbursements of Loans and Grants to Developing Countries, 1965–69 (Millions of Dollars).

Area	(1) Debt payments	(2) Loan disbursements	(3) Loan & grant disbursements	(4) Ratio (1)/(2)	(5) Ratio (1)/(3)
Africa	2,748.9	4,529.6	8,262.0	60.7	33.3
Middle East	1,605.2	3,284.4	3,805.8	48.9	42.2
South Asia	2,445.0	7,077.7	10,398.4	34.5	23.5
East Asia	1,399.4	3,995.3	5,856.8	35.0	23.9
South Europe	2,349.4	3,938.6	4,142.0	59.7	56.7
Western Hemisphere	10,127.9	12,858.0	14,927.8	78.8	67.8
Total	20,675.8	35,683.6	47,392.8	57.9	43.6
Selected countries					
Argentina	2,209.4	1,717.5	1,821.9	128.6	121.3
Chile[a]	545.9	994.1	1,145.1	54.9	47.7
Colombia	511.6	900.7	1,073.6	56.4	47.7
Mexico	3,549.7	3,787.9	3,858.7	93.7	92.0
Peru	571.3	1,033.2	1,178.2	55.3	48.5
Uruguay	191.9	271.4	302.5	70.7	63.4
India[a]	1,597.6	3,948.2	6,089.5	40.5	26.2
Pakistan	587.7	2,271.4	2,985.0	25.9	19.7
Philippines[b]	342.7	533.2	839.0	64.3	40.8
Korea[a]	126.5	984.7	1,646.4	12.8	7.7
Tunisia	155.0	387.1	579.5	40.1	26.7
Zambia	95.3	103.0	127.1	92.5	75.0

Source: IBRD and OECD (see IBRD, *Annual Report*, 1971, pp. 68–75).
a. Data for four years, 1965–68.
b. Does not include transactions of Philippine private debt guaranteed by the government, about $600 million principal.

The second part of Table 12 was constructed to show the situation of certain countries, though the data may not be strictly comparable to the area data, since the grants are on a "received" rather than a disbursed basis. The error probably is not great, except possibly in the cases of India, Pakistan and Korea, which were large grant recipients.

Argentina, the East African community, Rhodesia, Rwanda and Sierra Leone appear to be the only debtors which paid more in debt service than they utilized in loan disbursements. Rhodesia has not received much in loans recently, but has paid service on its debt. The East African community in 1968 paid off one security issue and replaced it by a smaller one. Sierra Leone and Rwanda paid off suppliers' credits, but received loans from governments which have been only partly utilized. Only Rwanda and Rhodesia have reduced their outstanding debt.

Argentina has for several years been rolling over its debt by issuing securities or borrowing from banks or others. When this practice is followed, both debt payments and disbursements of debt appear as larger amounts than in the case of countries which have borrowed more at longer term from governments and international organizations. In the Argentine case, disbursement of loan proceeds of $1.72 billion was only slightly larger than amortization payments of $1.70 billion. The total debt disbursed and outstanding at the end of 1969 was $1.78 billion. That is, in the 5-year period almost the entire debt was rolled over, but Argentina met interest payments from exchange earnings. It appears to illustrate Case 1 above.

Mexico, whose debt is about half bank loans, security issues and supplier credits, paid $2.1 billion in principal (of a total debt disbursed and outstanding at the end of 1969 of $2.5 billion) but used new loans in greater amount than it paid in principal and interest. While debt service has been mounting rapidly, Mexico has lengthened the term of its debt, so that amortization on old debt will be lower in coming years. It has steadily increased the total debt, even though new borrowings have added only a small fraction to total resources.

Only a few countries have reached or are approaching the point where debt service has caught up with new borrowing. Most have increased their total indebtedness. There has been considerable shifting in the form of debt in some countries, replacement of high-service private debts by credits from governments and organizations. The break-even point has been pushed forward in this way. The debt crises which have arisen have resulted partly from other factors.[22]

Exports and Debt

Table 13 brings up to 1970 certain significant results shown by the World Bank.[23] Developing countries as a whole had substantial trade deficits of between $2 billion and $4.2 billion in the period 1960 to 1970, but the totals included the oil producers which had trade surpluses of $3 billion to $5.5 billion in these years. The trade deficits of the non-oil producers have had annual average amounts of about $7.7 billion, increasing to $10.3 billion in 1970.

Both exports and imports of the non-oil-producing countries increased sharply from 1968 to 1970 in comparison with the period 1960–68. Exports in 1970 were 196 percent of 1960; in 1968, 153 per-

22. Cf. chapter 4.
23. *Annual Report,* 1966, p. 32. The report for 1968, p. 51, has a similar table but the country coverage differs.

Table 13. *Trade Balances of Developing Countries, 1960–70 (Billions of Dollars).*

	1960	1961	1962	1963	1964	1965	1966	1967	1968	1869	1970
Developing countries[a]											
Exports (f.o.b.)	.27.5	27.8	29.6	32.2	35.3	37.8	40.4	41.6	45.2	50.8	56.4
Imports (c.i.f.)	−31.5	−32.5	−33.2	−34.8	−37.9	−39.7	−43.5	−45.4	−49.5	−53.9	−59.9
Trade balance	−4.0	−4.7	−3.6	−2.6	−2.6	−1.9	−3.1	−3.8	−4.2	−3.1	−3.5
Developing countries excluding major petroleum exporters[b]											
Exports (f.o.b.)	21.7	22.0	23.0	25.4	27.4	29.4	31.5	31.0	33.4	38.1	42.6
Imports (c.i.f.)	−28.7	−29.7	−30.4	−32.2	−34.8	−36.7	−39.4	−39.5	−42.6	−46.9	−52.9
Trade balance	−7.0	−7.7	−7.4	−6.8	−7.4	−7.3	−7.8	−8.5	−9.2	−8.8	−10.3

Source: IBRD. *Annual Report*, 1966. p.32; IFNS. Aug. 1971, pp. 36–39.
a. Including southern European developing countries other than Spain.
b. Middle-East oil producers and Venezuela (Saudi Arabian imports and exports have been in part estimated).

cent of 1960. Imports, however, also increased relatively, 184 and 148 percent respectively of 1960. In terms of compounded rates, exports increased from 1960 to 1968 at 5.54 percent, from 1960 to 1970 by 6.98 percent. Imports also increased considerably from annual (compounded) rates of 5.06 percent, 1960–68, to 6.31 percent, 1960–70.

The rise in prices of exports and imports accounts for a good part of the growth. At deflated prices, the export growth rate between 1960 and 1968 was 5.14 percent, and to 1970, 5.52 percent.[24] But a 14.6 percent increase in exports in deflated prices over a 2-year period is by no means negligible. While almost all countries increased their exports, a few had very sharp increases in volume, notably, Brazil, China (Taiwan), Hong Kong and Korea. Imports increased at rapid rates also in terms of deflated prices, i.e., at rates of 4.7 percent in 1960–68, and 5.39 percent in 1960–70. Some of the increases in export receipts went to reserves (e.g., in the countries whose volumes expanded most rapidly), some to increased imports and some to debt service.

As a matter of interest, algebraic projections were made from the table data to determine when the non-petroleum producers would have exports equaling imports. On the basis of 1968 current dollar values for exports and imports, projected at the growth rate, 1960 to 1968, balance would be reached in 53.7 years. Projecting 1970 figures at rates 1960–70, the deficits would disappear on the average in 34.4 years. These results project rates of price increases as well as exports and imports. If the current trade data are deflated by the respective index numbers, balance on the 1968 trade data would be reached in 64.5 years. On the basis of 1970 data and 1960–70 rates, the deficits would disappear in 244 years. This curious result follows from the more rapid increase in imports (deflated) in the later years than in the earlier.

These computerized algebraic results should be regarded merely as such. They are not a forecast. They may serve as a note of caution to model builders who project steady and disparate growth rates. Compound rate calculations of trade data implicitly assume the independence of imports and exports, when in fact they are not. Moreover, results follow from the particular numbers in the table. The inclusion or exclusion of a single country, or selection of a particular base year, as indicated, show widely differing results.

The 1970 IMF *Annual Report* presents data on the trade balances of primary-producing countries, a classification which is broader than

---

24. Export and import figures were deflated by the U.N. index of export prices, excluding petroleum, and the import price index, with country weights based on transactions in 1963.

Table 14. Trade Balances of Primary-Producing Countries, 1965–69 (Billions of Dollars).

	1965	1966	1967	1968	1969
Total primary-producing countries	−7.7	−7.7	−7.9	−7.6	−7.2
Excluded countries[a]	−4.7	−4.2	−4.0	−3.8	−4.0
Developing countries	−3.0	−3.5	−3.9	−3.8	−3.2
Oil producers[b]	4.8	5.2	5.8	6.4	6.7
Non-oil producing developing countries	−7.8	−8.6	−9.7	−10.3	−9.8

Source: IMF, *Annual Report*, 1970, pp. 66, 69, 71; IFNS (figures have been rounded).
a. Finland, Iceland, Ireland, Spain, Australia, New Zealand and South Africa.
b. Middle-East oil producers, Libya and Venezuela.

the OECD-DAC classification of developing countries. An attempt is made in Table 14 to show data comparable to the preceding, though apparently the Fund data are more inclusive. On the Fund basis, the non-oil-producing countries showed rather larger deficits. While the LDCs' total deficits decreased by some $600 million in 1969 as the consequence of increased exports of oil, ores, metals and some other exports, the trade balance of the countries not primarily oil producers improved by $400 million, with higher prices for metals and some other products as well as a drop in imports by India.

Revised data for 1967 to 1970 in the 1971 IMF *Report* (p. 78) indicate somewhat smaller trade deficits for the non-oil-producing developing countries for 1967, 1968 and 1969, but an increase to $10.6 billion in 1970.

Precise annual changes in aggregate deficits are of minor importance for the analysis of the debt problem. It is significant, however, that the non-oil producers have large annual deficits, the oil producers, generally, large surpluses. The non-oil countries with surpluses were mainly exporters of minerals, e.g., Zambia, Congo, Chile and Peru. The non-mineral surplus countries were Argentina, Ghana, Nigeria and the Ivory Coast. (Nigeria's increased exports were mostly new oil production; Peru's largely fish products.)

The value of exports depends on production levels and world prices, which, in turn, are related to production and prices in the industrial countries. Import levels are set in part by what may be regarded as "autonomous" factors—population, income, consumption standards and prices. In part, import levels are the result of borrowing and aid received. The deficits will vary in the same direction as the amount of external resources provided varies.

The non-oil countries have received aid on loan and grant terms. The oil countries have not been heavy borrowers or grant-aid recipients.

"Autonomous" imports are themselves conditioned by export receipts. Monetary reserves can be a buffer; IMF drawings and other credit can help cover a short-fall. From a long-run point of view, per contra, imports of capital will lead to an expansion of exports if investment is directed to potential export production. With the complex interaction of the factors affecting the exports and balance of payments positions of the debtor countries, the future is not predictable except in the broadest terms. It seems a fair inference, however, that non-oil exporters are not likely to increase their exports sufficiently to keep up with their increased debt service (see Table 15). Among these countries, the mineral exporters have done better than those primarily exporting agricultural goods.

Table 15 shows the increase in debt service in the last 10 years compared with export receipts. Column (4) is the ratio of total debt service to exports for all LDCs, including the oil producers. Column (5), debt service as a ratio to export receipts of non-oil producers, can be somewhat misleading since the debt service of oil-producing countries is included. The parenthetic figures represent a correction made for known payments of principal and interest of the main oil countries.

Table 15. Exports and Debt Service, 1960–70 (Billions of Dollars).

	(1) Exports LDC	(2) Exports non-oil LDC	(3) Debt service LDC[a]	(4) Ratio (3)/(1)	(5) Ratio (3)/(2)[b]
1960	27.5	21.7	—	—	—
1961	27.8	22.0	2.3	8.3	10.4
1962	29.6	23.0	2.6	8.8	11.3
1963	32.2	25.4	2.7	8.4	10.6
1964	35.3	27.4	3.2	9.1	11.7
1965	37.8	29.4	3.4	9.0	11.6 (11.2)
1966	40.4	31.5	3.8	9.4	12.0 (11.6)
1967	41.6	31.0	4.0	9.6	12.8 (12.4)
1968	45.3	33.4	4.5	10.0	13.6 (12.9)
1969	50.8	38.1	5.0	9.8	13.0 (12.5)
1970	56.4	42.6	6.0[c]	10.6	14.0 (13.5)

a. IBRD Estimates for 80 developing countries, including oil-producers. The combined debt service of Iran, Iraq and Venezuela increased from about $121 million in 1965 to $211 million in 1969.

b. Numbers in parentheses are estimates for the debt service ratio of non-oil producers. Ratios have been calculated from unrounded figures.

c. Projected.

They are, at best, approximate. The ratios shown here are somewhat higher than the normally computed debt service ratio, based on receipts from goods and services.

Debt service has been increasing at 10 percent[25] compounded annually over the last 10 years, a rate considerably higher than the growth rate of exports of all the developing countries, and particularly of the non-oil producers, which are the principal debtors. Debt service has become an increasing charge against export earnings. The denominator in the debt service/exports rate increased sharply with the rise in prices in recent years. The numerator has been less affected since grace periods have not yet run out on new loans, but higher interest costs were reflected in the payments of countries which had rolled over debt, e.g., Mexico and Argentina. On the other hand, principal payments were reduced for some countries as the result of refunding at longer terms.

Compounded rates should not be projected far into the future, since debt service will depend on the level of borrowing and the terms applicable as well as price levels. Aid levels and terms are unpredictable.

The aggregates of debt service and exports are heavily weighted by the figures for the larger countries. Sixteen countries account for almost three-fourths of the debt,[26] but debt service has increased for most LDCs as a ratio to their exchange receipts. Some of the heavily indebted countries, e.g., Korea and Brazil, have greatly increased exports (and imports). Other debtors, India and Pakistan, have shown only moderate increases.

For the LDCs as a whole, excepting the oil and mineral exporters, there seems little prospect that they will attain a position of current account surplus, a necessary condition for *net* repayment of debt. For most, as their debt service increases, their problems will become more acute.

Export potential is not the only factor in ability to service debt. The debtor country may not generate or mobilize internal savings in sufficient amount to pay the local currency equivalent of debt service through voluntary savings or taxation. Investment financed through foreign loans may not be productive of net revenue, either in local currency or exchange. Inflation is a factor not only in discouraging

25. Calculation of growth rates at compound interest formulae depends on the years selected, so that similar data can yield different rates. The IBRD, *Annual Report,* 1971, p. 50, reports a 14 percent compound rate between 1956 and 1969 and a rate of 9 percent in the 1960s. It recognizes that the earlier data were less adequate.

26. Ibid., pp. 50, 64.

internal savings, but in the investment of external capital as well as the misdirection of production. Overvalued exchange rates are a further factor. Political events are often important, e.g., coups d'état affect revenue collection, induce a flight of capital, disrupt trade, and are likely to induce new waves of inflation. The East Pakistan situation (1971) will adversely affect both Pakistan and India. Political considerations may direct resources to military purposes or to conspicuous public consumption, e.g., presidential palaces, ornate public buildings or to ill-advised and improperly planned highways and other labor intensive works in election years (where they are important) or as means of alleviating chronic underemployment. When these elements are combined with heavy debt service, they may precipitate crises.

THE DEBT SERVICE RATIO

Current Ratios

The percent ratio of payments of interest and amortization in a given year and the country's receipts from exports of goods and services, has, in the last 20 years or so, become a convenient measure of debt burdens, and a factor in determining lending policies. Table 16 shows the debt service ratios for all countries whose ratios exceeded 8 percent in any of the years 1965 to 1969. (Ratios are not given for a few countries, notably the U.A.R., whose data are regarded as confidential.) It is significant that there have been multilateral or bilateral refundings of the debt of most of the countries with ratios over 10 percent. The important exceptions are Mexico, Israel, Iran, Korea and Colombia, which have high ratios but have been able to handle their debt problem satisfactorily.[27] Minor reschedulings have occurred in other cases of countries with high ratios, e.g., Afghanistan, Costa Rica, and Ethiopia. Per contra, there have been refunding arrangements in some countries, e.g., Liberia and the Philippines, which have relatively low ratios. Pakistan is currently servicing only part of its debt. In sum, the 10 percent ratio should not be regarded as a critical ratio,[28] though it does point to problems.

The significance of the debt service ratio has sometimes been questioned. Certainly, it does not tell the whole story. As computed by the

27. Cf. chapter 4.
28. The data used are not always precise, and IBRD computations for various countries made at different times have changed as better data have become available.

Table 16. Debt Service Ratios, 1965–69, Selected Countries.[a]

	1965	1966	1967	1968	1969
Chad[b]	n.a.	n.a.	2.9	11.5	9.9
Ethiopia	4.9	7.6	9.5	9.2	10.6
Gabon[b]	5.0	5.4	5.8	8.0	8.2
Ghana	18.8	6.5	7.2	12.3	9.9
Guinea[b]	n.a.	n.a.	n.a.	8.9	n.a.
Liberia	8.6	6.0	6.0	6.8	6.4
Malagasy R.	n.a.	3.8	8.7	6.1	5.8
Mali	11.8	11.8	16.1	14.5	23.2
Morocco	4.7	6.8	6.6	7.2	8.5
Sierra Leone	6.1	7.6	8.7	6.1	7.0
Sudan	5.7	6.5	5.4	7.1	9.3
Tunisia	7.4	14.2	20.1	22.4	20.4
Uganda[c]	n.a.	4.4	5.5	8.4	9.7
Upper Volta[b]	3.4	3.7	4.5	7.5	8.7
Turkey	24.5	17.6	14.7	13.9	16.7
Yugoslavia[d]	14.0	13.1	12.1	13.0	14.6
Iran[e]	8.6	7.6	7.8	10.5	13.8
Israel	21.4	20.3	14.5	16.2	16.5
Syria	n.a.	n.a.	6.8	7.5	8.8
Korea	2.7	3.6	5.6	7.5	12.4
Afghanistan	7.9	8.9	16.6	16.6	20.0
India	16.5	19.8	22.6	20.3	22.0
Indonesia	11.0	9.1	7.0	9.1	5.9
Pakistan	11.0	12.9	16.8	19.4	21.7
Argentina	20.1	25.3	26.8	27.2	23.9
Brazil[f]	n.a.	n.a.	n.a.	20.9	17.9
Chile	15.3	13.2	12.4	16.0	15.9
Colombia	14.4	16.5	14.0	12.8	11.2
Costa Rica	10.3	12.0	11.9	12.1	10.5
Dominican R.	19.3	12.6	7.2	7.8	8.7
Ecuador	6.3	6.4	6.3	8.3	10.4
Guatemala	5.0	5.5	9.8	8.5	8.7
Mexico	24.7	21.2	21.5	25.1	22.4
Nicaragua	4.3	5.3	6.1	6.7	9.1
Paraguay	6.6	5.4	7.2	9.4	8.8
Peru	6.8	9.7	10.6	22.0	13.8
Uruguay	6.7	12.3	20.3	19.2	18.8

Source: IBRD.

a. Debt service payments on external public and publicly-guaranteed debt as percent ratio of export of goods and services. Payments on short-term (under one year) debts are excluded. Countries listed are all for which data are available whose ratio in any year was more than 8 percent.

b. Exports of goods only. Ratios would be lower if data on invisibles were available.

c. Includes one-third of the debt service of the East African Community.

d. Excludes debt service on nonguaranteed debt of the "social sector" contracted after March 31, 1966.

e. Iran ratio based on oil exports.

f. Includes some debt service on nonguaranteed debt.

World Bank, the numerator is the service of public and publicly guaranteed debt. The balance of payments of the debtor nation must provide the wherewithal to service private debt as well. In countries with a predominantly private economy, private debts are large proportions of the total, e.g., in Argentina, Brazil, Colombia and the Philippines. If private debt service were included, the ratios would be, say, from a fourth to a third higher. Many of these private obligations have been covered by exchange assurances, though not guarantees. In Yugoslavia, the ratio does not include the debts of nonguaranteed enterprises, though they are not exactly private. There can be a shifting between public and private accounts, particularly in the case of supplier credits. In many cases the amount of private debt is not known to the authorities, and its service may appear in IMF balance of payments tables as part of errors and omissions.

The ratio expressed in terms of goods and service receipts is more useful than one in terms of exports only for countries with appreciable income from tourism (Mexico), shipping receipts (Greece) or earnings of workers abroad (Turkey). The measure will be less reliable if the debtor receives relatively larger amounts of unrequited transfers, gifts and grants, remittances or reparations. Even export figures may not be adequate when a country receives only part of the proceeds of the earnings of concessions.

The simple debt service ratio measures two significant variables for a given year. As a liquidity ratio, it measures vulnerability of the debtor country to decreases in export earnings, or to variations in the net inflow of capital. With a low ratio, a moderate contraction of imports may be sufficient to enable the debtor to maintain its credit. There are limitations to belt-tightening, or as the Ghanaian Prime Minister quoted a local proverb, "the debtor still must eat."[29] With a high ratio, it is more difficult to pay debt by contracting imports needed to maintain production and consumption standards. Under adverse circumstances, the debtor may default (old style) or request refunding (new style).

Whether a ratio of 5, 10 or 20 percent is prudent from the point of view of either debtor or creditor is debatable. It has been said that the IBRD at one time regarded a 10 percent ratio of public debt service as a criterion of credit-worthiness and the Ex-Im, 15–20 percent of debt service on private and public debt.[30] Obviously, other factors must be

29. *New York Times,* Jan. 30, 1970, p. 50.
30. O.A.S., *Financing of Economic Development in Latin America,* (Pan American Union, 1958) pp. 125, 135.

taken into consideration. Neither institution has, as far as known, officially stated a crucial ratio, and certainly in recent years they have, and the IDB as well, made loans to countries with considerably higher ratios, e.g., Argentina, Brazil, Mexico, India and Pakistan, to mention only the larger countries. The bank staffs, however, generally show the debt service ratio as a significant factor in appraising loans.

Before their defaults on bonds in the 1931–33 period, the Latin American countries on the average had debt service ratios between 11 and 13 percent in 1929[31] and these ratios increased sharply during the depression years with the drop in exports. The variation among countries was considerable. At the extreme in 1932, Chile's contractual debt service was 102.6 percent of its exports. At the time of their depression defaults on bond issues, the debt service ratios of individual Latin-American countries ranged between 16.3 and 28.4 percent.[32] While 1930–33 data on bond defaults may not be quite appropriate today, it has been noted that most of the countries whose debts have been refunded in recent years have had ratios above 10 percent.

The debt ratio for a single year can be misleading as an indicator of future debt troubles. A drop in exports in a given year for whatever reason will raise the ratio for that year, only to fall in the following year if exports increase. The ratio may be high, exports constant, because a maturing debt, say, a bond issue, has been paid off in that year even though sinking funds had been built up in prior years. (This possibility is not important for most countries.) Countries with medium-term debts to banks may have a continuing high ratio, even though as one note is paid off, a new one is given. As long as credit is good (e.g., Mexico) they may renew without a net payment of principal. A regularly increasing ratio, especially with increased exchange earnings, may indicate trouble ahead.

The IBRD has been concerned with the rapid rise in debt service in comparison with the exchange earnings of the LDCs,[33] and has computed the debt service ratios. The general trend has been upward, and most of the instances of decreased ratios result from the reduction in payments accorded in refundings. Averages and aggregates are heavily weighted by the larger debtor countries. The ratios have increased also for smaller countries whose debt in the aggregate is small, but whose

31. By two different methods of estimation (U.N., *External Financing in Latin America*, 1965, pp. 28, 201); Dragoslav Avramovic, *Debt Servicing Capacity and Post War Growth in International Indebtedness* (Baltimore: Johns Hopkins Press, 1958) p. 194.

32. R. F. Mikesell, *U.S. Private and Government Investment Abroad*, p. 383.

33. Cf. IBRD, *Annual Report*, 1965–66, pp. 33–37; 1968, pp. 35–38; 1970, pp. 49–53.

exchange earnings are also small, e.g., African countries (not oil producers).

To use the current debt service ratio as an indicator of future debt troubles implicitly assumes that the present conditions will continue. This needs qualification. Countries with a high proportion of medium-term debt will have higher ratios than countries with longer-term debt. If maturing debts have been paid in a given year, the ratio will fall later. If they are banking debts, they may be rolled over with no change in the numerator of the ratio. On the other hand, a country may have a low ratio at present, but the ratio will rise in coming years as grace periods run out. The DAC has recently used an adjusted average debt service ratio to try to deal with this factor. Neither form of the ratio takes account of indebtedness to be incurred in the future.

The denominator will also change. Korea has increased exports from $175 million in 1965 to an annual rate of $968 million at the end of 1970. In the same period, Israel moved from $430 million to $811 million. Large percent increases were shown by some other heavily indebted non-oil producers such as Brazil. It is doubtful that these rapid increases in exports will continue indefinitely. To make a forecast of the future problems of countries, some hazardous assumptions must be made.

Another construction noted below tries to forecast by making a range of assumptions on exports and the rate at which debt will be incurred.

Adjusted Average Debt Service Ratio

The 1969 and 1970 DAC reviews of development assistance have introduced a variation on the simple debt service ratio by taking into account the total debt service due over the next 15 years. The "adjusted 1 to 15 years average debt service ratio" (1970) divides the mean of 15 years contractual service (less monetary reserves in excess of two months' imports) by exchange receipts on goods and services account for the latest year.[34] By including service over a longer period than a single year, it takes account of the situation of countries whose ratios now may be low because of grace periods, but whose service costs will mount in the future as grace runs out. The ratios so computed are generally higher than current ratios for countries which have received larger amounts of concessional aid at long term, and the ratios are

34. DAC, *Development Assistance*, 1970, pp. 154–56.

lower for countries which have borrowed at shorter term from institutions, banks and suppliers. The computation includes only debt now on the books.

The DAC report plots these ratios against per capita GNP figures, without stressing the doubtful character of these figures when used as more than a very rough yardstick.[35] With some appropriate caveats, the *Review* concludes that countries with low ratios and higher per capita GNP "do not raise serious problems," and conversely, low income and high debt ratio countries face difficulties and should seek aid on lenient terms. As an argument for giving aid on easy terms to poor countries (DAC's raison d'être), this construction is relevant.

It is more doubtful as a predictive measure of debt difficulties. Most of the countries with an adjusted debt ratio of about 10 percent or more have had their debts refunded multilaterally or bilaterally (except Mexico and Korea) or are currently in trouble (e.g., Pakistan) whether they are relatively rich (Argentina, Chile) or poor (India, Indonesia). On the other hand, some countries with lower adjusted ratios (Uruguay, Yugoslavia, Liberia and the Philippines) have also had to refund, largely because of the shorter-term character of their debt. The DAC adjusted average ratio is less satisfactory than the simple ratio for such countries. It may indicate a problem in the future for countries such as Korea, whose simple ratio (7.5) for 1968 is not high, but has been increasing to 12.4 in 1969.

The Frank Projection

An econometric study by Frank and Cline[36] concluded on the basis of past experience that three variables had significant predictive value: the simple debt service ratio, the amortization/debt ratio, and less importantly, the imports/reserve ratio. Reserves of the LDCs generally are sufficient to cover only a few months imports and those with relatively larger reserves (e.g., Libya) are often not heavily indebted. Reserves, however, may be crucial if a country is regularly rolling over relatively short-term debt. The amortization/debt ratio for one year or the related average maturity of debt will be reflected in the num-

35. Among the qualifications to these figures may be mentioned the calculation of GNP in countries where a large part of the economy is nonmarket, conversion into dollars at official exchange rates in inflationary situations, and projections of population on the basis of dubious initial data. DAC annual reviews use these data to measure growth of the LDCs, e.g., 1970, pp. 90–92. The justification may be that there are no better figures.

36. Charles R. Frank, Jr. and William R. Cline, "Debt Servicing and Foreign Assistance: An Analysis of Problems and Prospects in Less Developed Countries," *AID Discussion Paper*, no. 19 (June 1969).

erator of the simple debt service ratio, so that they are not, however, independent variables.

Debt service ratios are computed on currently outstanding debt and current exchange receipts. In practice, both parts of the fraction will change over time as new debt is incurred and exports increase (or decrease). The problem for the future is the relative rates of change. To forecast statistically it is necessary to make assumptions about the rate of new borrowing and the terms of the debt and the rate of increase in exports. Frank has made such projections on alternative assumptions, that exports increase at compound rates of 4 or 8 percent and that debt increases either by constant gross amounts at present terms or at increasing amounts to provide constant net aid (gross aid less amortization). He concludes that one group of countries (India, Indonesia, Pakistan and Tunisia—what may be regarded as "hard-core" aid recipients) are likely to have debt troubles for most of the next 25 years. A second group, the larger Latin American countries plus Israel, Korea and Turkey, are likely to be in trouble a good part of the time, but Bolivia, Iran and Nigeria are likely to avoid debt crises.[37] He concludes, however, that his results may be optimistic. Terms of aid have been hardening; new aid may not in fact be net; countries must also service private debt not included in the ratios of official debt.

The Frank and DAC studies shed additional light on the debt problem of less-developed countries, particularly in directing attention to prospective problems in some countries which have not had debt crises. Mexico has been able to roll over its debt quite successfully. Other countries, e.g., Tunisia, Colombia have been aided in ways that have avoided sharp crises, but may find things more difficult if program aid is not forthcoming in the amounts needed. Projection of exchange receipts and rates of increase on the basis of the recent past may prove over-optimistic, if the industrial countries generally, not merely the United States, bring their inflations under control. On the other side, exchange adjustments have been helpful in the Argentine and Brazil and could benefit other heavily indebted countries. Political factors are important, but scarcely predictable.

DEBT BURDEN, PRICE LEVELS AND EXCHANGE SYSTEMS

For more than two centuries it has been recognized that rising prices

37. Charles R. Frank, Jr., *Debt and Terms of Aid* (Washington: Overseas Development Council, 1970) pp. 34–37.

favor the debtor by enabling him to pay debt with money of less real value in commodity terms. As Adam Smith put it, "when the coin is debased, a debt of twenty shillings is then paid with ten."[38] In simple algebraic terms the real value of a dollar paid in 2011 in amortization of an AID loan made this year would be worth 45 percent of the dollar loaned, if inflation continues at 2 percent per annum compounded. If inflation is at 3 percent, as in France and the United States since 1964, the real value of the dollar repaid in the 10th year would be 74 percent and in the 40th year 31 percent of present purchasing power. At 4 percent inflation as in the U.K. since 1964 the corresponding amounts would be 68 and 21 percent respectively. Algebra and B.L.S. and similar index numbers apply directly when the obligor and the creditor use the same currency. International debt payments involve two or more currencies, rates of inflation and the balances of payments of debtor and creditor countries.

It may well be argued that the rate of inflation in the creditor countries is likely to be such as materially to reduce the burden of repayment so that the argument of the preceding sections may be overstated. That is, while debt service will increase at some compound rate, the compounding will be offset by the diminishing value of the money required for interest and amortization. The debtors surely gained relatively in repayment in currencies of creditor countries which were inflated in the two world wars and their aftermath. On the other hand, the burden of debt increased greatly during the depression of the 1930s and was a significant factor in the general defaults in international debt at that time. Under present conditions with debt service increasing at a compound rate in the neighborhood of 10 percent, the rate of inflation in the creditor countries is not likely to be that high. There may be some offsetting, but not enough to give much consolation to the heavily indebted.

Relative exchange rates of debtor and creditor currencies may be taken as a first approximation. Balance of payments effects are more involved. While the dollars paid in 1970 under the Anglo-American Financial Agreement had a purchasing power of about half of the dol-

38. *Lectures on Justice, Police, Revenue and Arms* (1763), ed. Edwin Cannan (Oxford: Clarendon Press, 1896), p. 188. *The Wealth of Nations*, bk. IV, chap. III, gives various examples. The same argument was advanced by some of the French financial writers in the preceding fifty years. As a practical device in a period of paper inflation, the colony of Massachusetts in 1747 established a crude tabular standard for the payment of debt. See Irving Fisher, *The Making of Index Numbers*, (Boston: Houghton Mifflin, 1927), p. 458. In fact price index numbers owe their origin largely to proposals for tabular standards as a device for equity in long-term debt and rent contracts.

lars loaned in 1945, the British budget had to provide 68 percent more in sterling to make the payment. (The 1971 payment was somewhat less costly.) If the creditor currency is devalued with the debtor currency unchanged, debt repayment, in money terms at least, is easier. An Australian could pay a debt of £1000 with A$2143 in 1968 as opposed to A$2500 before the 1967 devaluation. New Zealand debtors gained no currency advantage since their dollar followed sterling. (The balance of payments effects in these two countries would require special study.) Conversely with the revaluations of the Deutsche Mark, debts denominated in that currency became more burdensome in terms of debtor currencies, e.g., some of the loans by the IBRD and IDB. No doubt in some of the debtor countries with rates pegged to the dollar (or sterling) the increased cost was partly offset by rising prices at home so that the payments in local currency represented lower real costs.

Devaluation of the debtor currency, with no changes in creditor pars, requires the debtors to provide more in local currency from earnings or budgets to meet their payments. The situation of the individual, say, private, debtor will be different than that of the government or central bank. For the individual debtor the effect will depend on domestic prices and earnings. For the government the question is partly a budgetary problem and partly a balance of payments problem.

The rate of inflation has probably been generally higher in the debtor countries in recent years than in the industrial countries, particularly those with the heaviest debts.[39] Fixed rates of exchange have in many (or most) instances lagged behind price levels. Floating rates have also tended to lag behind inflation, though there is probably no theoretical way of establishing what rate would reflect purchasing power.[40]

To service international debt the local currency equivalent must first be realized by the debtor. An exception would be the debt of a

39. A satisfactory statistical comparison is difficult. The principal indices that can be compared are of consumer prices computed in various ways. These indices may not be adequate to measure local costs of living and may not be representative of commodity prices. They may have only a limited relation to the value of exports. In the industrial countries consumer prices have generally increased more than wholesale prices.

40. Floating rates are controlled by central bank intervention, so that they become administratively controlled rates. Central authorities tend to be optimistic about the future course of the balance of payments and so intervene to check the rise in the rates of foreign currencies until their reserves run low. The theoretical issues in the purchasing power parity theory are passed over here. The internal purchasing power of a currency (which is important for the private debtor's situation) may not be related to the prices of exports in a direct way, and at a minimum, the balance of payments includes invisibles.

concessionaire, which may be permitted to service its debt from retained exchange earnings. In some multiple currency systems exporters may have a similar privilege.

Inflation is generally advantageous to the private borrower, obviously when he borrows on the domestic market and interest rates are not high enough to compensate for the price rise, but often also when he borrows abroad. In Chile, for example, real interest rates have been negative for decades. Even the present discount rate of 20 percent in Chile and Brazil may not be enough to restrain profitable private borrowing. When the private firm borrows abroad on export credit terms, for example, the interest rate is low. As prices go up, sales proceeds increase faster than the cost of sales. If the exchange rate is fixed, amortization and interest cost can be met easily from profits. If the exchange rate floats, with a lag behind prices, the borrower has to pay more in local currency for his foreign exchange requirements, but he still has an exchange advantage (at the expense of the central bank) as well as an interest advantage. Various devices can be used to reduce or eliminate these advantages, such as the imposition of higher rates on dollars for debt payment than for imports, or exchange trading in dual markets. (In Chile recently, the dollar cost more than twice as much for invisible than for trade transactions.) Of course, administrative action can restrict private borrowing abroad.

The governmental or public utility borrower may not have these advantages. Utility rates generally lag behind the inflation of the general price level, so that costs may go up more than receipts. Public revenues also tend to lag. Taxes may be specific; customs duties, even if ad valorem, will lag since the unit price of imports will not rise as fast as domestic prices (e.g. Chile, Portugal, Philippines, Korea, but the contrary in Venezuela); taxes on personal and corporate income are based on a prior accounting period. Hence the budgetary deficit is likely to increase so that borrowing from the central bank increases and feeds the inflation. When the government buys exchange at a favorable rate the rise in prices may not be fully reflected in the local currency cost of servicing foreign debt, at the expense of the exchange authorities.

Foreign debt, public and private, must be serviced through the balance of payments of the debtor country. Inflation is likely to increase payments deficits though not necessarily in proportion. Some countries export a limited range of products, whose prices may be determined on international markets. Local costs may have little effect on these prices which depend on demand in the industrial countries and the production of the same commodities in other areas, e.g., copper, cacao, coffee. Inflation in one producing country may reduce its production and export of a particular commodity, and so worsen the balance of payments. But a fall in world market prices may also increase the deficit without regard to local inflation. The more diversified the production and exports of a given country the closer is the relation between its internal prices and its exports.

On the import side inflation increases the demand for foreign goods. Rising nominal incomes are spent in part for imported goods. The effect is probably most pronounced in countries which import a high proportion of their consumption goods, and demand increases particularly for the goods consumed by those who benefit from the inflation.

In general, then, it appears that the governmental debtor under inflationary conditions faces both internal and external difficulties in servicing its debt. It may not be able to raise revenues in the requisite amount and its balance of payments is likely to deteriorate. The budgetary problem can exist without regard to inflation. The level of savings in the less developed countries is low. Voluntary savings cannot readily be tapped for noninflationary public financing of development and debt service. Involuntary saving through taxation is hampered by tax structures and policy.[41] Inflation exacerbates these difficulties. The balance of payments deficits may be financed by additional borrowing, as they have been, but debt service increases until the lenders call a halt.

The preceding discussion has been in terms of a single developing country. Most of the argument applies as well to the industrial countries—need it be said—though they have greater flexibility in fiscal and monetary policy, which they may be reluctant to employ. In recent years there has been inflation in both creditor and debtor countries, with consequent disruption of their balances of payments. The sharp increase in prices in the industrial countries from 1967 to 1971, and also in the developing countries, led to a rapid increase in the value of exports by the latter group, whether petroleum producers or not.[42] Imports increased as well. The deficits of the non-petroleum developing countries continued. The situation of individual countries

41. IBRD, *Annual Report*, 1970, pp. 53–55, has a brief discussion.
42. Cf. pp. 57–60 above. Export prices for LDCs increased more rapidly than import prices. The composite index numbers may be regarded as statistical approximations.

varied with the commodity composition of their exports, the amount of aid received, and inflation.

If inflation is arrested in the industrial countries or reduced to a moderate rate of one or two percent for a period of years, without serious curtailment of output, the volume of exports of the LDCs is likely to increase. The consequences for the value of exports are less sure. Equilibrium in the United States balance of payments will require the reduction of imports, though the drop is likely to affect U.S. imports from the industrial countries more than from developing countries. Other countries will have smaller dollar receipts and so may reduce their imports from LDCs. The complex interaction on the balances of payments of the world are scarcely predictable.

The short-lived period of floating exchange rates has been followed by agreement on a new set of "central rates" and the allowance of wider margins. Some of the LDCs will maintain existing relations with the dollar, some with sterling. The currency cost of debt service will not change for the former group for their dollar debt. The currency cost of service in DM will increase. Most of the existing debt is denominated in dollars. The effects of the dollar devaluation and revaluation of other currencies on the balances of payments of the debtors will not be clear for several years. The immediate future of world payments is even less predictable than it was when the world economy was so heavily financed by a steady net outflow of dollars. Some individual debtors may find that they will be in a better situation to service their debt, others will be worse off.

The one safely predictable consequence of inflation in the creditor countries, particularly the United States, is that what they receive in payment of amortization of existing debt will have less real value than what was originally lent. While the debtors can pay in depreciated money, there is no assurance that payment will be easier. The course of commodity prices in international trade and the balance of payments consequences are too uncertain. If inflation persists even at a low compound rate, however, the cost of additional borrowing will increase. Many of the debtors are repetitive borrowers. As prices increase in the creditor countries they will have to borrow larger amounts to obtain a given quantum of development goods or commodities used for consumption. Debt will increase at a faster rate or development programs will be curtailed. A price factor will be added to the compounding of debt service costs.

The reverse problems which would arise if prices fell seriously in the creditor countries will not be elaborated here. Falling prices do not seem likely short of a world-wide depression, and governments will not wittingly adopt measures that would result in sharp drops of employment and production.

SUMMARY

To reduce debt a country must pay a larger amount in amortization of old debt than it borrows currently. It can do this by achieving a surplus of its export and other exchange receipts over its imports, current debt service, and other invisible payments, or using its exchange reserves, which generally, however, are not large enough to reduce debt as well as cover financing requirements for current account purposes. The amount of net debt repayment in recent years has been insignificant. A few countries have reduced their debt in some years, but borrowed more in following years. Some others have held their external debt fairly constant in principal amount and have covered interest costs from current receipts. Most have regularly increased their borrowings at rates which have exceeded payment of debt service.

Debt service has been increasing at a compound rate of about 10 percent per annum, a rate higher than the growth of export and invisible receipts for most countries except the oil producers. Their debt service ratios have risen accordingly. Debt service ratios have decreased for some countries because their exports have expanded rapidly; in some, concessional-term loans have replaced harder-term loans; in others, a reduced ratio has resulted from formal refundings.[43]

As net indebtedness increases, debt service becomes larger in proportion to new borrowings and may eventually reach the point at which new loans provide no net resources unless the amount of new borrowing increases at some compound rate larger than debt service. This process can continue as long as the creditor countries are willing to lend (or grant), particularly in ways which facilitate debt payment.[44] The creditors in this way help pay off debts to themselves, their nationals and others. If the amount of new resources decreases, the difficulties of the debtors, whose economies have become dependent on foreign assistance, are likely to become more acute.

Recent experience does not indicate that the countries which are

43. Cf. Table 15 and Table 16.
44. Cf. chapter 3.

heavily indebted, relative to the size of their economies, are likely to attain the balance of payments surpluses which would enable them to stop the spiral of debt and debt service. The oil producers have had substantial surpluses, but they are generally not heavily indebted. Iran and Venezuela have, however, increased their debt. For the non-oil countries exports have increased by almost 7 percent compounded over the last decade in current prices and at a rate of 5.5 percent at deflated prices.[45] The countries producing metallic minerals and some with textile and other manufactures (e.g. Hong Kong, Korea, Taiwan) have fared better than most. Some of the heavily indebted (e.g. India, Pakistan, Colombia) have had less than average export growth rates.[46]

To some degree the inflation of the creditor currencies may alleviate the burden of debt, but will increase the rate of debt accumulation, unless the transfer of real resources is to be curtailed. Moreover, inflation in the debtor countries worsens their balance of payments situation, and generally impedes the mobilization of savings to pay debt service in local currency, neglecting the transfer problem. The longer-run balance of payments consequences of the monetary adjustments of 1971–72 are not yet apparent.

It seems to follow then, that for the immediate future, say, 10 years, there will have to be adjustment of the debt obligations of some countries additional to those which have already had refundings, unless the creditors continue, as they have, the process of indirect refunding.

45. See above, p. 59.
46. Cf. IMF, *Annual Report*, 1970, p. 106.

3. METHODS OF DEBT REFUNDING

Debt relief has been provided by the creditors in a variety of direct and indirect ways. There is no generally agreed terminology, and specific arrangements have often involved the use of several devices as described below. "Refunding" is probably the broadest term and may be used for several of the direct relief methods. In the original IBRD-DAC terminology under the Expanded Reporting System (1967–68) three types of debt refunding were specified: consolidation, rescheduling, and refinancing; this terminology has been embodied in the Treasury regulation governing the reporting by U.S. agencies.[1] These methods of refunding are conceptually clear, but it is sometimes difficult to classify a particular transaction, as when a government refunds private credits that it has previously guaranteed or when an arrangement is made which includes several types of refunding in one "package." In the "club" arrangements discussed below, different methods have been used by the creditor countries to satisfy the requirements of a given situation. It has been proposed to extend the definition of "refinancing" to include the various types of relief treated here as "direct refunding," but this does not appear to be an improvement in terminology and has not been accepted.

DIRECT REFUNDING METHODS

Particular Rescheduling

In some cases, especially in the case of foreign private obligors, debt payments have been postponed by amendment of the terms of individual loan contracts. This may take the form of rewriting a loan originally made, say at 10 years, into a modified agreement with amortization over, say 15 years, or extending the grace period on principal for an additional term and extending the final maturity. There is, therefore, no cancellation of principal, generally no change in interest rates, but merely a reduction of the principal payments in the course of a year or number of years. In the case of private loans this may be practically necessary in that the original loan contract provided for a definite schedule of repayment through a series of notes, but delays in the construction or other factors make it practically impossible for the obligor to repay according to the original schedule. In the extreme

1. U.S. Treasury, "Department Circular No. 1080" (March 5, 1968); *Fiscal Requirements Manual*, pt. 2, chap. 4500.

case there have been a few instances in which the Ex-Im had notes falling due before there were any actual disbursements under the loan. On appropriate occasions the Ex-Im has extended maturities or lengthened grace periods on loans primarily for conditions affecting particular projects.[2]

The best known case of Ex-Im rescheduling because of the economic situation of the borrowing country is Haiti. The Ex-Im loaned $5 million for an agricultural development project (SHADA) in 1941, with interest at 4 percent and repayment over 10 years, including a 5-year grace period. In 1941 there was the first loan for the Artibonite project. The original $4 million was increased in a succession of steps to $27 million by 1955. Original terms were 4 percent and 18 years including 3 years of grace. Payments to the Bank under these credits have been spasmodic. The SHADA credit was refunded in 1950, 1952, 1958, and 1962 with a reduction of interest rate and waiver of interest for periods of years. In the Artibonite case, the interest rate was reduced and payments rescheduled, including a waiver of interest for some years, to a final maturity in 1990.[3] In 1965 these credits were again readjusted.

Dollar repayable loans by AID (or administered by it as successor agency) have been rescheduled in relatively few instances since principal payments will generally start falling due about 1970. The old DLF loans as well as Cooley loans are repayable in local currencies and so ignored here.

Loans to Turkey go back to 1948, but there have been only small dollar principal payments to date. Principal due from 1956 to 1967 on the earliest loans was deferred to June 30, 1968, but there have been further postponements. The Indian wheat loan of 1954 has had principal installments deferred three times—the last time as part of the 1969 consolidation—so that the payments due from 1958 to 1967 have been deferred to successive years beginning in 2002. Payments on the 1952 wheat loan to Pakistan due from 1958 to 1967 were deferred to years after 2012. Accruing interest has been "capitalized" on loans to governments in Ghana, Tunisia, Brazil, Guinea and Indonesia.[4]

The deferment of payments at the option of the debtor, sometimes

2. Of Ex-Im loans outstanding March 31, 1969, $480.7 million or 9.5 percent of the total of $5,053.9 million "was attributable to loans which at one time or another have been rescheduled or refunded." The figure includes both rescheduling and consolidations, but does not include past transactions which have been fully paid off (House Subcommittee on Appropriations, "Foreign Assistance and Related Agencies Appropriations for 1970," pt. 1, p. 33).

3. Ex-Im, *Report*, June 30, 1965, p. 15.

4. That is, as interest payments fall due they are accounted for as paid and the amount is added to the principal of the loan.

referred to as a "bisque clause," in the loan under the revised Anglo-American agreement and the parallel Canadian loan agreement, is a built-in rescheduling mechanism.[5] A similar clause is included in the 1970 consolidation for Indonesia.

Somewhat similar is the provision in the IBRD Articles (IV, 4.(c)) permitting it to reschedule or to accept the borrowing member's currency for service payments for a period up to 3 years, subject to appropriate repurchase. This latter provision has not been applied in any case. Some of the loan agreements made under the European Recovery Program contained similar provisions for acceptance of borrower currencies by agreement or at the borrower's option and also permitted rescheduling by agreement.

The IBRD has rescheduled loans in only a few cases. In the case of India the IBRD postponed for 10 years the equivalent ot $30 million of principal payment in Indian fiscal years ending March 31, 1968 and 1969.[6] This was part of the general debt relief exercise of the Indian consortium.

In a number of minor instances, largely related to changes in the project, the World Bank has revised loan terms with a repayments schedule appropriate to the revised project.

The 1951 loan of $5 million to Paraguay for agricultural development was to be amortized in 6 semiannuals, since expenditure was to be largely for agricultural implements and supplies. In 1954 the World Bank approved a Paraguayan request to change the project to financing imports of road construction and river improvement equipment, and in 1958 extended the final maturity to 1964 on the basis of 14 semiannuals beginning in 1958. Difficulties with coal mining projects in Chile (earthquakes, strikes, market overestimation, increased costs) financed by two Bank loans in 1957 ($21.8 million) resulted in a merger of the companies (Lota-Schwager), a revision of the loan project, the postponement of some of the principal repayments, and the extension of the repayment schedule by three years and a reduction of payments in the earlier years. In fact, one of the loans had repayments falling due before the work was completed. The financial difficulties of the Peruvian Railways resulted in the World Bank's cancellation of the undis-

5. This appears to be the only instance of this arrangement before 1970. In this connection the following story told in the Treasury may be of interest. When the staff was explaining to the late Secretary Humphrey the statistical and other difficulties in deciding whether the U.K. was entitled to the waiver of payment under the original agreement, he said, "Why not simplify the business and give them a couple of 'bisques.' " The staff members looked confused, so the Secretary explained the sports usage of the term.

6. *Annual Report*, 1969, p. 27.

bursed portion of the loan and its application to the first installment of principal. Ex-Im, a parallel lender, also extended the maturity of its loan by a year.

To the present the IDB has not had occasion to reschedule debts.[7]

While there is no reduction of principal in loan reschedulings, this does not mean that it involves no cost to the lender if the loan has previously been disbursed. The lending institution is generally financed by borrowing so that it continues to pay interest and amortization on its borrowings, while the expected return of principal is not forthcoming, so that if it is to continue its lending program, it must borrow additionally. A payment postponed for 5 years at 6 percent discount has a present value of 75 percent and for 10 years 56 percent, and at 10 percent, 62 and 39 percent respectively, the difference being the equivalent of a grant to the debtor. To the debtor the amount postponed in any one year frees exchange for other purposes. Simple rescheduling has the advantage to both debtor and creditor of being inconspicuous and specific instances can often be traced only by a comparison of loan statements at successive dates, or footnotes to balance sheets. Rescheduling may require the rewriting of numerous loan agreements when relief is general.

Refinancing Credits

In the IBRD-OECD nomenclature, the term "refinancing credits" applies to loans whereby an official agency "takes over" credits previously extended by private creditors. The intent of the definition is clear enough—the replacement of private claims by obligations to a public institution. The devices used by various countries differ, and in fact, many of the "consolidations" (see below, next section) have been partly "refinancing."

In the instances of the general "consolidations" in Turkey, Argentina, Brazil and Chile, the European credits involved were mostly trade credits or suppliers' credits to the government or private businesses in the debtor country, which had previously been guaranteed or insured by a governmental institution, in the creditor or debtor country or both. Under the multilateral arrangements (detailed below) the central banks of the debtor countries assumed the obligation of paying off the loans, under the revised shcedule, to the central banks of the creditors. The precise mechanisms used to pay off the creditors appar-

---

7. There have been two defaults, Lutcher in Brazil and Vialsa in Argentina, which are in litigation. The IDB has had partial recoveries on these loans.

Table 17. Export-Import Bank Refinancing Credits (Millions of Dollars).

Country & obligor	Date	Description	Auth'd amount	Outstanding June 30, 1971
Argentina				
Consortium of commercial banks	1951	Refinance purchase of equipment	125.0	—
Brazil				
Banco do Brasil	1961	Refinance U.S. purchases	168.0	102.4
Banco do Brasil	1961	Refinance U.S. purchases	484.3	114.4
Chile				
Central bank	1961	Refinance U.S. purchases	15.0	—
Government	1963	Refinance U.S. purchases	15.0	3.0
Colombia				
Central bank	1957	Refinance U.S. purchases	60.0	—
Central bank	1958	Exchange credit	78.0	—
Venezuela				
Government	1960	Finance dollar obligation	75.0	—

ently varied somewhat among the countries.

The Ex-Im has over the last 20 years made loans to "bail out" American private creditors (banks or exporters) of Latin American countries or their nationals, in most instances after arrearages had reached considerable amounts. Table 17 is illustrative rather than complete. In these cases the Ex-Im extended a dollar line of credit to the government or central bank of the country, which drew dollars to pay off arrearages or to make payments on the private credits as they fell due. Ex-Im had no direct relation with the individual creditors, though it received evidences of payment to them. By the central bank becoming the obligor on a new loan generally covering principal and accrued interest on the old obligations, payment is stretched out for an additional period of years, often at lower interest rates than the older credits.

The refinancing credit may in practice differ little from general balance of payments assistance except that it provides new finance for past exports, while balance of payments or program credits provide financing for future imports by the borrower. Funds are freed for current imports. In some of the refinancing credits, both old and new imports were covered as payments came due. In several instances not listed in the table—Argentina, Brazil, Mexico ($90 million, 1961, 1963, 1965, 1966) and Uruguay—the Ex-Im authorized refinancing credits which were not drawn upon, presumably because the debtor obtained other financing.

The refinancing credit constitutes a budgetary cost to the Ex-Im, and, since the exports refinanced were accounted for in earlier balances of payments, it is analagous to a portfolio loan offset in the balance of payments, however, by the payment to the private creditors. The refinancing credit can be of great help to the debtor country generally by spreading relatively short-term payments over a longer period so as to reduce strain on its balance of payments and reopening normal channels of financing of its import requirements. Refinancing, of course, may also apply to medium-term supplier credits. Refinancing may be almost a necessary condition to stabilization and exchange reform measures, as discussed below with regard to particular countries.

Consolidation Credits

A consolidation credit in the OEC-IBRD terminology is a rescheduling of maturities, funding of arrears or of future payments, as they fall due, of principal or interest on loans previously made by the same public creditor or group of creditors.[8] Generally, the refunding applies to a number of outstanding credits to which the revised terms apply, hence "consolidation." The consolidation may involve the cancellation of outstanding credits and the substitution of a new credit instrument with a new schedule of interest and maturity. The consolidation, however, may be partial, i.e., only part of the maturing principal and/or interest (see Argentina and Chile below, chapter 4) is rescheduled and the remainder continues to be paid under the original terms. In such cases the old credit instruments remain in effect and accruing payments are funded in a new credit. The consolidation may be bilateral or multilateral (Hague Club, Paris Club, OECD and IBRD consortia and consultative groups). The current trend is in the form of multilateral consolidation of part of the debt with the retention of the original credits but with changes in the terms. (As noted, "refinancing" and "consolidation" arrangements may be intermixed.)

Probably the best known case of a straight consolidation is the refunding of World War I debts by the United States. During World War I the allied European countries, and some others, contracted

8. There can be private consolidation credits as well, but they are not considered here.

debts to the Treasury for munitions and other supplies needed. Some of these transactions were made under the express authority of the the Second Liberty Bond Act, as amended, which authorized the Treasury to lend to foreign governments at the same rate at which it was borrowing from the public. Consequently, the debts contracted were of varying maturities and rates of interest. After the war the United States established a Debt Refunding Commission, of which the Secretary of the Treasury was chairman, which was authorized to renegotiate the outstanding debts, subject however to the approval of Congress. While the terms of the refundings varied—the complaint has often been made that those who negotiated first got the worst terms—new agreements were made which cancelled the earlier obligations. In the refunding the consolidated debts generally had a longer term and a lower rate of interest than the original obligations so as to make payment easier. There was no cancellation of principal. On the basis of "present values" of the original obligations and the refunding obligations, the total debt was cut approximately in half, though the terms varied with countries. These are the credits which have for the most part been in default since the Hoover moratorium of 1931.

The Export-Import Bank has consolidated payments on a number of its own loans. Its procedure currently is to establish a line of credit on its books to the central bank of the debtor country and as payments fall due in the agreed percentage, it charges the line of credit with the amount falling due and credits the old loans by that amount. The old credits continue on the books as before. The Ex-Im generally carries these consolidation credits on its books as "defer transfers." In several instances, as in Brazil, the Bank has consolidated debt due at the same time that it has refinanced the obligations of American private creditors. Under the current Ex-Im consolidation procedure there is no charge to the lending authority of the Bank since it has not obligated any new money, and there is no direct budgetary outlay to the Ex-Im or the government. The terms vary somewhat. The Ex-Im arrangements in the case of Chile, for example, provide that if a private debtor meets his obligations from funds not obtained through Chilean exchange authorities, the Ex-Im pays dollars to a bank account of the Chilean central bank for the amount paid over and above the 70 percent of principal covered by the agreement. Table 18 shows some of these consolidation credits as they have appeared on the Ex-Im books in recent years.

In some of the earlier operations of the Ex-Im older credits were

Table 18. Export-Import Bank Consolidation Credits (Millions of Dollars).

	Date of consolidation	Scheduled final paymt.	Original amount	Outstanding June 30, 1971
Argentina	1963	1970	72.0	0.0
	1965(M)[a]	1972	15.4	4.6
Brazil	1961(M)	1979	79.6	49.9
	1963	1966	19.4	0.0
	1964(M)	1972	66.2	12.7
	1964	1967	6.6	0.0
Chile	1965(M)	1974	40.0	18.1
Costa Rica	1962	1972	2.6	0.5
	1965	1972	2.5	0.5
Indonesia	1967(M)	1979	30.6	Ref.[b]
	1968(M)	1976	14.0	Ref.
	1969(M)	1977	12.8	Ref.
	1971(M)	2000	96.9	95.1
Liberia	1963(M)	1978	13.2	9.9
	1969	1976	4.6	4.6
Yugoslavia	1965	1971	3.5	0.0

a. (M) indicates consolidation as part of multilateral arrangement.

b. "Ref." In 1971 the outstanding amounts of these consolidation credits were refunded along with accruals on other credits in the new consolidation arrangement.

extinguished and accounted for as paid while an entirely new credit covering refunded principal and/or interest payments was put on the books. This was done in 1961 in the case of Brazil and additional balance of payments assistance was provided through a new credit. These credits were, however, subsequently reconsolidated.

The retention of the old obligations has certain advantages over the cancellation of the old obligations and the establishment of a new credit. For example, if the underlying loans involved mortgages or limited the declaration of dividends in the case of a private borrower or special conditions such as prepayment determined by earnings, they are retained, while if the old obligations were cancelled by the new credit, many of these conditions could not be made part of the new obligations. When principal payments only are consolidated the original interest rates continue in effect. When a government or central bank becomes the obligor on the refunding obligation, it generally collects interest and amortization in local currency from the original private or public agency obligors and services the consolidation debt in foreign exchange.

Multilateral Consolidations

Most of the recent consolidations have been multilateral since the number of creditors has increased in recent years, and the immediate debt problem has been related largely to the hump in the repayment schedule for a period of years, generally resulting from a large proportion of relatively short-term debt, whether suppliers credits, financial credits or other obligations, superimposed on longer term obligations. The recent situation differs from the earlier period, say before 1955, when there was one predominant creditor country for a single debtor.

Multilateral consolidations have taken two main forms, consolidation through a creditors' club (e.g. The Hague and Paris Club arrangements for Argentina, Brazil and Chile) or in the framework of aid consortia or consultative groups. While the procedures differ somewhat in these two classes, there are certain common characteristics. The club participants agree on refunding of debt on substantially the same terms, so that the debtor may not pay off some creditors before the others. In the club arrangements generally there has been an agreed percentage to be consolidated, while in the consortium arrangements the consolidation of debt has been related to the aid pledges of the donor countries. The European countries have generally favored multilateral club-type consolidation since the governments or central banks were acting on behalf of their agencies guaranteeing exporter credits

For the debtor, multilateral consolidation is generally advantageous in that a proportion of all of the obligations of the agreed type is postponed promptly and generally on similar terms of "consolidation interest" and maturities of the consolidated debt. If the debtor has to negotiate with the creditors individually, time is lost and the crisis may deepen. The creditors may insist upon different terms, the postponement of debt payments may involve retention of the original interest rates or, in some cases, as in the Peruvian arrangement of 1968, payment of higher interest rates, as the result of market conditions, on the refunded obligations than on the original. In individual negotiations the creditor and the debtor may be faced with the alternative of complete default, which neither side favors. When all of the creditors have to make a common arrangement, they are more likely to be liberal in their terms. It may be noted here that no two of the consolidations have been identical since the circumstances and the composition of the debt of the countries involved have varied. Individual cases are discussed in chapter 4 under country headings.

Multilateral consolidations occur when a country has been in arrears on its payments (Turkey) or has accumulated large debit balances under various bilateral arrangements (Argentina and Brazil) or has a large amount of debt due in a short period. The debtor usually asks for a joint meeting with the creditors at which it proposes a list of debts which it wishes to have refunded. Usually these requests have covered obligations with maturities over one year having large principal payments accruing in the current or immediately following years. The arrangement has, therefore, applied most commonly to various exporter and medium-term credits extended by the European countries and, to some extent, Ex-Im credits. Consolidation arrangements have generally not applied—India and Indonesia are the exceptions—to long-term obligations such as AID loans, international agency credits or other bilateral loans which have long grace periods or long maturities. Short-term credits, usually for current imports with a maturity of less than one year, have generally not been included in the multilateral refundings except where arrears of short-term debts have been refunded at longer term. Moreover, consolidation arrangements have generally not covered credits extended to private entities without government guarantee in the debtor country or without insurance or guarantees in the creditor country. To these purely private credits the principle of caveat creditor has been applied with a few exceptions, and to the extent that they have been refunded it has been by special arrangement outside the club or consortium arrangements.

In the general consolidation[9] procedure the representatives of the creditors generally agree among themselves on the terms to be offered or accepted in the settlement. One of the principal problems is the agreement on the inclusion or exclusion of certain classes of debt since this will determine how much of the burden falls on the respective creditor countries. In fact, one of the principal problems has been to determine the amount and terms of the debt under consideration. (One of the values of the Expanded Reporting System of the IBRD-DAC may be to shorten the period of negotiation of future debt refundings.)

Under the procedure for the club arrangements there is usually an "agreed minute" setting forth in general terms the type of obligation to be refunded, the proportion of debt payments to be deferred and the period of deferment. There may also be agreement on the interest to be charged, if any, on the payments deferred, (consolidation inter-

9. For a brief discussion of the procedures see OECD, *Development Assistance Efforts and Policies, 1967 Review*, pp. 84–86.

est). The arrangement may involve some compounding of interest, but at least at a lower rate. The agreed minute may also take account of the undertakings by the debtor governments on its financial policy, generally as part of IMF standby arrangements and drawings. In several instances the Fund has acted as a central source to which the debtor supplies information on its program, as well as its payments or agreements to pay with the respective creditors. Arrangements with each creditor on a general MFN principle have had to vary in detail. In some cases the creditor is a government agency such as the Ex-Im, while in other instances the government has been acting for public or private agencies which have guaranteed individual private suppliers or other lenders, and so has to make special arrangements.

In the multilateral consolidations where the debtor government has not been itself the obligor or guarantor of the refunded obligations, the central bank with the guarantee of the government becomes the obligor on the consolidation credit and makes payments to the creditors through the creditors' central banks. The central bank of the creditor in turn pays its government or the credit insurance agency which has previously paid off its assureds. These arrangements necessarily vary from country to country. In Germany the payments to the individual creditors are made by Hermes, but the international guarantee operations are at the risk of the government, which receives the guarantee fees as they are collected and makes payments through Hermes to the individual exporter. In the case of France COFACE has used its reserves to pay off the creditors, but has also apparently been given government allocations to reimburse it in the case of some of the consolidations. In Italy special arrangements have had to be made with the various quasi-public entities which have been involved in guaranteeing credits. In the case of Ex-Im when it has been party to multilateral arrangements, the debtor central bank usually pays to Ex-Im directly. In the case of Turkey, however, where the settlement affected numerous private American creditors, the amount of reimbursement under the consolidation was screened by the Department of Commerce while payments were made by the Central Bank of Turkey to the New York Federal Reserve, which paid the creditors.

In the consortium arrangements the debt problem has been one aspect of the aid program to a given country. The aid consortium originated in 1958 when India faced a severe balance of payments crisis, resulting largely from inflation, an increase in imports, a decline in exports, and a loss of reserves over several years. The United States had been supplying aid to India on concessional terms, including loans repayable in local currency, P.L. 480 sales for local currency, and grants, while some other countries had been assisting the Indian Development Program with loans on harder terms, including supplier credits. The IBRD had also made large loans to India on its usual terms. Without additional aid on relatively easy terms the Indian development program would have had to be drastically curtailed.

The IBRD called a meeting of the interested countries to secure the needed aid. Since then under IBRD chairmanship the consortium has met annually with each country pledging, in the U.S. case usually subject to appropriation of aid funds, a specific amount toward the planned deficit in the balance of payments resulting from the development program. The effort in the consortium has generally been to obtain softer terms for aid to be provided, and the two refundings of Indian debt in 1968 and 1969 were agreed in part, at least, as alternatives to further lending on concessional terms, which would have assisted India in maintaining normal service on its debts. In the consortium debt refunding, however, the percentage of outstanding debt refunded varied with the donors and the terms were adjusted to the particular circumstances.[10]

The relative success of the Indian consortium in getting aid at better terms has resulted in the formation of a similar consortium for Pakistan under IBRD chairmanship. The OECD heads the consortium for Turkey. It is difficult, however, for countries to give firm "pledges" of aid. AID generally has not had its funds appropriated at the time of the meeting. There are budgetary problems in other donor countries and difficulties in specifying the amount of loans which may be made by private or quasi-public agencies. In the "consultative groups" for Colombia, East Africa, Korea, Tunisia, relative magnitudes of aid to be forthcoming are indicated without a formal pledge. Less formal aid coordinating arrangements are used for Ceylon, Ghana, Guyana and Indonesia, countries to which various donors have been giving aid and which also have significant debt problems. In the case of Ghana, the IMF took the lead and secured a debt adjustment and further aid, in relation to a Fund standby which assisted the stabilization effort.

INDIRECT REFUNDING

Formal refunding as described has occurred in a limited number of

10. See below, chapter 4, section on India.

countries, detailed below in chapter 4. In other countries debt has been paid off by incurring new indebtedness, either in the market or at concessional aid terms. If a country is regarded as "credit worthy" by the lenders, this rolling over of debt may go on almost indefinitely, or at least until the creditors become worried. Short-term bank credits are commonly renewed, and if bank A for whatever reason does not renew its credit, bank B often will increase its line. Medium-term bank credits are often similarly treated, though a renewal of exporter credits is more difficult. New security issues and some other inflows of capital are alternatives. Rolling over credits in these ways has been the practice of some of the developed debtors such as Canada and Japan, and among the less developed, Mexico. In these countries a good part of the debt is private.

The more closely new borrowing or aid approaches untied cash, the more readily it can facilitate payments on past debt. If a country issues general obligation bonds, the underwriters give it cash in convertible currencies which can be used to make debt payments, pay for imports, or finance projects. Security issues in the American or the Euro-market have, for a few countries, enabled them to meet their obligations, though this device is barred for most countries because of their past debt history or present situation. They may, however, get cash from banks and occasionally other sources. For the most part, the countries have depended on loans from governments, institutions and suppliers, which are tied to use for an agreed purpose (project or program), often in procurement. The greater the restrictions on use required by the creditor, the less easily can the new loans in practice free other resources for debt payment. As the extreme case, if a loan is made for the purchase of a particular piece of equipment from a given firm, there are no additional resources made available for debt service unless the borrower would otherwise have paid for the equipment out of its current exchange earnings.

For a very large number of developing countries, as their indebtedness and debt service have increased, the forms which aid has taken have facilitated payments on previously incurred debt by financing part of their balance of payments deficits.

While economic assistance in any form, grant or loan, project or balance of payments financing, adds to the resources available to the recipient and, unless wasted, to its productive capacity in the long run, it is the contention here that some forms more readily facilitate the servicing of debt than others. These are (1) direct balance of payments financing, by whatever name used in formal or accounting descriptions,[11] (2) the financing of costs in the recipient's currency through foreign exchange provision, and, of course, (3) drawings of foreign currencies from the IMF to meet balance of payments deficits, in part occasioned by heavy debt service over a short span of years.

Balance of Payments or Program Loans

The imports of a country that is a regular aid recipient, assuming no change in reserves, equal its exports of goods and services, plus aid or loan disbursements minus debt service and other invisibles. To the extent that foreign sources finance a portion of "normal" import requirements, earned exchange is freed to service debt. It could, of course, hold down its imports of non-aid or loan financed goods to the amount of its current earnings minus debt service and net invisibles. With debt service increasing at a faster rate than exports, as is the case with most of the debtors, its import program from its own resources would steadily decrease. On the other hand its import requirements would generally increase over time with the expansion of population and GNP. The gap would tend to widen unless part of its import requirements for food, materials, supplies and capital goods were financed by borrowing.

If, however, foreign assistance, under consortium arrangements or otherwise, is intended to meet a payments deficit of a planned or agreed amount, assistance would have to increase as debt payments rise, since the deficit would result in part from these payments. To the extent that assistance finances imports which the recipient could not readily curtail without impairment of its consumption standards, its earnings can be freed to service debt. In practice the relationship may not be precise, or even expressed. Development programs are flexible in conception as well as performance; import requirements are estimated in part in the light of expectations of what is likely to be received —somewhat overestimated, perhaps, to allow for the almost inevitable shortfall. The broader the list of commodities that can be financed under the program (small negative list or large positive list) the greater

11. For the present purpose loans called by various names, whether balance of payments, program loans, import program loans, etc., have been put in one category, essentially nonproject finance. In practice, it is difficult to distinguish some of these transactions in the accounts of the lending agnecies since the terminology varies with the vagaries of legislation, executive boards, accountants and loan officers, i.e., substantially similar transactions may be carried on the books of a given agency under different names at the same time, or the same transaction may appear under different names at different times.

is the fungibility between normal imports and goods needed for development.

Perhaps the closest to an official recognition of the relation between program lending and debt service is the following quotation from the testimony of the then AID Administrator to the Senate Foreign Relations Committee:

Now, when these reschedulings have been made the result is, of course, of part of the future balance-of-payments picture of that country, and it is against that future balance-of-payments picture, among other things, that we will be considering with the country how much assistance might be needed and of what kind, and in that sense certainly there is a relationship between the obligations not only to American private creditors but also the Export-Import Bank, for example, as to what the AID program in a country will be.[12]

A somewhat more direct connection was made in the findings of the 1971 Consultative Group for the Philippines. The debt problem in that country is largely a matter of medium-term bank credits,[13] which had been stretched over additional time. The Group said in part: "It was also recognized that while the Phillipines had the capacity to service this debt, it would do so only by foregoing opportunities for growth. The Group was therefore of the view that there was need for quick disbursing aid and the Philippines merited assistance from capital exporting countries and international institutions on as liberal terms as practicable."[14] In short, by providing balance of payments loans on easy terms the governments could help the Philippines in paying off the obligations to the banks.

In contrast, the relatively large project loan, when limited to foreign exchange costs, does not give the borrower any leeway in dealing with its debt. The power plant, say, will constitute an additional import, but will not substitute for other imports unless it is provided on a "turn-key" basis, in which foreign exchange will pay some local currency costs. The distinction between project and program loans will be questioned by some students of economic development for various reasons, including the difficulty of definition and the fungibility of resources.

There are many arguments advanced in favor of program (or the

12. David E. Bell in Senate Committee on Foreign Relations, *Hearings*, "Foreign Assistance, 1965," p. 598. The creditors may also include the IBRD, and foreign public and private lenders.
13. Cf. chapter 4, Philippines section.
14. IBRD, press release, April 23, 1971, "Meeting of the Consultative Group for the Philippines."

related sector) loans which have considerable cogency. General balance of payments assistance is almost indispensable when a country undertakes a stabilization and exchange reform; a country may reach a stage in its development when it needs additional infrastructure and capital projects less than it does supplies and materials needed to keep existing plant in effective operation. [15] Program loans are readily and cheaply administered; they constitute "quick disbursable aid," and so may help in meeting aid targets of one percent of GNP, and they give greater leverage to the donor country in influencing the policies of the recipient. [16] It is not denied here that balance of payments assistance is desirable under certain circumstances, merely that it facilitates refunding of debt more readily than more restricted types of lending. It is perhaps significant that as debt service has become more onerous, program lending has had more advocates, including the Pearson Commission, presidents of the World Bank, and students of economic development.

AID non-project loans. Whatever the economic or political theoretic argument may be, the fact remains that the bulk of AID (and predecessor agencies) program loans from development loan funds, i.e., excluding supporting assistance, has been made to countries which have had their debts refunded one or more times in the last 10 years. Program assistance from 1949 to June 30, 1970 aggregated $5,640.1 million out of a total of $10,952.9 million of loans authorized. India, Turkey, Indonesia, Ghana, Argentina, Brazil and Chile (refunded countries) accounted for $3,739.9 million or 66.3 percent of the total. Pakistan, Ceylon, Colombia and Korea, whose debt service is heavy but which have not had refunding, received $1,548.5 million or 27.5 percent. In FY 1970, program assistance, excluding supporting assistance (to Southeast Asia, Congo and Nigeria), amounted to $499 million, of which the first group of countries received $235 million (47 percent) and the second group $183 million (36.7 percent). [17] Some of the countries listed are relatively advanced developing countries which have built up their economies with the aid of past project loans at conventional terms or supplier credits, which are in part responsible for their debt difficulties. They are also countries which use program

15. Cf. *Pearson Report* for a strong statement of the general argument (pp. 177–79) and its application to India particularly (p. 301).

16. Jacob J. Kaplan, *The Challenge of Foreign Aid* (New York: Praeger, 1967), p. 293.

17. AID, *Operations Report*, June 30, 1970, pp. 31, 43–56. The totals are heavily weighted by the program loans to India, Pakistan, Brazil, Colombia and Turkey. (Data are on a commitment basis.)

assistance for needed supplies and materials which they cannot well afford from their exchange earnings.

Agricultural surplus, (P.L. 480).[18] From the standpoint of the recipients P.L. 480 transactions are a form of balance of payments assistance tied to the import of specific agricultural commodities, which the United States supplies on concessional terms. The principal aid recipients, some of which have the most serious debt problems, are also the largest recipients of P.L. 480 assistance in the form of sales for local currencies or long-term dollar-repayable loans on easy terms. (CCC credit transactions, on the other hand, are analagous to exporter credits.)

Sales for local currencies from 1954 to end of fiscal 1970 (agreements signed basis at market value for the commodities) have aggregated $10.4 billion, of which $9.5 billion was for country use. India received $3.5 billion for country use, Pakistan $1.2 billion; Turkey, U.A.R., Brazil, Korea were other larger recipients among the LDCs. The countries mentioned above as having debts rescheduled received $4,447.8 million, 46.6 percent of the total; the second group $1,851.1 million or 19.4 percent.[19] In the transition to long-term credit sales for dollars the proportion of these countries has been 44.8 and 13.4 percent respectively,[20] though this lower proportion is affected by continued provision of P.L. 480 to India on local currency sales terms for about half of its requirements in FY 1969, and for more than a third in FY 1970.

It may well be argued that P.L. 480 assistance is additional to normal import requirements and so cannot provide indirect debt relief, since agreements are "to safeguard usual marketings of the United States" and are not "unduly" to disrupt "normal patterns of commercial trade."[21] These statutory requirements, however, admit of considerable flexibility in their application to particular countries. The food needs of the aid recipients have been increasing (population), so that additional "food for peace" or "food for freedom" may readily be additional to the usual imports in earlier periods.

18. The Agricultural Trade Development and Assistance Act of 1954. (Public Law 83-480) has been amended many times.
19. These calculations are on the "country use" basis, since the portion for U.S. uses may be currently or subsequently used for the purpose of the government, which would otherwise have to expend dollars. Private trade and special donations and grants are here ignored.
20. $1,014 million and $305 million respectively of a total of $2,263 million (AID, *U.S. Overseas Loans and Grants July 1, 1945-June 30, 1970*, 1971).
21. Sec. 103 of P.L. 480, as amended.

IBRD-IDA. The IBRD has concentrated on projects since the reconstruction period, but it has made program and general development loans of $637.7 million of which $223.8 million have been to countries of Asia, the Middle East and Africa, with the balance going to developed countries in Europe and Australia. IDA, however, has provided $680 million in program credits (out of total credits of $3,340.4 million)—to India, $605 million, and to Pakistan, $50 million for industrial import programs.[22]

Ex-Im balance of payments credits. The Export-Import Bank has at various times given balance of payments loans, often in conjunction with stabilization programs of the recipient country. Prior to the establishment of the IMF these credits were extended on a bilateral basis, generally after discussion between the United States and the country concerned. More recently such loans have been extended generally to supplement resources made available by the IMF, particularly when drawings under the quota would not have been adequate to sustain the stabilization effort. In the "package deals" there have been agreed Fund drawings, Ex-Im credits, AID credits, and Treasury exchange agreements. As shown in Table 19, these credits have been either completely or largely paid off.

Local Currency Expenditures

Loans of foreign exchange to finance expenditures in the recipient's currency may also assist indirectly in meeting the burden of previously incurred debt. A loan made to support the budget of the borrowing government is equivalent to straight balance of payments assistance, or could even directly provide exchange to service debt. The borrower may use the exchange for imports by selling it to the central bank which covers some foreign payments for imports, indirectly freeing earned exchange for debt, or it may directly pay its debt from the loan proceeds. There have been relatively few direct budgetary support loans made by AID, (e.g.. Argentina, 1963; Dominican Republic, 1962; Ecuador. 1961, 1962, 1966; Guatemala, 1960; Panama, 1960, 1967). They are too frankly political and run counter to the principal of tying aid to assure exports, and do not appear to have been closely related in most instances to external debt problems, though they may have assisted in meeting short-term obligations. Conversely, balance

22. *Annual Report,* 1970, pp. 110–11; 1971, pp. 108–09. Recent reports classify as program loans, some loans which in prior years have been included under other headings, e.g., industry.

Table 19. Export-Import Bank: Selected Balance of Payments Loans[a] (Millions of Dollars).

	Purpose[b]	Original amount authorized	Outstanding June 30, 1971
Argentina			
1948	Essential imports (f)	24.8	0.0
Brazil			
1939	U.S. agric. & industrial products	19.2	0.0
1961	Finance U.S. purchases (in part)	454.2	114.4
Chile			
1939	Industrial products & machinery	15.8	0.0
1941	Agric. & industrial prods.	4.2	0.0
1949	Purchase of equipment	25.0	0.0
1957	Capital goods	12.5	0.0
1958	Capital goods (f)	15.0	0.0
1959	Capital goods (f)	25.0	0.0
Colombia			
1940	U.S. agric. & industrial products	10.0	0.0
1961	Finance U.S. goods & serv. (f)	44.9	0.0
Honduras			
1942	Materials & equipment	2.7	0.0
Peru	Finance essential imports (f)	40.0	0.0
China			
1938	U.S. agric. & indus. prods.	25.0	0.0
1940	Raw materials & equipment	20.0	0.0
1940	U.S. agric. & indus. prods.	25.0	0.0
1940	U.S. agric. & indus. prods.	50.0	0.0
India			
1958	Capital equipment for development prog.	150.0	37.5
1960	Appropriate to purpose (f)	50.0	22.5
1962	Subject to approval (f)	25.0	11.5
1964	Various for private & public (f)	25.0	15.6
1968	Finance of capital equipment (f)	20.0	19.2
Indonesia[c]			
1950	Various allotments	100.0	Ref.
Greece			
1946	U.S. products & serv.	25.0	2.9
Yugoslavia			
1946	Materials & equipment	55.0	0.0
1961	Various allotments	50.0	23.6

a. Loans marked (f) were made in conjunction with or approximately at the same time as IMF standby or drawing arrangements.

b. The purposes as listed here were those originally stated (see *Foreign Credits*, Dec. 31, 1970). In 1971 most of the outstanding credits were rephrased as "Multiproject Assistance."

c. The outstanding balance of the credit to Indonesia was consolidated in 1971.

of payments support may help meeting budgetary deficits since the government or central bank sells exchange, or in practice draws a-gainst letters of credit, to importers who pay in local currency, which may be used to finance current budgetary deficits or to fund development projects—what is sometimes referred to as "generating local currency."

More importantly, project loans for local currency expenditures, wholly or in good part, provide exchange, some of which can be used to service debt. Examples would be loans for agricultural development, land reform, rural credit and other items not involving imports to a great extent, housing developments, education, irrigation, and water supplies and sewerage. Many of these projects require some foreign exchange, but largely local labor and materials. In terms of development these credits may finance work which is more important in the long-run than "monuments." A given sum may have a higher marginal utility in education or agriculture than it would have in in-cremental power facilities or establishment of high-cost industrial enterprises. Programs of this sort, however, are not likely to be self-liquidating in foreign exchange, while incurring foreign debt adds to the payments problem of the recipient. Accordingly, they have been funded in large part by highly concessional loans. IDA credits have been committed largely for program loans and purposes requiring large local currency costs, some $1.8 billion of a total of $3.3 billion (to June 30, 1971), including $680 million in general development and program loans. The IDB has used the Fund for Special Operations and the Social Progress Trust Fund mainly for water and sewerage systems, agriculture, education and housing. U.S. bilateral support for projects of this sort comes from AID project loans, and more recently through loans for development programs including educational, agricultural and similar projects. An amount of exports equivalent to the local currency expenditure may be assured by special letters of credit for imports by the recipient which draws against them as local costs are disbursed. If these imports were always "additional" to normal imports they would not help in dealing with debt, but additionality cannot in practice be assured and the policy has now been abandoned.[23]

Even project credits with international competitive bidding may provide significant local currency financing if the successful bidders

23. Specifically for Latin America and by implication elsewhere, cf. President Nixon's foreign affairs report, "United States Foreign Policy for the 1970's; A New Strategy for Peace," *Weekly Compilation of Presidential Documents* (Feb. 18, 1970), 6, no. 8: 209, 225.

are in the borrowing country. Local firms may be the low bidders because of cost factors or location, or other conditions. IBRD loans to Japan and Yugoslavia have had successful local bidders, so that the loans of dollars and other currencies financed local expenditures, though there were some imports. It may be noted in passing that both countries have had heavy external debt mainly to creditors other than the IBRD. A device which is important in the industrially more advanced developing countries, Argentina, Brazil, Colombia, India, which can produce some of the equipment or materials needed for projects financed by the IBRD, is the allowance of a differential of an agreed percent to local bidders, to compensate for tariffs.[24] A local supplier or contractor may receive the award if his bid does not exceed by the agreed percentage, usually, 15 percent, the lowest bid of the foreign suppliers. If this percentage does not exceed the applicable tariffs on the imported goods, the cost to the borrower is no higher, but the IBRD finances local expenditures. This differential rule was useful in dealing with the Brazilian debt problem in 1965, when the IBRD did not modify the terms of its outstanding loans when the other creditors consolidated. Instead it granted new loans to Brazil under which a good portion financed local currency procurement.[25]

Development Finance Companies

Loans to development banks or finance companies in the developing countries, whether private, public, or mixed, serve somewhat the same purposes as balance of payments loans, though they are smaller in amount than program loans and are less directly related to the over-all needs of the recipient economy. Typically these companies make loans to local private firms for expansion of their operations, either by providing foreign exchange for their requirements of imported equipment or by lending local currencies for purchase of locally available materials or working capital. They can be most important in the development of the economy since they finance requirements of the private sector, while project loans go mostly to infrastructure, which is either publicly owned, or so affected with a public interest, that governments will guarantee loans or request them from the lenders. For the present purpose the significance of external loans to development banks lies in the provision of foreign exchange by the IBRD, the Ex-Im, and to a lesser extent, the IDB and the ADB, for

24. IBRD, *Policies and Operations, The World Bank, IDA and IFC* (1971), p. 37.
25. See below, chapter 4, Brazil.

purposes which would otherwise have to be financed through official exchange, which might be more difficult to get in competition with public requirements if it were not specifically earmarked. Generally the loans are shorter term than loans to governments, and substitute in part for supplier credits. The IBRD has committed $1,292 millions to such companies, 8 percent of its cumulative loan commitments to June 30, 1971. Companies in India and Pakistan were the largest borrowers. In the Asian Development Bank $105 million of total loans authorized of $341 million from ordinary capital resources was to development finance corporations (December 31, 1970). The Ex-Im has outstanding $86.2 million (June 30, 1971) to such corporations in developing countries. The IDB (to end of 1970) had loaned from its three windows $377.6 million for relending in industry and $445.2 million for relending in agriculture to various development finance institutions. These amounts, however, included considerable portions in the borrowing country's currency, which could not be used to finance imports.

International Monetary Fund

The Fund has had an influence on member policies in connection with their stabilization efforts and debt adjustments far out of proportion to the amount of balance of payments assistance supplied, because drawings have been conditional upon undertakings by the member on appropriate policies, and secondly, because it could supply exchange that could be used without strings, once the drawing or standby is agreed. Moreover, its regular consultation with the members, and particularly discussions before and after drawings, have given it the strategic advantage of information, consultation and follow-up procedures.

IMF drawings are made to assist in meeting current balance of payments deficits for the members within the limits set by their quotas. Current transactions are defined by the Articles of Agreement (XIX (i)) to include: "(1) All payments due in connection with foreign trade, other current business, including services, and normal short-term banking and credit facilities; (2) Payments due as interest on loans and as net income from other investments; (3) Payments of moderate amount for amortization of loans or for depreciation of direct investments." Accordingly, a country having difficulty in meeting payments due on either short- or long-term debts has a prima facie right to draw on the Fund. The Articles also, however, provide that within a 12-

month period the member may not draw more than 25 percent of its quota unless the Fund waives the condition. It is IMF policy that drawings above the gold tranche (i.e., the currency equivalent of the member's gold subscription) are not automatic. The Fund's attitude to drawings in the first credit tranche (i.e., the next 25 percent) is liberal, but larger amounts require substantial justification and are favorably received when they are to support a "sound program aimed at establishing or maintaining the enduring stability of the members' currency at a realistic rate of exchange."[26] When countries have undertaken stabilization programs by adjustment of their exchange rates or other changes in their systems as well as certain domestic financial policies, they have usually required funds to tide them over the stabilization period in amounts considerably larger than their gold tranche or the first credit tranche. To provide these amounts larger drawings are indicated, and in a considerable number of the stabilization arrangements Fund drawings have been supplemented by U.S. Treasury exchange agreements, Ex-Im credits and AID program loans, particularly in Latin America.

The Fund standby arrangement is agreement by the Fund in advance to permit drawings of the specified amount generally without further challenge in the Fund's Board. In Fund procedure the country concerned usually presents a program for stabilization including undertakings on the extension of credits by the central bank, fiscal policies on the part of the government, and increasingly, limitations on the amount of foreign debt to be incurred during the life of the standby, usually one year. Subsequently, after further discussion a new standby may be arranged. These conditions are specified generally in letters to the IMF from the finance minister or central bank governor or both, which set forth the precise program in considerable detail. These conditions are generally arrived at after more or less extended discussion by the Fund staff mission and the country, a factor which may explain the remarkable similarity stylistically among the letters of intent of finance ministers in all parts of the world.[27] While the Fund formally may not propose an adjustment of the member's exchange rate, the staff may informally suggest devaluation or even floating rates in its consultation. While the conditions precedent

26. IMF, *Annual Report,* 1959, p. 22.
27. For a general discussion of the standby procedure and the conditions in stabilization programs, see Emil J. Spitzer in IMF, *The International Monetary Fund 1945–65,* vol. 2, chaps. 20, 21, and Joseph Gold, *The Stand-By Arrangements of the International Monetary Fund* (Washington: IMF, 1970).

to the standby are not contractual in a formal sense, the members undertake not to draw if they are unable to fulfill them.

In recent years most drawings by developing countries have been made under standby arrangements. In the IMF FY 1971, about three-fourths of drawings by developing countries were under these arrangements, the rest largely in gold tranche drawings. About half of the arrangements made over the years specified limitations on external debt.

Where the member countries' difficulties have arisen from heavy payments on debt, the undertakings have specified the limits on debt, generally under 5 years but occasionally of longer term which the country may have outstanding. These conditions vary with the situation. They sometimes specify that maturities of more than 1 year and under 5 or 8, should not exceed a specified amount, or the amount at the time of the agreement, or should not exceed that amount by a specified percentage; in an extreme case, Ghana undertook not to incur debts of more than 1 year and less than 12 without the specific agreement of the Managing Director. These undertakings on additional borrowings of the type that has frequently created the debt problem have been a consideration in the agreements by the creditors in the refunding arrangement, and the agreed minute has sometimes specified that the debt relief was to be conditional upon the continuance in effect of the Fund standby arrangement. In other instances the debtor country, e.g., Brazil, 1964, agreed to inform the creditors through the Fund of actions taken under the arrangement, including as appropriate statistical information on debts incurred, debts paid off and the terms of the specific bilateral agreements to implement the agreed minute. The Fund has in this way to a degree "policed" the agreement. In many of the multilateral debt renegotiations the Fund has supplied the parties with authoritative information.

Procedures of this sort are probably necessary to make the stabilization and debt refunding programs effective. If there were no limitation on the member's authority to borrow it could use the Fund drawing to meet arrears or accruing payments on previously incurred medium-term debt, while at the same time continuing to borrow on supplier credits or other medium-term debt, so that at the end of the period it might find itself in the same debt situation that it was in the beginning. Under the circumstances there would have been little improvement and the member would scarcely be in a position to repurchase its currency within the 3 to 5 year period normally required under Fund drawings policy. Since the Fund to preserve its own liquidity must revolve its resources through the repurchase of drawings, undertakings of this sort are necessary not only in the member's interest in the long run but in the Fund's. Repurchases from the Fund in 5 years impose a rather heavy burden on the members' balance of payments, comparable to commercial credits, but as appropriate the Fund has effectively extended the period of repayment by allowing new drawings of currencies as older drawings are repurchased, generally under revised standby arrangements.

DIRECT VERSUS INDIRECT DEBT REFUNDING

The problem for the future is the rate of increase in the external debt resulting from development programs or ordinary balance of payments deficits. Since most development assistance is on a loan basis the capital sum may be expected to increase annually by several billions of dollars, though annual service may not increase proportionately, depending on the terms of the loans. If all development loans were on AID terms, the point at which debt service would equal the amount provided, assuming a constant annual amount of aid, would not be reached for about 25 years;[28] if it is on DAC terms the period could be shorter.

If aid is provided in annually increasing amounts the point of no "net aid" would be postponed, and advanced if aid decreases. This time period might be sufficient to enable recipient countries to develop and to export enough to meet debt service so that they could begin to repay and so reduce burdens. Whether or not this happy situation will be reached, say, by 2000 is, or course, unknown. AID or DAC terms would preclude any IBRD, IDB (ordinary capital) or Ex-Im loans as well as commercial credits and much of the assistance provided by European countries and Japan to the countries with programs of long-range developmental borrowing. Without these credits on harder terms, the tempo of development would be greatly slowed. Moreover, the harder credits have financed many worthwhile projects important in the long run. There also seems to be little likelihood of all credits being on soft terms, even to the countries whose debt burdens are now fully apparent.

The issue should be faced squarely by the donor-creditor countries

28. Cf. p. 53 above.

and the multilateral institutions. Should they more readily agree to refunding, or should they continue to postpone the evil day by soft program loans, which may now provide "net aid?" Their decision will depend upon various budgetary and balance of payments considerations as well as institutional factors including the "announcement" effects.

Budgetary Considerations

In the rescheduling of particular debt obligations there is generally no direct budgetary outlay, though there are indirect budgetary effects. Similarly, when consolidation credits are given there is no cash outlay if they are handled by the device of crediting the old loans and debiting the consolidation credit on the books of the lending institution. Under U.S. budgetary procedures, then, there is no budgetary outlay directly attributable to the refunding arrangement. (The new accrual system does not change this result since receipts of principal are not accrued, in accordance with usual accounting procedures.) Interest earnings, however, directly affect the income and expense statement of the lending agency. This is probably an important reason for limiting the refunding to principal. It obviously makes little difference in fact, e.g., in the Chilean case, whether 70 percent of principal payments are deferred or 65 percent of principal and accruing interest (at about 5 percent), though the former looks better in the accounts.

There is, however, an indirect real effect on the budget of either a rescheduling or consolidation, since anticipated receipts are not forthcoming, so that a net deficit is increased or a net surplus reduced. The lending agency, say, Ex-Im, if it is to continue its lending operations at the same scale, must borrow enough to cover the decrease in the cash flow occasioned by the postponement of receipts of principal. Increased borrowing from the Treasury or the public would not, however, affect the budgetary surplus or deficit. If refunding were to become widespread, the cash flow to the Ex-Im would be drastically reduced, and it might have difficulty in accommodating itself to the changed situation, since its borrowing and lending authority is limited by statute. At current rates of interest, however, new money costs more than the interest rate applying to the refunded obligations.

The same argument applies to the international lending agencies since they also obtain their funds largely by market borrowings. A refunding of interest would also affect their current earnings, and the institutions prefer to show a profit on their operations.

Indirect refunding by providing new loans represents a definite budgetary outlay for U.S. agencies, whose funds are provided either by appropriation or borrowing authority included in the over-all budget.[29] This also applies to foreign creditor countries, particularly since loans at concessional rates are generally made from funds appropriated to a government department rather than being provided by a lending agency which must cover the cost of its borrowings.

The net effect on the budget of the government may not over a period of time be very different for either method. In the short run, however, direct refunding involves no direct outlays compared with the definite expenditure under the indirect refunding methods.

When private credits are refinanced the effects on the public budget are the same as of other new loans.

From the standpoint of the borrowing country's budget, deferment of principal repayments represents an immediate reduction in outlays. In some cases the additional borrowing on a program loan might even be treated as a budgetary receipt.

Balance of Payments

Consolidation of debt is essentially untied balance of payments assistance to the debtor, generally on a repayment basis, with a considerable "grant element," in the DAC terminology, equal to the difference between the payments due and the present value of the future payments agreed. The consolidation permits the debtor to spend anywhere exchange earnings, which otherwise would have been paid to the creditors as service on loans, which for the most part had been tied in procurement. This would not apply to international agency loans which have been for the most part untied, or at least with less stringent limitations on procurement than national loans. A rescheduling of particular loans has the same balance of payments effect on the debtor. Refinancing credits also free earned exchange for imports or invisible payments including other debts by stretching repayment over a longer period than the original loans.

General balance of payments credits which may indirectly aid in refunding debt are generally tied in form. Even when these credits are extended specifically to deal with debt problems, as in India, they have sometimes been tied to purchases in the creditor country.[30] Direct

29. The outlay would be offset by receipts of principal and interest on the old loans.
30. Limits to the effectiveness of tying have been recently discussed on the basis of British experience by Bryan Hopkin et al., "Aid and the Balance of Payments," *Economic Journal*, 80 (March 1970): 1–24.

refunding may be regarded by some as preferable to the indirect methods in part because it is untied assistance.[31]

From the point of view of the creditors' balances of payments, the
effect of the different refunding techniques is essentially the same. The
creditor does not receive the expected receipts of principal (or interest
in a few cases). There is likely to be some partial offset in exports, paid
for by the exchange freed by the refunding, which would not otherwise have been sold. The offset would be complete if the debtor purchased imports in an amount equal to debt relief and in proportional
amounts for the creditors. This is probably the main reason for tying
when the refunding is covered by new commodity credits, e.g., some
of the U.K. refunding arrangements. The tying would be more important for those creditors whose share of the debt relief is larger than its
proportion of the debtor's imports, and vice versa. The real cost to the
debtor and the offsetting effects on the creditors' balance of payments
depends on relative costs of imports and their pattern.

Without refunding the debtor would have to restrict imports, if it
paid service, so that the creditors' exports would be reduced, since the
debtors secure a large part of their requirements from the industrial-
creditor countries.

In refinancing arrangements, when the creditor "bails out" its own
nationals, there is a capital outflow in the balance of payments offset
by the inpayments to the suppliers or banks. In debt consolidation
payments are credited to the old loans as the new credit is debited so
that there is no net change in the capital accounts. If the debt payments
are rescheduled, the creditors do not receive expected returns in the
period during which payments are postponed, but future receipts are
increased. New balance of payments credits are offset by exports as
they are disbursed. If the credit does not finance debtor imports which
would otherwise be paid from its resources, it does not give debt relief.

Announcement Effects

The strong preference for indirect refunding of debt on the part of
governments and international lending institutions is largely a matter
of the differences in the "announcement effects" of the alternatives.

Program loans do not call attention to the debt difficulties of the
recipient, while a formal debt rescheduling or consolidation, particularly when arranged at a multilateral meeting, sooner or later calls to
the attention of everyone that the borrower is having difficulties in

31. Cf. *Pearson Report*, p. 160.

meeting its contractual obligations. Borrowers may feel that lenders will regard them as less "creditworthy" after a refunding so that no new loans would be forthcoming, or at least the creditor's exposure would be reduced. If the borrowers received loans only at irregular intervals this might be the consequence. It is less likely to occur when they are regular annual borrowers under an aid program, or when the creditors, national or international agencies, believe, mainly for political reasons, that the economy of the refunded borrower must be sustained. While governments and international bodies have provided soft loans under these circumstances, they have also continued to supply credit on "hard" terms, though probably in smaller amount or proportion. The IBRD has made project loans to India since the refunding, as have some of the other creditors, though with longer grace periods than in earlier loans. Ex-Im has made substantial loans, mostly to private entities, after the consolidation of the debt of Argentina, Brazil and Chile. Private lenders, perhaps confident that creditor governments would somehow come to the aid of the debtors, have also continued to provide supplier and other commercial credits, and the borrowers would continue to borrow on these terms if they were not restrained by the terms of IMF standby arrangements. The recurrent Turkish debt difficulties have occurred in periods subsequent to the well-known refundings. American private lenders used to expect that the Ex-Im would bail them out in any case. Moreover, as long as aid programs can be assumed for the future, the private lenders can expect to be covered indirectly by soft program loans.[32]

The program loan has the advantage to a lending agency in showing an increased level of activity in its reports and press releases, while a consolidation arrangement or rescheduling of particular amortization payments is effected unobtrusively. In any event it may not be good advertising for the lending agency, since it calls attention to the fact that loans previously made on the assumption of reasonable prospects of repayment have not in practice paid off as contemplated. This may appear to reflect a possible error in judgment on the part of the governing board. This is probably one reason why the institutional lenders have been reluctant to be parties to consolidation arrangements, since this might reflect on their public image and so make it more difficult to

32. If I may introduce a personal note, I might illustrate by a conversation with two old friends, responsible officers of American banks making loans to India at 5- and 7-year maturities at the time that India's debt burdens had become well known. In response to the inquiry as to whether they were concerned with the Indian debt burden and debt service ratio, one responded, "We're not worried, India will pay." The other said, "Do you suppose that the U.S. will stop aid to India before seven years are up? As long as aid goes on we're covered."

borrow on the market or to secure appropriations from congresses and parliaments. The IBRD has generally been reluctant[33] to be a party to consolidation arrangements even after other creditors had refunded or were refunding, since it depends for its funds on borrowing in financial markets. While the Ex-Im has agreed to refundings in many more cases[34] its ability to secure lending and borrowing authority from the Congress has rested in part on its reputation for making sound loans which have been paid off according to contract, with relatively few delinquencies. The same probably applies to corporate lending institutions in other countries which depend either on direct appropriations from budgets or borrowing in the market with the direct or implicit guarantee of their governments.

A new program loan also involves new exports. Individual exporters may benefit and banks get new business even if total creditor exports do not increase. They might therefore give more support to an aid program somewhat as they have generally fully supported the lending program of the Ex-Im in the U.S. and the guarantee and export financing agencies in other countries.

In the debtor country, on the other side, the program loan may be advertised by the recipient government as evidence of confidence or approval of its policies by foreign countries or international bodies, perhaps an important factor in view of the instability of government in many of the developing countries. It may also be favored by the recipient governments as providing commodities which can be sold profitably by those who obtain the imported goods, particularly where there is an overvalued currency or a multiple rate system. Of course, when a formal refunding becomes necessary it is relatively easy to blame the situation on the incompetence or corruption of a predecessor administration. This may not, however, be as convincing to the public.

CONCLUSION

The heavy debt service burden of some of the aid recipient countries has been greatly alleviated by the provision by the creditor countries

---

33. Cf. chapter 4 below, India and Brazil.

34. As noted above, p. 78, as of 1969 about 9.5 percent of the loans on the Ex-Im books have at some time been refunded or rescheduled. The Ex-Im *Annual Report*, June 30, 1971, p. 24, in discussing delinquencies in payment, said, "when conditions justify, Eximbank will revise repayment schedules on a reasonable basis."

and international agencies of assistance on a loan basis in forms which have relieved pressure on the recipient's balance of payments, so that earned exchange can be used for debt service. These forms of balance of payments aid have, with rare exceptions, not been specifically directed to providing exchange for debt payments, but rather to supply goods needed for the development program[35] or to encourage desirable development activities in education, agriculture, etc. Both creditors and debtors have preferred this course to direct refunding.

Debt refunding has occurred with the increasing difficulty of getting budgetary allocations for program aid, not only in this country but in other countries as well. Refunding may not require direct budgetary outlays and can often be arranged without seeking additional legislation or appropriations or the equivalents in other creditor countries, since a lending institution normally has legal authority to amend its loan agreements. It may not like to, but it may do it. This may have some appeal in the future. In other instances, without prior aid programs, the refunding has been precipitated by the unusually large payments due over a short period, when the creditors have preferred to settle on an arrangement of debt rather than face default, continued delinquency and also an interruption of trade with the debtors.

The circumstances of and arrangements for these countries refunding are outlined in the next chapter.

35. "Mr. Fountain. What percent of the total aid going to India and Pakistan goes toward debt service payments on foreign loans?

"Mr. Williams. Well, none of the aid goes toward it directly. I will come back to the question, but none of the aid goes for debt payment. Our aid goes for very specific things, like fertilizer and raw materials, which are used directly in the development program. In 1967, worldwide, the return flow of payment of interest and capital on past loans, paid out of their own foreign exchange earnings, was about 50 percent of the level of aid being received from all sources. In India debt service now represents somewhat less than 40 percent of gross aid disbursements. In Pakistan less than 40 percent of gross aid disbursements." (House Committee on Foreign Affairs, *Hearings*, "Foreign Assistance Act of 1969," pt. 4, p. 765.)

4. CASE STUDIES

The countries selected here for specific analysis illustrate a variety of debt problems. No two cases are identical, though there are features common to the various groups. To the general reader the discussion may appear too detailed, to the country specialist too summary. Several countries have required successive refundings of their debt and some are likely to be candidates again. Hence the discussion of the conditions producing debt crises or stringencies, and the specifics of the relief given should be useful to those who will have to be concerned with the problem in the coming years, both in creditor and debtor nations. Once in debt difficulties requiring concerted action by the creditors, it is not easy to get out of them. It is a pity, but it is a fact. With the relief given, Liberia may stay in the clear. Argentina and Brazil may also be able to avoid further readjustment. The recurrence of debt stringencies is not merely that the refunding measures were temporizing actions. It is the persistence of the underlying economic and political conditions which occasioned past crises.

The cases arising from relatively short-term credits from suppliers, exporters and contractors have received the most attention in the past, e.g., Argentina, Brazil, Chile, Ghana, Liberia and Turkey, since in these instances there were multilateral arrangements. Heavy debt, inflation and balance of payments deficits have also been prevalent in the countries whose adjustments were made bilaterally or by agreement of a group of banking creditors, e.g., Peru, the Philippines and Uruguay. In the Peruvian case certain supplier-type credits were also converted into financial credits.

Indonesia and Ghana have in common the accumulation of debt by prior regimes and the settlement of these obligations as part of programs of rehabilitation and stabilization of their economies. Debt to the Soviets and other CMEA countries has been an important factor. A somewhat similar situation exists in Mali but information is lacking. Egypt has made bilateral refunding agreements with suppliers and others, but the precise terms have not been made public. Obligations to U.S. agencies had been in default for several years until December 6, 1971, when a refunding arrangement was agreed covering the total principal of $108.4 million and arrearages of interest of $37 million. These amounts are to be paid off in installments extending from 1972 to 1978. Arrangements with the creditor agencies vary somewhat. In the Yugoslavian case, the terms of refunding, except by the United States, do not appear to be available.

India, Pakistan, Tunisia and Turkey are among the countries whose balance of payments deficits, in part arising from their development programs, have been met by foreign aid largely in the form of commodity credits provided under consortium arrangements. In the Indian case clearly, and somewhat less clearly in Turkey, debt refunding has been an alternative to provision of more balance of payments assistance. Some of the consortium countries have in practice refunded their earlier harder-term credits by giving easy-term loans for commodity imports. The Pakistan unilateral moratorium of May 1971 was replaced a year later by an understanding on short-term relief extending to June 30, 1973. A more permanent adjustment may then be possible. In the Tunisian case there have been some minor adjustments but debt service as well as other elements in the payments deficit have been covered by soft loans and grants from the United States and France.

Brief treatment is given here by way of comparison to the debt situation of Colombia and Mexico. Neither has had a debt refunding in recent years, though their situation is in many ways similar to that of some countries which have required it. Colombia's balance of payments deficit has been met for many years by foreign aid under the consultative group understandings. Colombia's debt is in more manageable form than that of some other countries and consists largely of obligations to international organizations and to the United States, largely on AID terms. Mexico, on the other hand, is more heavily indebted to private entities but has successfully rolled over its accruing payments by voluntary agreements with banks and by the issue of bonds. Israel has followed the same practice with heavier reliance on bonds, which, however, are purchased in large part for noneconomic reasons. The paucity of the available data precludes analysis of the recent period.

Various minor refundings and adjustments of particular loans are not discussed here as of less general interest.

I. ARGENTINA

Background

Since 1956 there have been three multilateral refundings of Argentine debt, with additional bilateral arrangements. Since 1965 Argentina has been rolling over its public debt by new borrowings in the bond market and commercial banks as principal of old debt becomes due. Interest cost has been met from exchange earnings and reserves. The outstanding public debt is about $2.3 billion ($1.8 billion disbursed) with annual debt service near a half billion. In addition the economy must service a private debt of $1.2 billion including some debt under one year. More than half of this debt was due in 1970, but has also been rolled over. The refunding of Argentine debt to suppliers and banks in the last 20 years followed refunding of the earlier bonded debt. The Argentine national government, however, maintained service on its bonds through the depression, a factor which probably affects its ability to borrow on the bond market in recent years.

Argentine debt problems arise in good part from the endemic inflation which has persisted for most of this century, though with several periods of only moderately rising prices. Prices are (October 1971) about 182 (1963 = 100) times the level of 1948 and the cost of living 187 times. The dollar now costs more than a hundred times the 1948 peso amount. In 1967, after a succession of years in which the price level and cost of living had gone up about 30 percent each year, a stabilization program was adopted and the peso devalued. The price spiral was slowed for 3 years (index numbers of 235.3 at end of 1967 and 283.2 March 1970). It has risen more rapidly since, about 2.5 percent per month compounded. The cost of living has gone up at a rate of almost 30 percent annually.

A second factor in the debt problem has been the direction of Argentine trade, with exports mostly to European countries whose currencies were inconvertible for 20 years, and a regular trade deficit with the United States, though debt to the U.S. economy was heavy after 1920. While balance of payments data are not available for earlier periods, it would appear that Argentina generally had a trade surplus in the early part of the century which enabled it to service its debt and to increase monetary reserves. From World War II to 1962 there was generally a deficit on trade account, since then a trade surplus, though since 1968 the current account has been in deficit, with a reduced trade surplus and heavy debt payments.

To deal with the inflationary situation, the inconvertibility of the currency of the major trading partners, and the deficits on international account, including the service of its heavy debt, Argentina developed a network of bilateral trade and payments agreements as well as complex multiple currency arrangements, which, however, during the Peron regime particularly, discouraged exports and increased local consumption of meat and wheat. A series of exchange crises resulted in rescheduling of debt and the insistence by the creditors (and later the IMF) on the adoption of policies intended to arrest inflation and to modify the exchange structure.

Earlier Refundings

Argentina began to borrow abroad soon after independence, mainly in England, which invested heavily in subsequent years in railways and public loans. There were intermittent debt service difficulties in the period 1830 to 1900 and several issues were refunded after default or threatened default. Finally there was a general refunding in 1897–1900 with a reduction of interest to 4 percent. This refunding covered national, railway and some provincial bonds.

Between 1914 and 1931, the Argentine government borrowed or guaranteed borrowings in the American market to a total of $824 million, and Argentine corporations borrowed an additional $100 million. Full service was met throughout the depression on the national government debt, though the province of Buenos Aires defaulted as did some other debtors. With lower interest rates in 1937, the old 6 percent dollar bonds were converted to 4 and 4.5 percent issues ($132.2 million) which stretched the debt out an additional 35 years. In 1946 the dollar and Swiss franc bonds were paid off—Argentina had earned dollars during the war in excess of purchases—and in 1953 the sterling debt was retired. Public bonded debt outstanding is now about $480 million. It consists of issues in the U.S. market and in Europe at varying dates from 1961 to 1971.

The relatively short-term dollar commercial debt was also refunded in part in 1934 by the issuance of dollar notes maturing serially over 4 years ($16.5 million) at 2.5 to 4 percent. There was also refunding of commercial debt to Europe in 1933 by the issue of sterling and Swiss franc obligations.

Refinancing, 1950

By 1950 the Argentine had accumulated large arrears in its commercial debts to American suppliers and banks. The reserves acquired during the war had been used to pay off external debt rather rapidly, to purchase the railroad system from British investors, and to cover balance of payments deficits. The Ex-Im in 1950 provided a loan of $125 million to a consortium of Argentine banks, guaranteed by the central bank, to pay off the arrears to American creditors, at 3.5 percent, repayable in 4 years after a 3-year grace on principal. Only $96.5 million was actually disbursed.

Refunding, 1956 [1]

The overthrow of the Peron regime (1946–55) led to an attempt to regularize Argentine financial relations with other countries, and to begin formulation of a development plan. Additional foreign credits were needed. The most urgent problem was the consolidation of the debts to Europe under the bilateral trade agreements, about $353 million. The agreement of these countries to consolidate the outstanding clearing debts and to multilateralize payments among them constituted the "Paris Club," (May 1956). The main creditors (Germany, U.K., Italy and France) agreed to payments over 8 to 10 years, apparently in equal annual installments. The debt to the Netherlands was to be paid in 5 years, while the smaller countries did not consolidate their claims. The installments were to be paid from the proceeds of Argentine exports. [2] Details of the individual country agreements varied. Japan joined the group with a similar consolidation. The original terms of payment were further extended by the creditor countries in 1960 and 1963.

The U.S. did not participate in the Paris Club meetings. As noted, the Ex-Im had refinanced American credits in 1950. After the conclusion of the European Agreement, however, the Ex-Im gave two credit lines (September 10 and November 11, 1956) aggregating $100 million to finance "equipment and services" and "transportation equipment," which further eased the balance of payments situation. In December 1958, a group of American banks agreed to lend $54 million for financing arrears on exchange operations.

In 1959 there was another group of credits intended to assist the attempt at stabilization. The IMF made a standby arrangement for $100 million, the Treasury extended the period of repurchase under its exchange agreement of $50 million, a consortium of 9 U.S. commercial banks provided a $75 million loan to finance arrears, and an equal amount was provided by a consortium of 54 European banks. The European credits were specifically conditional upon the IMF standby. Drawings under these credits in 1962 were largely repaid by mid-1963, but in June 1963 the European and American banks re-

1. IDB, *European Financing of Latin America's Economic Development* (1966), p. 100.
2. Under the "club" arrangement each member agreed to accept payment in any other member's currency, so that a surplus with any one of the members could be used to pay others.

funded the amounts outstanding ($18.75 million to be repaid in 1965). [3]

Refunding, 1962–63

The refundings of 1962–63 and 1965 were part of larger programs intended to deal with the inflationary problem and the exchange policy of the Argentine. The government put into effect measures to restrain inflation and to devalue the exchange rate, and received support for the program from the IMF and the U.S. Treasury and AID as well as a refunding of debts due to the Ex-Im and other creditors.

Under the 1959 arrangements Argentina had unified the previous dual exchange system, and maintained a relatively stable rate by central bank intervention in the market despite the internal inflation. In April 1961, after exchange reserves had been sharply reduced, the bank stopped intervention. In this year there was a trade deficit of about $500 million as well as heavy scheduled debt repayments. [4] Argentina had had from 1958 to 1961 annual standby arrangements with the Fund with appropriate undertakings on fiscal and monetary policies. The Treasury supplemented the Fund arrangements with related stabilization agreements. The 1961 IMF standby was cancelled at Argentine request in May 1962, and further drawings were not made under the Treasury parallel agreement. [5]

The 1962–63 debt refunding was a rather different matter than the 1956 arrangement. The funded Argentine public debt, which stood at $575 million in 1955, had risen to $2,649 million in 1962 and there was about a billion dollars of private unguaranteed debt. [6] Service on the public debt alone probably took a fourth of exports. The debt consisted of medium-term supplier credits extended largely by European firms, debts to American and European banks, international organizations and numerous Ex-Im credits to public agencies and private entities. Probably the full extent of indebtedness and the terms on which it had been contracted were known only approximately even by the Argentine authorities. The various creditors obviously were anx-

3. IDB, *European Financing*, pp. 138-39. In 1959 about $64 million in Japanese credits and commercial arrears was also consolidated bilaterally.

4. In July 1961 Argentina issued $25 million in serial bonds to refinance short-term debt owed to European and U.S. creditors and also long-term bonds, $114 million, for the acquisition of Segba (Servicios Electricos del Gran Buenos Aires).

5. See IMF, *Annual Report*, 1963, pp. 15, 158–59; Argentina, Banco Central, *Memoria Anual, 1962*, pp. 64–65.

6. Oficina de Estudios Para la Colaboración Económica Internacional, Buenos Aires, *Argentina Económica y Financiera* (1966), p. 302. The source does not explain how the data were compiled; they are probably not consistent with other reports.

ious not to give more favorable terms of refunding than other creditors would. Debt relief was contingent upon the IMF standby and the specific undertakings of Argentina as part of the arrangement. Negotiations, started early in 1962, were protracted.

While the Fund made a new standby ($100 million) in June 1962 under which Argentina undertook to take new measures "for reduced government spending, tightened control of credit and some increase in taxation,"[7] and the Treasury made a new exchange agreement ($50 million), there were no immediate drawings pending appropriate action. Obviously without a scaling down of debt payments the exchange resources provided would have been quickly dissipated, with little advance in the "orderly exchange system" which was the objective of the U.S. government as well as the Fund. After further discussions, the Fund, on July 26, announced that Argentina had not exceeded the ceilings and would try to operate under the agreement. The State Department the next day announced (1) that AID would continue disbursements under prior commitments (i.e. the $20 million balance of payments loan in February 1962), (2) that the Treasury Agreement was in effect (drawings could be resumed), and (3) that Ex-Im would consider a rescheduling of amounts coming due from governmental and private borrowers.[8]

The Ex-Im began rolling over maturing principal on some Argentine debt in August 1962 and the Paris Club in October agreed in principle on consolidation of part of the maturing principal on supplier credits, subject to the continuance in effect of the Fund standby and the credit limitations agreed. The Ex-Im was represented by an observer at this meeting, but subsequently agreed to similar debt relief. The creditors agreed to refinance about half of the $270 million due on principal of credits arising from the procurement of capital goods. The European governments or their agencies advanced funds to the Argentine government (or central bank) sufficient to cover half of the principal falling due in 1963 and 1964, i.e. $108 million. Japan made a similar arrangement, apparently $20 million, so that there was a refinancing of $129 million. The consolidation credits were to be repaid on a sliding scale—5 percent in 1965, 15 percent in 1966, and 20 percent annually in 1967, 1968 and 1969. The creditors also agreed to defer to 1966 25 percent of the amount due in 1962–63 on the earlier refundings

7. IMF, press release, June 7, 1962; U.S. Treasury, press release, June 7, 1962; NAC, *Report*, Jan.–June 1962, p. 34. Banco Central, *Memoria Anual*, 1962, p. 65.
8. U.S. State Department, *Bulletin*, Aug. 13, 1962, p. 253.

($15 million). Details of the bilateral agreements signed in mid-1963 varied somewhat.[9]

The tentative Ex-Im refunding of 1962 was formalized in an agreement of June 1963 to consolidate $72 million falling due between November 15, 1962 to October 1, 1964. Of this amount $67.5 million was used. Repayment terms were the same as for the European creditors. This credit has been repaid.

The roughly 50 percent devaluation of 1962 was followed by a sharp reversal of the balance of payments, mostly through a reduction in imports. While the Europeans granted no additional debt relief in 1963, the U.S. decided to give additional bilateral support in conjunction with the IMF. The new package deal included (1) reactivation of the Fund standby to make possible drawings of $25 million, (2) reactivation of the Treasury Exchange Agreement with another $25 million, (3) an AID balance of payments loan of $20 million and (4) an additional $20 million Ex-Im refinancing of debt. The $29 million new Ex-Im credit was to refinance U.S. supplier credits, but was not in fact used. The U.S. private creditors apparently refinanced their arrears by other methods. AID moreover provided $19.9 million in budget support (June 3, 1963) shortly after the Ex-Im refunding arrangement was agreed.

Refunding, 1965

The 1962–63 refundings proved only a temporary solution. The budgetary deficit continued with central bank financing, and prices continued to rise at about 25 percent a year. The exchange adjustment produced an export surplus, but current account "balance" was maintained by arrearages in payment for imports. In 1964 arrearages on current payments reached $70 million and by 1965 were $140 million, including agreed payments not made to the oil companies for the settlement of their property and other contractual claims.

Argentina's external debt had been reduced from $3.2 billion in 1963 probably including private debt to $2.9 billion at the end of 1964. About a third of this debt was in the form of supplier credits to state enterprises and private firms, largely with government or central bank guarantees. These debts required heavy amortization. Argentina requested a new refunding in 1965.

The U.S. participated fully in the meeting of the Paris Club in June

9. Banco Central, *Memoria Anual*, 1963, p. 57; IDB, *European Financing*, pp. 101–02.

1965 and the terms of settlement for the U.S., the Paris Club members, Japan and other countries were put on MFN terms. As part of the deal, Argentina agreed to let the unitary exchange rate float, to take internal measures to restrain credit and work toward budgetary equilibrium, to continue to limit new supplier credits to the amount paid off in a given period, and not to use pesos received for payment of foreign obligations for budgetary purposes.

The creditors agreed to provide financial relief equal to 60 percent of the principal due in 1965 on guaranteed supplier credits and project loans, to be repaid over 5 years beginning January 1968. Payments under the earlier refunding arrangements of 1956 and 1962 were to be continued as originally scheduled. That is, the 1965 rescheduling applied only to debts contracted after these agreements. [10]

The amount consolidated in 1965 was about $75.7 million, equal to 60 percent of the principal accruing to the creditors in FY 1965. The European countries and Japan, whose claims were mostly on guaranteed exporter credits, agreed either (a) to reimburse the Argentine central bank for 60 percent of the payments received (France, $7.9 million; Italy, $18.3 million; Japan, $10.2; Switzerland, $2.8; U.K., $9.8), or (b) to accept 40 percent payment by it (Germany, $8.1 million; Netherlands, $0.7 million). The consolidated amounts were to be repaid in 5 years after a 3-year grace period. Payments in the first year were to be 15 percent of the deferred amounts, in the second, third and fourth years, 20 percent; and in the fifth year, 25 percent. Some of the agreements provided for semiannual installments.

The Ex-Im, which had numerous small loans to private enterprises on its books and a few large loans to the government and its agencies, agreed to provide equivalent relief ($18 million—60 percent of the total payments of principal) by consolidating 100 percent of the principal of certain loans to the government and agencies. The agreement provided that if payments were not made on the private loans as scheduled the consolidation of the government loans would be correspondingly reduced. On receipt of interest payments the bank charges a note of the government or agency concerned for the corresponding principal. A total of $15.4 million was debited to the note, of which $6.3 million is outstanding (December 31, 1970). Subsequent lending to Argentina by Ex-Im has been for larger project loans, airplanes, steel mill and electrical facilities. To date, Argentina has met the required schedule under these refunding arrangements.

10. Cf. IDB, *European Financing*, p. 102.

Sequel

Argentine inflation continued to mid-1967 when a new stabilization program was adopted and received support from a $125 million IMF standby, a Treasury exchange agreement of $75 million, and standby credits of $100 million from American banks and $101.4 million equivalent from banks in Europe, Canada and Japan.[11] The banking credits were utilized but there were no drawings from the Fund or the Treasury, which in 1968 renewed their agreements. In fact Argentina repurchased pesos to repay previous drawings and pesos were used in part for drawings by other countries so that Fund holdings have been reduced to 75 percent of quota (February 29, 1972).

The 1967 stabilization program included a devaluation on March 13 from M$N250 to M$N350, when "virtually all restrictions on payments and transfers were eliminated." Import duties were reduced, import prohibitions lifted and export subsidies eliminated. Internal measures included tax increases, reduction of government expenditures, and limitations on wage increases.[12]

Since 1965 Argentina has been rolling over debt as it fell due. Payments of principal to DAC governments, largely the refunding credits, have exceeded utilization of government loans by about $140 million. Outstanding supplier credits have also been reduced. Correspondingly indebtedness to banks and bondholders has increased so that there is little change in the outstanding disbursed external debt. The interest rates on some of these issues have been higher than on the debt they replaced. Bonds have had interest rates either fixed at the time of issue or floating with the Euro-money rate. For example, the 7-year issue of 1970 pays 1.5 percent above the Euro-rate, initially 9.62 percent. Bank loans have also had differentials above prime or Euro-rates. Interest costs have risen about 37 percent above the 1965 figure. These costs must be met from earnings or reserves. Reserves are now less than half what they were at the end of 1968.

The outstanding public and private external debt, requiring heavy amortization in 1970, will constitute a crucial problem for the next few years. Obligations under the earlier refundings have been met and are scheduled to be paid off by 1972. The outstanding external debt of the government, central bank and other agencies, payable in convertible currencies, stood at $1,991.2 million at the end of 1969. Almost half consisted of commercial credits to governmental authorities. The

11. Banco Central, *Memoria Anual*, 1967, pp. 66–67.
12. Fund, press release, May 1, 1967.

central bank estimates 1970 amortization of public debt at $395.2 million, and $282.1 million in 1971.[13] Interest payments will be $110 to $185 million. Total service on public debt is almost $500 million, 28 percent of Argentine exports in 1970. In 1968, debt service was $482 million, a third of exports in that year, or 27.2 percent of exchange receipts (IBRD ratio).

Private debts at the end of 1969 were stated as $1,234.5 million, of which $807 million was in the form of bank credits and $390 million in commercial credits. Of the total of private debt, $737.4 million had a maturity of 180 days to 5 years, and contractual amortization in 1970 was set at $654 million,[14] i.e., the bulk of the debt had a maturity of 180 to 360 days. Without a renewal of bank loans and other credits, the contractual payment of the Argentine economy would be over a billion in 1970, compared with exports of $1.8 billion in 1970.

In sum, the solvency of the Argentine economy depends on its ability to renew banking credits and issue securities. The formal refunding credits will have been paid off in 1972, but there will be continued service on the debt which has replaced them. The inflation continues and the balance of payments has deteriorated. With an effective stabilization the balance of payments could improve to the extent that the net burden of debt could be reduced.

II. BRAZIL

Introduction

The multilateral consolidations of Brazilian debt in 1961 and 1964 were merely the most recent of a series of adjustments effected since 1898. The more recent consolidations of Brazilian debt were arranged in conjunction with various undertakings in the financial and exchange fields, by which successive finance ministers hoped to stabilize the Brazilian economy, or at least its foreign exchange situation.

The overthrow of Dom Pedro in 1889 has been followed by a series of dictatorships and intermittent periods of constitutional government. Political instability has been an important factor in the inflation

13. Banco Central, *Boletin Estadistico*, March 1970, p. 42.
14. Ibid., June 1970, p. 77. Bank of London and South America, *Review*, May 1970, p. 266; Sept. 1970, p. 490, gives slightly different figures based on releases of the central bank.

and foreign exchange difficulties which have persisted.[1] Along with the inflation, the exchange rate has depreciated, though generally with a lag, and periodically Brazil has accumulated delinquencies in its current payments of such magnitude as to require refinancing.

Bond Issues

Brazil met the payments on its outstanding sterling debt from 1824 to 1898 despite the internal political and economic difficulties resulting from increased borrowing and inflation. In 1898, however, Brazil was unable to meet payments of interest on its sterling bonds and gave the bondholders new bonds for the equivalent of the interest due 1898 to 1901. Sinking fund payments on all debt were suspended. Interest was paid from 1901 to 1914, and then interest was defaulted. There was a refunding issue, but the sinking fund payments were not met from 1914 to 1927, when they were made for a period of 4 years.

By 1930, total Brazilian public debt (including subordinate governmental units) reached $1,266.5 million equivalent, of which $373.5 million was denominated in dollars and the balance almost entirely in sterling.[2] Annual debt service was about $100 million, roughly 23.5 percent of export receipts.

In 1930–31 Brazil defaulted on the bulk of its sterling, franc and dollar debt. Under the unilateral offers made in 1931–32 and 1934 (Aranha Plan) fractional interest payments (40–50 percent) were made, the fraction depending on the security involved and the original coupon. In 1943, a new refunding (de Souza Costa) was negotiated with the bondholders' councils in the U.S. and U.K., and received the blessing of the State Department. Debt then amounted to $837 million in nominal principal, of which $286 million was in dollars, the balance mostly in sterling.[3] The bondholders were given the option (a) of taking a fractional interest payment (an average of about 2.5 percent),

1. With the rapid rise in prices and changes in the base years of index numbers, it is rather difficult to measure precisely the rate of inflation. Wholesale prices in June 1971 were about 162 times the level of 1953, and about 479 times the level of 1944. The exchange cost of the dollar for imports is about 138 times the 1953 level and about 384 times the 1944 rate. In the last year the rise in prices has been at about 20 percent per annum (see *Conjuntura Econômica*, Fundaçao Getulio Vargas, June 1970. Benedito Ribeiro and Mario Mazzei Guimarâes, *History of Brazilian Banking and Financial Development* (Rio: Pro-Service, 1967), pp. 114–73, outline developments since 1889.

2. George Wythe et al., *Brazil, an Expanding Economy* (New York: Twentieth Century Fund, 1949), pp. 295–96.

3. The outstanding Brazilian debt was extraordinarily complex. The national government had assumed responsibility for servicing provincial and local external debt, most of which had preceded the government in default. Debt had been contracted recklessly largely for budgetary

roughly a third of the contractual rates, on the original principal, but with amortization stretched out from 1.5 to 10 times the original period, or (b) accepting a reduction in principal of 20 to 50 percent with interest at roughly half of the contractual rates (an average of 3.75 percent) and a stretch out of amortization by relatively shorter periods. [4]

Under the 1943–44 refunding arrangement the annual debt service was reduced to probably about a fourth of the original amounts, though a precise figure cannot be obtained without an elaborate calculation. Interest payments have been made on the stamped bonds, and principal was rapidly reduced; the issues were retired in 1968. The sterling debt was retired in 1953 when a Fund drawing ($28.5 million) in sterling financed the payment. In 1956, the French franc bonds were also retired.

Brazilian Refunding: 1936–60

In view of this debt history, Brazil could not borrow at long term in financial markets and could finance development only by loans from public institutions, largely the Ex-Im and, to a lesser degree, the IBRD. The Brazilian government and Brazilian companies, however, financed a large volume of imports of equipment by short- and medium-term borrowings from exporters and commercial banks, which also loaned to meet balance of payments deficits. The Ex-Im up to June 30, 1960 authorized $1 billion in numerous exporter credits, project loans and balance of payments financing. The persistence of inflation and exchange difficulties led to frequent accumulation of arrearages on short- and medium-term transactions, which were refinanced several times before the general refundings of 1961.

At the beginning of 1935 approximately $30 million was overdue to American exporters. The borrowers had paid in local currency to the Bank of Brazil which, however, lacked dollars to make payments on the contracts. The National Foreign Trade Council, representing the U.S. exporters, negotiated an agreement for the payment of the arrears. Small claims were paid in cash, the balance, through the

reasons, at high interest rates and large discounts from nominal principal (see Valentim F. Bouças, *Finanças do Brasil*, vol. 19). The flotation of these securities in the United States in the 1920 period provided some of the provocation for the Johnson and Pecora hearings in 1932–34. In the Aranha and de Souza Costa refundings the outstanding obligations were divided into eight broad classes, each of which was settled on a different basis.

4. The Bondholders' Protective Council was unwilling to make a recommendation as to which alternative the bondholders should choose.

issuance of 5-year notes which the Council requested the Ex-Im to agree to purchase from the holders. In November 1935 the Ex-Im committed $17 million to purchase 60 percent of the notes received by each exporter, and subsequently raised the sum to $27.8 million to permit purchase of 100 percent. With the Bank's agreement to purchase, apparently the exporters were able to discount the notes with private banks or were willing to hold them, so that in practice only $1.7 million of the notes was presented to the Bank for purchase and this amount was paid off within 6 months.[5]

Three years later Ex-Im provided $19.2 million to the Bank of Brazil for current imports, to be repaid in 2 years' time, but only $4.5 million was actually disbursed on this credit at the risk of the Ex-Im. In 1941 a similar loan of $1.2 million, with repayment in 5 years, followed. The Bank also committed a credit of $12 million to the government of Brazil but this credit was not used. There were also no drawings under a $10 million credit committed in 1944.

In the following years Brazil borrowed from commercial banks and the New York Federal Reserve Bank (with gold as collateral) to meet immediate import requirements. These credits were, however, repaid in 1949, when coffee prices were rising, and when there was expectation that the Brazilian situation might be stabilized. Debt service in 1949 took about 30 percent of Brazilian exchange receipts.

The balance of payments surplus of 1950 turned into a deficit of $250 million in 1951 and $600 million in 1952, when total exports amounted to $1.4 billion. At the end of the year commercial arrears to all countries were in the neighborhood of $900 million to $1 billion. In 1953 the U.K. and Brazil agreed on a refinancing of $158 million equivalent. Other creditors in Europe may also have made arrangements. The arrears to American creditors were about $450 million. The Ex-Im provided a credit of $300 million partially to liquidate the arrears, and commercial banks provided the balance. The Ex-Im credit at 3.5 percent probably reduced the interest cost to about half the former rates. The loan was originally to be repaid in monthly installments over a 2-year period after a grace period of a year and a half. In 1954, however, the Ex-Im extended this loan for an additional 5 years. Monthly payments were reduced from $13 million to $4.2 million, with a proviso for larger amounts to be amortized from Bra-

5. Statement of Hawthorne Arey, Assistant Director. Export-Import Bank, in Senate Banking and Currency Committee, *Hearings*, "S. Res. 25, Study of Export-Import Bank and World Bank" (1954), p. 89.

zilian dollar earnings above $1 billion in any one year. At the time of
the 1961 consolidation the $70.4 million still outstanding was included
in the new financial arrangement.[6]

As the result of drought in Argentina, the usual source of Brazilian
wheat imports, Brazil bought wheat in the United States from 1952 to
1954, and in the later year the Ex-Im authorized a loan to the Bank of
Brazil of $15 million for wheat imports, repayable in 15 months, of
which, however, only $10.4 million was disbursed. In 1955, following
conversations in Rio by representatives of Ex-Im and the State and
Treasury departments, there was an Ex-Im loan to refinance purchases
of equipment manufactured in the United States of $75 million to be
repaid in 1961–62,[7] and in 1958 there was a similar credit of $100
million to be repaid in monthly installments after 1962. The outstanding balances on these loans were consolidated in the 1961 arrangement.

The IMF provided assistance to Brazil in a series of drawings with
repurchases between 1949 and May 1961, under which the net drawings outstanding stood at $237.4 million. The Treasury Department
also provided exchange agreements in 1958–61 in connection with
the Fund standby.

1961 Consolidation

In 1961 Brazil, in consultation with the IMF and the United States,
undertook a new exchange reform under which the rate was to float.
To assist in financing the reform the IMF provided a standby credit of
$160 million, which, in effect, refunded previous drawings outstanding
and allowed some new credit. The Treasury provided $70 million in an
exchange agreement, and AID provided a $100 million program loan,
and P.L. 480 local currency sales agreements provided $70 million in
1961 and $102.2 million in 1962.

An adjustment of external debt was essential to the exchange measures. Total Brazilian debt at the beginning of 1961 was about $3.8
billion, of which $2.8 billion was outstanding to American public and
private creditors. Some 40 percent of the principal was to be repaid in
1961 and 1962 and 78 percent between 1961 and 1965. Of the total debt
about a billion was relatively short term. Some $400 million was due

6. Cf. Arey, *Hearings*, "S. Res. 25," p. 117; Ex-Im, *Semiannual Report*, July-Dec. 1953, p. 31;
Jan.-June 1954, p. 11.
7. Ex-Im, *Report*, Jan.-June 1955, pp. 18–47.

to European export creditors and $300 million to U.S. private exporters and banks.

The consolidation of the commercial debts to European countries, due between May 1961 and December 1962, was arranged through the "Hague Club." Under this arrangement the proceeds of Brazilian exports to the European creditors were used in part to pay a portion of the debt outstanding, but 80 percent of the obligations falling due in 1961 was to be refunded, 70 percent in 1962 and 1963, 50 percent in 1964, and 35 percent in 1965. The total amount of European refinancing was $135 million. As in other "club" arrangements the bilateral agreements differed in detail, but repayment generally was to be made in installments between 1966 and June 1971. Brazil, however, again accumulated commercial arrears with these countries on its trade in 1963 and 1964 so that some of the participants suspended the 1961 arrangements, and they were included in the consolidation of 1964–65.[8] At the time of the 1961 consolidation there were new European credits of about $110 million which facilitated payment of amounts not consolidated.

The United States was not a party to the Hague Club arrangement, so that the Ex-Im made its own arrangements for refinancing commercial arrears, refinancing of earlier credits, including the earlier consolidation credits of 1953, 1955 and 1958, and also project credits on which payments were falling due between 1961 and 1962. While the Ex-Im authorized credits aggregating $731.8 million, not all of the amounts were needed. A loan of $168 million was authorized ($162.4 million disbursed) to pay off commercial arrears, with repayment over 14 years after 6 years' grace on principal. A second loan of $484.3 million ($454.2 million disbursed) refinanced the earlier consolidation credits and provided funds for new imports. In this case, the older refinancing credits were extinguished and the amounts due included in the new loan. This loan was to be repaid in 16.5 years after 1.5 year's grace. A third credit of $79.6 million was authorized to cover payments on various project credits as they fell due. This consolidation credit was to be repaid over 18 years. On June 30, 1971, $263.3 million was outstanding.

Some of the American private creditors also rolled over the amounts due them, but the precise terms do not appear available. Japanese credits were also refinanced. Total refinancing arrangements with public and private creditors aggregated about $2 billion.

8. IDB, *European Financing of Latin American Economic Development*, pp. 103–04.

1963–64 Consolidation

Brazil was unable to meet its obligations under the 1961 refunding arrangements or its undertakings under the IMF standby. Inflation continued, about 50 percent in 1962, and further arrears were accumulated from current transactions.

The United States was greatly concerned about the state of affairs in Brazil, and at the end of 1962 President Kennedy, who had earlier discussed affairs with President Goulart, announced that the United States would be unable to help Brazil further while the inflation continued. Brazil took some measures, and the Finance Minister, San Tiago Dantas, came to Washington for discussions. The resulting Brazilian undertakings and the proposed U.S. assistance were published in the Dantas-Bell correspondence.[9] In addition to internal measures to check inflation, raise revenues, restrain wages, etc., the program included an exchange adjustment and negotiation of refunding arrangements on debt to Europe as well as to the United States.

The U.S. government proposed a "package" of $395.8 million to assist Brazilian efforts. Immediate resources to be available included $33 million from Ex-Im, $25.5 million from the Treasury and $25.5 million from AID. Subsequently, Ex-Im was to refund debt payments of $44.5 million falling due June 1, 1963 to May 31, 1964; AID was to provide $100 million in program loans and $100 million in project loans, and P.L. 480 was to supply $70 million.

In the 1964 Hague Club consolidation the United States participated fully and agreed to a refunding of credits substantially on Hague Club terms. The 1964 Hague Agreement provided for the refunding of $250 million in arrears accumulated since 1961. The 1961 consolidation arrangements were to be continued in effect and were not included in the 1964 agreement, with the exception that payments due in 1964 and 1965 under the 1961 arrangement were reduced from 70 percent of the agreed amount to 50 percent for 1964 and to 35 percent for 1965. It was further agreed to refinance 70 percent of the obligations falling due between January 1, 1964 and December 31, 1965 to the extent that they had been registered with the Brazilian authorities before the end of 1963. That is, 30 percent only of the principal was to be repaid in 1964 and 1965 and that the balance would be amortized over a 5-year period beginning January 1, 1967 for 1964 obligations and beginning January 1, 1968 for 1965 obligations. The additional refunding credits

9. On March 25, 1963, the White House released the correspondence embodying the results of the discussions (State Department, *Bulletin*, April 15, 1963, pp. 557–61).

by the European countries amounted to about $62 million.[10] American and European banks provided additional finance of $80 million and $58 million, respectively.[11]

In accordance with this understanding the Ex-Im in two transactions consolidated $73 million. Payments on the consolidation credits to the Ex-Im and the European creditors have been made in accordance with the agreement.

The IBRD did not refund the obligations of Brazil due to it. Brazil's outstanding debt to the Bank was $193.3 million ($4.8 million undisbursed, June 30, 1964). Interest rates varied between 4.25 and 6 percent and maturities ranged from 15 to 25 years, so that annual payments of principal and interest were about $20 million per annum in 1965 and the following years. Instead of refunding, the Bank made new loans in 1965 and 1966 amounting to $229.1 million. These long-term loans had grace periods of 5 to 6.5 years so that principal repayments would not be due until 1971, corresponding with the period of beginning repayment on the Hague Club arrangements.

Had the IBRD loans been entirely for foreign exchange costs they would not have provided debt relief. These loans were primarily for power production, and allowed a preference to local bidders in lieu of customs duties so that a good part of the construction work and equipment was provided by Brazilian producers. The Bank loaned dollars to cover local currency costs, and the loan agreements specifically provided "withdrawals from the Loan Account in respect of expenditures in the currency of the Guarantor or for goods produced in (including services supplied from) the territories of the Guarantor shall be in dollars or such other currency or currencies as the Bank shall from time to time reasonably select."[12] Likewise the livestock development loan of $40 million (1961) financed an agreed percent of the cost of loans to livestock producers. A considerable portion of the goods supplied was probably of local origin and, to the extent that it consisted of imports, they were imports which had previously been paid for or otherwise financed. A 1968 loan for highways ($26 million) covered 40 percent of the cost of construction of roads by Brazilian states. In effect then, without formally rescheduling the Brazilian debt to the Bank, the large amount of local currency payments financed by

10. IDB, *European Financing*, p. 104.
11. Banco do Brasil, *Relatorio*, 1965, pp. 55–56.
12. See Loan Agreement between IBRD and Central Electrica de Furnas, 1965 (Loan 403 BR). Similar provisions were included in other Brazilian power agreements, e.g. Loans 475, 476, 477, 478 made in 1965 and 1966, and in subsequent agreements, e.g. in 1968 Loan 565 BR.

the Bank's loans subsequent to 1965 has indirectly refinanced these credits for an additional 20 years.

Current Situations and Prospects

An attempt to appraise the Brazilian debt situation is complicated by the lack of comparable data. The distinction between public and private obligations is blurred when some private indebtedness has been guaranteed by public authorities and much of it has been contracted under assurances of exchange availability, though not of the applicable rate. Since the private debt now on the books has been contracted at various times under different regulations, there is probably considerable legal uncertainty as to the government's obligation.

The available data are summarized in Table 20, but they should not be regarded as definitive or consistent as explained in the notes to the table. The higher figures for 1970 in column A include some $1.6 billion "capital loans" to private firms,[15] which are relatively short term. Ordinary short-term commercial and banking credits outstanding to American concerns alone were about $400 million at the end of 1969.

As of the beginning of 1970, bilateral governmental credits were reported as $1,989 million, as part of the $3.5 billion shown in column B. U.S. agency credits including undisbursed as of that date were $1,852 million. These credits included private obligations which had exchange assurances. Of the disbursed outstanding of $1,455.6 million, $789 million was AID, $101 million in dollar repayable P.L. 480, $522 million of Ex-Im, and the balance military and CCC credits. As of the end of 1970, the total disbursed outstanding to U.S. agencies was $1,504 million.

Debt service in 1971 is of the order of $400–600 million, depending on inclusions and exclusions. On the basis of balance of payments figures, amortization of government and central bank debt was $405 million in 1969, and of private long-term debt, $188 million. Interest was about $206 million for both. These gross amounts were offset by disbursements of $419 million on loans to government and $469 million to private firms.[16] Part of these amounts was new credit and

13. See IBRD, *Annual Report*, 1971, p. 65.
14. Bank of London and South America, *Review*, Feb. 1971, p. 93.
15. These are loans to supply working capital, denominated in foreign currencies but converted into cruzeiros, with guarantees of repatriation, but not of rates. For a brief statement of conditions see IMF, *Exchange Restrictions*, 1971, pp. 57–58.
16. IMF, *Balance of Payments Yearbook*, vol. 22, Feb. 1971.

Table 20. Brazil: Approximate Principal of Debt and Debt Service, 1956–70 (Millions of Dollars).

	A		B	
	Principal	Service	Principal	Service
1956	1,400			
1962	3,800			
1963		396		
1964	3,167	381		
1965	3,257	400		441
1966	3,051	465	2,773	474
1967	3,201	559	3,103	580
1968	3,469		3,426	391
1969	4,310		3,496	388
1970	[4,403]	[550]	3,522	n.a.

Source: IBRD, and Bank of London and South America, *Review,* Feb. 1971, p. 93. From the available data, it is impossible to construct a complete or consistent time series on Brazilian public debt. Column A, from IBRD data, includes undisbursed debt and includes some or all of the private debt, whether or not fully guaranteed. Column B data, a recent IBRD revision, include nonguaranteed debt of the private sector. Undisbursed amounts of U.S. government credits are included, but undisbursed amounts of supplier credits and loans by other governments to the public sector are excluded. As of Dec. 31, 1969, about $800 million of credits was undisbursed. The figure given in column A for 1970 is based on data from the exchange authorities, but may not be consistent with other figures. As of June 30, 1970, the reported figure was $4,907 million and debt service was estimated at $600 million. The figures may include some shorter-term debt.

part probably a roll-over of bank credits. Most of the consolidation debt of 1965, except the Ex-Im credit, has been paid off.

As noted, Brazil has met service requirements on its debt since the 1965 consolidation. The U.S. government has provided (June 30, 1965 to June 30, 1970) in AID program loans $566.6 million and in P.L. 480, $111.9 million. This balance of payments assistance helped pay debt service. Total credits and grants to Brazil in this period were about $1.6 billion.

The Brazilian economic situation has improved considerably since 1966. GNP at constant prices has grown. Exports in 1970 were $2.3 billion, $560 million higher than in 1966. The trade balance has been positive ($300 million in 1969 and 1970). The large current account deficit ($502 million in 1970) was partly a matter of debt service and remission of profits. Foreign exchange reserves have increased from $368 million in December 1966 to $1,477 million in January 1972, thus providing some cushion against adverse developments. Exports of iron ore and minor products have increased and there has been some improvement in coffee prices.

Inflation has been the principal factor in Brazil's exchange and debt problem. While the rate has decreased from earlier periods, it still is

20 percent a year. Governmental and private borrowing has risen rapidly. If inflation can be controlled and the program of gradual stabilization proves successful,[17] the Brazilian economy can further develop its resources, and with appropriate devaluation, its exports. Its debt will be more manageable, even though the debt service ratio is likely to be quite high, say 20 percent. Steps have been taken to control the increase in debt. Some of the debt can be further rolled over at a price. The AID portion will require only small service. Unfavorable political or economic conditions could check the flow of capital and aid, and could adversely affect debt-servicing capacity. For the immediate future there appears to be no need for further refunding.

III. CHILE

Economic Situation

Chile has had a long history of debt difficulties related to the persistent inflation and recurrent balance of payments deficits, financed by incurring greater debt.

Inflation has continued for well over a hundred years, though halted for brief periods by several attempts at stabilization. The rate of inflation cannot be precisely measured. Roughly prices (home and import goods, 1963 = 100) were in July 1971 about 360 times the 1948 level and 13 times the 1961 level. Consumer prices were about 380 times the 1948 and 12 times the 1961 levels. In the 12 months to July 1971 prices had increased by almost 10 percent and consumer prices by 28 percent. Between the end of 1970 and March 1972 consumer prices had risen by almost 39 percent and general prices (to January 1972) by 21 percent.[1]

The inflation has resulted from unbalanced budgets (including the autonomous agencies) which have shown a deficit in almost every year over the last 30. Private sector borrowing has also contributed significantly, and has been facilitated by the negative real interest rate pre-

17. For a discussion of the program see Alexandre Kafka, "The Brazilian Stabilization Program, 1964–66," *Journal of Political Economy*, 75 (Aug. 1967): 596–631.

1. An attempt to relate price changes over a long period is rendered practically impossible by shifts in the base of the index numbers, and splicing is particularly unsatisfactory when the index number on a given base is very large or very small in comparison with the index number on another base.

vailing for many years. Periodic escalation of wages, savings deposits, mortgage payments and social security, with changes in the cost of living index, has been a built-in factor for further inflation.

The Chilean balance of payments depends in large part upon copper export receipts which form two-thirds to three-fourths of the total receipts. With the heavy investment program the goods and services account has been in deficit annually, at least since 1955, though there were surpluses on trade account in 1959 and 1965–69. Heavy payments of interest and amortization and the remission of earnings of foreign enterprises have been important factors in this deficit. The deficits have been met largely by new borrowing. In the recent period to 1969 the rise in the price of copper and the increase in production favorably affected Chile's exports,[2] but debt service also increased. Chilean foreign exchange reserves increased from $162 million at the end of 1968 to $396 million in September 1970, but fell to $84 million in January 1972. They may now be as low as $45 million.

Chile has had a variety of exchange systems, but in recent periods there has been a "fluctuating" rate in a dual market, one for trade and government transactions and the other, for private invisibles. In the trade market the rate of exchange has increased from 7.67 escudos per dollar at the end of 1968 to 15.8 in February, and 25 in October 1972.[3] Over the 23-year period since 1948 the escudo (1,000 pesos) has fallen to about 1/1000 its earlier value.

Chilean Debt and Refunding

Bond refundings. Chile began to borrow abroad, principally by bonds floated in England, shortly after independence. These bonds went into default in 1826. In 1840 there was a readjustment of the old debt. From 1880 to 1884 there was a moratorium on all external debt. There were successive new and refunding issues, and prior to the depression Chile borrowed heavily in the American bond market. These issues defaulted on interest and principal in 1931. In the following years, when the bonds were selling at low prices, Chile used its available exchange to "repatriate" the bonds, rather than to meet contractual payments. In 1935 the outstanding amount was refunded to a 30-year issue with interest payments of from 0.6 to 2 percent. Half

2. In 1971, however, copper prices and production fell sharply.
3. The nontrade rate moved from 8.7 to 28 escudos per dollar as rates were bid up with the flight of capital. With the many changes in the exchange system a comparison of rates is practically impossible. The ratio in the text is based on the free market rate. On the official or trade market basis the ratio would be 1/488.

of the receipts accruing to the debt fund were to be used for retirement and half for interest payments. This arrangement was not satisfactory to the creditors, and in 1948 a new settlement was reached, with interest payments at 1.5 to 3 percent for various issues. The amount of bonded debt now outstanding, on which interest payments have been made (average of 2.3 percent) is about $82 million, of which about half is owed to American investors and the balance to British, Swiss and other holders.

Chilean debt problem, 1953–70. Over the last 15 years Chilean external public debt has increased from $322 million at the end of 1953 to $2.2 billion at the end of 1969, including undisbursed of $493 million. Excluded from this amount, however, are private unguaranteed debts of the order of $275 to $300 million.

The growth of the public debt and the increased cost of servicing are shown in Table 21. Debt service in 1968 was 172.6 million, 18.4 percent of exports and 16 percent of exchange receipts. With increased payment due in 1969 and 1970 under the refunding arrangements, total debt service was higher. President Allende Gossens is reported as placing the outstanding debt in 1971 as over $3 billion, with service in 1971 of $300 million and in 1972 and 1973 of $400 million, between 30 and 40 percent of exports.[4] The figures may not be comparable with the table data, and probably include short-term debt since long-term loans in 1970 were quite small.

Of the total debt (as of January 1, 1970) $1,192.6 million was owed to governments, of which $946.6 million was to the United States, including some loans to private entities, which may be unguaranteed. Debts to other governments included the refunding by the governments, in 1965, of debt owing to their nationals, most of which had been previously guaranteed. Supplier credits were about $364.3 million, bond issues, $82 million, and the balance of the private debt consisted of bank credits and other obligations. Total privately-held debt was about $709 million. The IBRD had outstanding loans of $152 million, the IDB, $79.7 million, and IDA, $19 million.

Refinancing, 1961–64. Prior to 1965, when there was a general debt refunding, Chilean debt was in part refinanced bilaterally, and funds were secured to meet accruing debt payments by further borrowing. For example, the Ex-Im in addition to many project credits has provided loans for "machinery and equipment" or capital goods, $62.5

4. *New York Times,* Nov. 10, 1971, p. 12.

Table 21. Chilean Public and Publicly Guaranteed Debt Outstanding, Including Undisbursed, and Debt Service, 1956–70 (Millions of Dollars).

	Debt	Debt Service
1956	351.0	50.0
1957	378.7	53.4
1958	417.1	51.2
1959	419.4	60.5
1960	541.6	78.3
1961	553.4	117.9
1962	751.6	127.0
1963	877.8	99.9
1964	992.9	122.9
1965	1,073.0	120.6
1966	1,138.2	129.7
1967	1,336.3	123.0
1968	1,830.5	172.6
1969	1,842.9	n.a.
1970	2,227.0	n.a.

Source: IBRD.

million in 1957–59; $15 million in 1964. Loans to refinance prior U.S. purchases were made in 1961 ($15 million, of which $12 million was utilized), and 1963 ($15 million, both repaid). Following the May 1960 earthquake, there was a sharp increase in the balance of payments deficit in 1961 to $286.7 million compared with $163.3 million in 1960. The United States financed import requirements for earthquake reconstruction to the extent of $110 million (AID, $100 million; Ex-Im, $10 million). In the same year the U.K. refinanced £2 million[5] and it is possible that other countries also made refinancing loans.

Consolidation, 1965. At the end of 1964 Chile requested its creditors to consolidate some of the outstanding loans for the ensuing years since the contractual payments due in 1965 on public and government-guaranteed credits amounted to $242 million, about 40 percent of foreign exchange earnings. In 1966 the total was $275 million. In addition to the Paris Club members, the United States, Japan and Canada participated in the Paris meeting in the middle of the year and joined in the multilateral refunding of the Chilean debt. The IMF, IBRD, IDB and the OECD participated in the discussions. As part of the understandings reached by the Chilean government with the creditor countries and the IMF, the Chilean government proposed restraints on borrowing from the central bank, holding down the rate of inflation by other measures, and limiting new supplier credits to the

5. Banco Central, *Memoria Anual*, 1961, pp. 177–80, 202–03.

amount paid off. Measures taken were to be reported to the IMF for the information of the creditors.

The multilateral arrangement provided for a consolidation of 70 percent approximately of the principal falling due in 1965 and 1966. The arrangement covered principally the credits over a year extended to the Chilean government or its agencies, or with its guarantee, by exporters from the participating countries whose loans had been guaranteed by their respective credit agencies and, to some extent, credits which had previously been granted by governmental institutions.[6]

The Paris agreement provided that individual arrangements were to be made by the Chilean government and central bank so as to adapt the consolidation to the requirements of the individual countries. The subsequent negotiations resulted in varying amounts of debt consolidated. The agreement contemplated that about $136 million of principal falling due in 1965 (of the total of $194 million) and $162 million due in 1966 would be deferred for repayment in 5 years beginning 1968 and 1969 respectively. Interest on the old obligations continued at the contractual rates, and varying rates were applied to the consolidation credits.

The specific bilateral implementing agreements gave Chile additional relief. While most refunded 70 percent of principal, the Ex-Im consolidated 75.4 percent of principal in 1965 and 72.8 percent of amounts due in 1966. The Export-Import Bank of Japan refinanced 100 percent; Canada, 88 percent for 1965 and 77 percent in 1966; Germany refinanced 70 percent of capital plus the accruing interest, and in addition provided other loans. Refunding procedures also differed somewhat. Most of the creditors extended new loans to the government or central bank in amounts equal to the deferred payments. In the cases of the U.S. (Ex-Im), Belgium and the Netherlands, the central bank paid 30 percent of the principal and the creditor debited the consolidation credit for the rest. In the Ex-Im agreement it was provided that if payments were made directly in full by the private obligors, the Ex-Im would pay to an account of the central bank with a U.S. commercial bank, the 70 percent refunded.

The net result of the renegotiation was that Chilean principal payments on the debts covered were reduced to $46.2 million in 1965 and $46.9 million in 1966. When payment was resumed in 1968, however,

6. For the terms of the Paris agreed minute and subsidiary agreements, see Banco Central, *Boletin Mensual*, Nov. 1965, pp. 1588–90; Dec. 1965, pp. 80–83, 135–49.

amortization increased by $27 million, and in 1969 and 1970 by about $57 million. The consolidation did not apply to long-term credits extended by the international institutions or the governments generally. Ex-Im, however, consolidated $40 million and AID extended the maturity of its $10 million program loan of 1958. Service on all long-term public debt was $120.6 million in 1965 and rose to $172.6 million in 1968. In 1970 debt service may have been about $200 million. A figure as high as $300–400 million has been reported as payable in 1972, but this may include short-term obligations and IMF repurchases due.

The Chilean stabilization effort was helped by a Fund standby of $36 million in 1965 and drawings in subsequent years. Drawings and repurchases have reduced the net credit from the Fund to $39.5 million (September 1971). In 1965 the Treasury provided $16.1 million in an exchange agreement, parallel to the Fund. American commercial banks gave a 4-year credit of $45 million (December 11, 1964) probably to refund short-term debt not included in the consolidation. British banks also gave new loans, and the K.f.W. provided $25 million.

Economic Assistance and Debt

Since the 1965 consolidation, Ex-Im loans to Chile have been for projects, largely to private copper companies, but also for steel, jet planes and chemical and industrial plants. The IBRD has given loans for power, roads, agriculture and education. IDB ordinary capital loans have been mostly to industry.

AID has provided a total of $340.2 million in program assistance of a total of $455.4 million (1963–70) in addition to the earthquake reconstruction loan of $100 million, which was used largely for balance of payment purposes. P.L. 480 has aggregated $261.9 million, of which $89.3 million is dollar repayable and the balance in grants or sales for escudos (pesos). By financing part of Chilean import requirements AID facilitated debt service, which, however, was considerably larger. Total U.S. assistance to Chile, (FY 1962–70) has been about $1.3 billion.

Current Situation

As mentioned above, the Chilean government anticipated a debt crisis in 1971 and later years, since debt service will take 30–40 percent of export receipts. Dr. Allende stated that Chile would continue to pay, but the creditors would be asked to "renegotiate the debt structure."

The Chilean economic situation has deteriorated rapidly in the last two years. Precisely how much is difficult to estimate for lack of data, some of which are not currently published. The money supply doubled between mid-1970 and 1971 as did government borrowings. The rise in prices is, however, not unusual for Chile. With the take-over of the copper mines, production was reported as sharply decreasing but has subsequently recovered. Copper prices fell about 25 percent in the last year. Undoubtedly the Chilean balance of payments has further deteriorated. The inflow of capital has practically ceased, though Chile has announced receiving credits of $250 million from socialist countries in the last year.

Chilean debt as of 1971–72 was more than double the 1965 figure. The total government and guaranteed debt to governments was about $2.6 billion, including some undisbursed amounts. There were several hundred millions of additional private obligations. Total debt figures as high as $3.7 billion have been reported, but there is no practical way of reconciling data. IBRD data as of the beginning of 1970 showed a total of $2.2 billion of long-term debt. More than half was to governments, $1.2 billion; supplier credits were given as $364 million; bank credits, $144 million; IBRD and IDB loans, $226 million; and other, $300 million. These figures are much lower than those discussed in the refunding meetings, though it is not clear how much debt may have been contracted in the interval. The intergovernmental refunding arrangement of 1972 applies to government and exporter credits, most of which have been guaranteed in the creditor countries. Bank arrangements were a separate negotiation.

The United States is the largest creditor. As of June 30, 1971 government disbursed credits stood at $869.9 million; Ex-Im, $307.5 million; AID, $497.9 million; CCC, $45.2 million; and military credits, $10.3 million. American private banks had short-term claims of $111 million and long-term of $97 million (April 30, 1972). Non-banking concerns had long-term claims of $126 million and short term, $48 million (December 31, 1971). Debt arising from nationalization is not included in the U.S. data.

Terms of the debt varied considerably. Based on reported service payments in 1968, supplier credits required annual payments of a third of principal; government credits from all countries, 8.1 percent;

and international institution loans, 13.4 percent. The Chilean government estimated contractual service of $300 million in 1971 and $400 million in 1972. This estimate seems reasonable.

The Paris Club met in February 1972 to consider the request for relief. The Chilean government was reported in the press as seeking a consolidation of amounts due 1972–75 with repayment over ten years starting 1976. It also asked for new credits to tide it over immediate difficulties.[8] Action taken was clearly a stopgap. The "memorandum of understanding" of April 19, 1972 recommended that the governments reschedule 70 percent of interest and principal falling due from November-December 1971 to the end of 1972. The rescheduled amounts are to be repaid over an 8-year period, including 2 years of grace. The creditors also stated their willingness to examine the Chilean request for a rescheduling of 1973 debt service "at the end of this year in the light of the Chilean economic situation."[9] The amount deferred is about $280 million for the 14-month period. Debt covered includes obligations to government agencies and supplier credits, which were mostly insured by public agencies. The governments will pay off, or have paid off, their nationals, and will receive payment in due course. Unlike 1965, accrued interest as well as principal is included. The "understanding" is not self-executing, so that Chile must make bilateral agreements with the creditors to cover relief on the variety of debts. France, Belgium and Spain have signed agreements. Others are likely to follow.

The United States wished to have the agreement contingent upon assurance of full payment for the nationalized mining and other property as well as Chilean agreement with the IMF on financial policies. Chile accepted the principle of paying "just compensation for all nationalization in accordance with Chilean and international law," a phrase which may lead to negotiation. What progress will be made toward stabilizing the Chilean economy remains to be seen.

A separate agreement was made between Chile and a group of 30 American banks, which gave loans aggregating $160 million to cover payments due them over a 15-month period to the end of 1974. Debts of public and private obligors are included. In 1972 and 1973 repayment will be 5 percent of principal, with the amount rising to 10 percent in 1975 and thereafter until the total is repaid.[10] Probably

7. U.S. Treasury, *Bulletin*, Oct. 1971, pp. 95–98, 105–08.
8. *New York Times*, Nov. 10, 1971, p. 12.
9. Paris Press Release, April 19, 1972.
10. Chile, Office of Information of the Presidency, *The Chilean Report*, June 1–15, 1972, p. 7.

other agreements will be made with banks in other countries and with governments not in the Paris Club.

Refunding of 70 percent of the debt service due to governments and the conversion of short-term banking loans to longer term will greatly relieve pressure on the Chilean balance of payments for the next few years. Settlement of the nationalization problem could possibly re-open the flow of private and public capital to Chile. There is little reason to expect that inflation will be halted for long or that budgetary difficulties can be avoided. The basic problems remain. While Chile has obtained financial assistance from other Latin American countries and from "socialist countries," these sources can offer only temporary relief. The creditor governments will in practice have to agree to successive refundings in the coming years or face outright default.

IV. TURKEY

Background

Aside from minor reschedulings, there have been 3 general refundings of Turkish external debt in the last 10 years, and additional action may be needed in the future.

Turkey has had a large current account deficit for the last 20 years, with imports exceeding exports by varying amounts, sometimes as high as 100 percent but generally about 50 percent higher. In 1970 the trade deficit was $262 million (f.o.b.) compared with exports of $578 million. Prices have risen steadily. The government budget has been in continual deficit, monetary circulation has increased with lending to the government by the central bank and expanding loans by the banks to the private sector. Despite the persistence of inflation and the payments deficit, the lira has been devalued only in 1946, 1959–60 and 1970, neglecting the multiple currency arrangements, 1953–59, which attempted to give an export incentive but retained a low rate for the dollar and other currencies for imports.

The Turkish development program has been directed to greater industrialization of an agricultural economy, partly through the establishment of state (or mixed ownership) industrial and mining enterprises, with considerable external finance and technical assistance. The task has been formidable, but results appear in the annual rise of about 3.5 to 4 percent in per capita GNP at constant prices, a relatively high rate in comparison with other developing countries (not oil producers) and many of the industrials. "The basic problem is that Turkish industry is by and large over-protected from foreign competition. This has led to costly, inefficient production, resulting in a product which is noncompetitive in the world market. Consequently, most Turkish industry has preferred to concentrate on the domestic market rather than to undertake the modifications necessary before export sales are possible . . . ."[1] The balance of payments continues to depend on the export of agricultural and some mineral products, and in recent years on the earnings of Turkish labor working abroad.

The massive economic assistance to Turkey by the United States and in recent years other NATO countries has obviously been related to strategic interests. U.S. aid has been on a grant or soft loan basis and the more recent European credits have been on easier terms than the earlier supplier credits which created the serious debt crises, though the recent European credits are in good part refundings of debt. Assistance has taken the form of loans for development projects, but almost as much for financing imports of consumption goods and materials and supplies needed to keep the economy going. European countries, the European Monetary Authority, the European Investment Bank and the IBRD have in the 6-year period, 1963–68, provided about $1.8 billion equivalent on a gross basis,[2] though this amount involves considerable double counting since it includes debt relief by the granting of new credits. Total U.S. aid to Turkey from 1946 to 1970 was $5.8 billion, of which $4.3 billion was in grants, including military grants of $2.9 billion. The loan portion was almost wholly on soft terms.

Turkish External Debt

The public and publicly guaranteed long-term debt of Turkey has mounted rapidly and is now almost 6 times what it was in 1958–59 when the first general refunding occurred. The present debt, however, includes a larger amount of concessional term debt, so that service is proportionally lighter, though still onerous in comparison with Turkish earnings of foreign exchange. Pre-1958 debt was largely on supplier credit terms though the United States had provided loans on

1. Maurice J. Williams (AID) in House Committee on Appropriations, *Hearings*, "Foreign Assistance and Related Agencies Appropriations for 1970" (1969), p. 1035.
    2. Ibid., p. 1036.

relatively easy terms (Marshall Plan terms) between 1948 and 1953, $85 million compared with grants of $140 million, and in the subsequent period prior to 1962, loans both for projects and import finance were made repayable in liras.

The growth of the Turkish debt is illustrated by Table 22, which shows the approximate principal outstanding (commitments less repayments) from 1955 to 1970 and estimated actual service payments. The data for principal are probably not entirely consistent (based largely on Turkish submissions to the IBRD), and the large changes in service payments reflect refundings, i.e., when a short-term debt is repaid and a new debt of equal amount (or an agreed fraction) is substituted, the payment of the old debt appears as amortization, as it is in accounting, even though the actual principal is unchanged.

Of the total of $2.2 billion of debt at January 1, 1970, $1.6 billion was owed to governments, more than half to the United States, with Germany and the U.K. as the other largest creditors; $462 million to international, mostly European regional organizations; and $73.2 million to suppliers and private financial institutions. The outstanding loans from the United States, Britain, Canada and Japan have relatively light terms, the others require service of between 10 and 20 percent per annum, though they are shorter-termed in form than in substance.

Total U.S. official credits disbursed and outstanding amount to $1,226.5 million (December 31, 1970), of which $759 million is dollar repayable and the rest lira repayable. Of the dollar-repayable Ex-Im is owed $17.2 million and P.L. 480, $45 million, and the balance is owed to AID and predecessor agencies. Payments of dollar principal have been made to Ex-Im and on the dollar repayable P.L. 480. Principal, except for some small amounts, and some interest, have been deferred on the AID-type loans.

Refunding, 1956–58

The modern[3] refundings of Turkish debt began in 1956 and 1957, when a number of specific obligations were rescheduled by the United

3. For a discussion of the earlier refundings of Turkish debt under the Ottoman Empire see William H. Wynne, *State Insolvency and Foreign Bondholders* (New Haven: Yale University Press, 1951), 2: 393–526. The older Turkish debt defaulted in 1875, was rescheduled in 1881, when it amounted to $252.8 million including interest, under an agreement to permit a foreign public debt administration to collect and administer the pledged revenues on behalf of the bondholders. This debt was readjusted in 1901 and payment was suspended to the Allies in 1914. The principal creditors were the French and British. The Lausanne Treaty and related arrangement

Table 22. *Approximate Turkish Public Debt Outstanding, Including Undisbursed, and Debt Service Payments, 1956–70 (Millions of Dollars).*

	Outstanding principal	Debt service
1956	249.0	
1957	241.1	11.5
1958	250.1	10.0
1959	363.6	8.9
1960	864.8	49.3
1961	813.0	172.4
1962	910.5	98.7
1963	941.4	83.0
1964	1,039.6	76.8
1965	1,198.9	147.8
1966	1,324.5	120.0
1967	1,562.5	106.4
1968	1,743.7	103.1
1969	1,979.4	134.1
1970	2,181.3	n.a.

Source: IBRD. Later figures are probably more nearly accurate than earlier. Principal is stated as of Jan. 1; service is for the calendar year. Principal and service on short-term debt is excluded. Principal increased by some $200 million in 1970.

States and some European countries. Some of these were plainly stop-gap measures. By agreement, some of the creditor countries withheld a portion of the proceeds of current Turkish exports to repay part of the accumulated arrearages, a procedure which left less free exchange to pay others. The EPU deficit was refunded as a loan. The United States postponed payments due under the Marshall Plan loans in 1958–63 to 1968—later postponed again. Credits were secured from central banks, secured by gold.

The situation was described at the time: "It became clear at the beginning of the year that Turkey's extensive and wasteful investments gave bad returns in the form of unstable money, inflation, high cost of living, disappearance of essential foodstuffs, low returns in agricultural and industrial production and general discontent."[4]

The Turkish external debt had mounted rapidly after 1950, and by January 1, 1958 it appears amounted to about a billion dollars, in-

of 1923 and 1924 assigned 66.2 percent of the debt of the Ottoman Empire to the Republic of Turkey. An agreement was reached on payments by Turkey in 1928, but Turkey in 1930 reduced payments to a third. In 1933, there was a new refunding issue by the Republic and in 1940 payment on the sterling issue was suspended. In 1958, the payments on the bonded debt were suspended along with commercial debts. Subsequently settlements were made with the British and French bondholders. The now outstanding bonded debt of Turkey apparently consists of Belgian, German and Italian loans made in 1964 to 1966 to refinance Turkish debts, though refunded Ottoman debt may be a part.

4. *Britannica Book of the Year*, 1959, p. 693.

cluding short-term credits. The payments due on this debt in 1958 were $371 million, an amount larger than total Turkish exports in 1957 or expected in 1958. Turkey suspended payment on its commercial debt ($476 million) in 1958 and called upon the creditor countries to refund payments coming due within the next 5 years amounting to some $400 to $450 million in commercial credits alone.

The 1958–59 Consolidation

Turkish negotiations with the Managing Board of the EPU and the OEEC, and consultation with the IMF ran from April to September 1958. It was agreed that as conditions to the provision of additional aid and refunding of debt, Turkey was to adopt a stabilization program and devaluation, which, however, became fully effective only in August 1960 when a par of 9 liras to the dollar replaced the 2.8 rate.

The OEEC Council sent a mission to Turkey in June of 1958, and a conference between Turkey and the thirteen members of the OEEC and the U.S. discussed financial assistance to Turkey and refunding of the debt from September 1958 to May 1959. The United States was not a member of the OEEC but was represented at this meeting, and the debt arrangements for the American creditors were substantially the same as for the Europeans. In the discussion of the debt, however, the European countries could act for their nationals since official agencies of the government had, for the most part, insured or guaranteed the commercial credits under their regular systems, so that the governments were obligated to make payment in any event. The American private credits were not guaranteed by the government, and the government could not make any agreement that was binding on its nationals.

The agreement applied only to credits arising from trade or services delivered before August 5, 1958 and which had payment falling due before January 1, 1964. Loans made by governments to Turkey and various other special transactions including barter deals were specifically excluded from the refunding. Central bank credits to Turkey were rolled over, and the EPU credit was refunded to an EMA credit. The refunding of short-term debts to longer-term obligations probably accounts for the rise in 1960, shown in Table 22.

The Turkish obligors were required by the agreement between Turkey and the OEEC governments to pay their debt in Turkish liras as it accrued between 1959 and 1964. The Turkish central bank and government agreed that they would transfer to the creditors $15 million in 1959, $20 million in 1960, $25 million in 1961, $30 million in 1962, and $35 million in 1963, and that in the sixth year payments were to be one-seventh of the amount then outstanding, and similar amounts for an additional 6 years. The payment period was in this way spread over a period of 12 years until 1969. Each of the creditor countries was to receive a percentage of the annual payments, the U. S. share being 18 percent, the German, 22.6 percent, the U. K., 28.3 percent, and smaller percentages for the other creditors. The post-poned payments were to accumulate interest at 3 percent per annum until the final settlement.[5]

The United States delegation to the Conference worked out the details of the settlement with the American creditors. The Turkish government (June 5, 1959) sent a note to the American Ambassador setting forth the terms of repayment, similar to those of the OEEC Agreement. In his response of the same date (note No. 2650) the Am-bassador welcomed this "statement of intentions" and indicated that the Department of Commerce would check the claims, and that pay-ments were to be made through the New York Federal Reserve. The total U. S. claims were approximately $60 million (later found to be $83 million) with 133 separate creditors. Under the schedule of the general agreement Turkey was to pay $2.6 million to the U. S. in 1959 and rising amounts to 1963. Of the amount paid by Turkey to the United States, there was agreement that the small creditors would be paid off in the first year, while the large creditors would grant an addi-tional year of moratorium. In this way all but a dozen of the claims were to be settled in the first year.[6]

Along with the debt settlement the OEEC members agreed to pro-vide assistance to Turkey in the form of balance of payments loans. The 5.75 percent loans were to be available for payments in the EPU monetary area and were to be amortized in 11 equal semiannuals beginning January 1964. The total provided by the participating mem-ber countries was $73 million equivalent. As part of the arrangement also the United States agreed to provide $100 million, of which $25 million was to be in grants and the balance in loans, one-half by the DLF and the other by Ex-Im. The EPU made a loan of $25 million and the IMF allowed drawings of $25 million, so that under these arrangements a total of $223 million in program assistance was pro-vided for. The United States, however, supplemented the original

5. OEEC, "The Work of the Conference on Financial Assistance to Turkey and on Turkish Debts," (Paris, 1959).
6. *Foreign Commerce Weekly*, June 15, 1959, pp. 2, 35.

assistance by a P. L. 480 local currency sale of $15 million, defense support of $75 million, and $44 million in the form of additional debt relief of the principal and interest on three ECA-MSA loans. The United States, therefore, provided about $190 million in commodities plus $44 million in the form of official debt postponement. (There was something of a numbers game of what to include in the columns of the tables and what in the footnotes.) Of the $73 million of bilateral credit from the Europeans, Germany provided $50 million and Germany was to receive 22.6 percent of the debt payments in each of the rescheduled years. The United States, on the other hand, provided 60 to 75 percent of the aid, depending on how computed, and received only 18 percent of the debt payments.

OECD Consortium and Debt Relief

After the 1958–59 consolidation it became quickly clear that the Turkish problem could not be regarded as a mere debt problem. The Turkish development program required the provision of external resources for projects, and there was no prospect that the current balance of payments would improve to the extent necessary to service the debt. While the United States had been supplying aid on concessional terms for 10 years, which helped to pay off such of the debt as was actually reduced, the OEEC-NATO countries, which were the main creditors, realized that they could properly expect to bear part of the burden of financing the Turkish program. The result was the formation of the OECD sponsored consortium in 1962 to coordinate aid and to secure, to the feasible extent, a softening of terms. Aid could be arranged in terms of the Turkish 5-year development plans, though any "pledges" had to be contingent upon legislative processes and institutional arrangements in other countries as well as in the United States. Consequently funds could not be provided simultaneously and Turkey has had to negotiate bilaterally the various project and program credits within the agreed targets. The donor countries as well as the IMF, which has had standby arrangements annually since 1961, had a natural concern with the policies of the Turkish government, inflation, inability to pay for current imports and the mounting debt, so that there has been a continual dialogue between Turkey and the donors and IMF, or through the meetings of the consortium[7]

7. For description, see W. F. Stettner, "The OECD Consortium for Turkey," *OECD Observer*, April 1965, pp. 1–7; John Hackett, "The Turkish Consortium of OECD," ibid., Oct. 1969, pp. 19–26.

three times a year, and the annual Fund consultation between the expiration of one standby and the agreement of the next.

Debt relief and economic assistance have been inextricably connected in these discussions, and it is in practice quite difficult to determine what the precise amounts were for any given year, though general action was taken in conjunction with the 1965 and 1968 meetings.

Beginning in 1964 Turkey was obligated to repay in part the loans extended as refunding in 1958–59. Supplier credits had also increased. By mid-1964 total debt had increased to $1.3 billion and service in 1965 was calculated as $216 million, almost half of Turkish exports in that year ($464 million). Debt service, which had been between 29 and 40 percent of exports in the immediately preceding 5 years, would decrease only moderately over the following years, neglecting increases in service for debt contracted subsequently.[8]

Since the European governments had succeeded to the claims of their nationals under earlier settlements, the 1965 situation presented the choice between additional program aid equivalent to debt service or direct refunding, or a combination. For the reasons outlined above,[9] individual countries took different measures. Some simply deferred payments due in 1964–69 to later dates. Others gave new program loans. The U.S. rescheduled payments due on Marshall Plan loans and provided $70 million in program assistance. The European Fund (EMA), whose earlier loans came due, was repaid but granted an equivalent in a new 5-year credit.[10] While the 1959 consolidation agreement was not modified, the creditors agreed to finance at least 60 percent of debt payments due them so that debt relief was about $50 million per annum in 1965, 1966, and 1967, and in 1965 the actual relief was about $77 million on the governmental credits and the consolidated supplier credits.

The original payment schedule of some of the bilateral credits was to be resumed in 1968, but further adjustments were made in 1967-69 by the consortium members, each in its fashion. The EMA has continued to roll over its credit and has provided additional credits at the easiest permissible terms, 5 years including 3 years grace.[11] The Bri-

8. Union of Chamber of Commerce, Industry and Commodity Exchanges of Turkey, *Economic Report*, 1965, pp. 114–16.

9. See chapter 3.

10. The European Monetary Agreement is subject to renewal every three years, so that its loans must be relatively short term. EMA, *Annual Report*, 1964, pp. 96–97; 1965, pp. 96–98; 1966, pp. 56–57. Cf. *Pearson Report*, p. 383.

11. *Annual Report*, 1967, p. 62; 1968, pp. 64–65; 1969, p. 37.

tish have granted "goods and services" loans annually since 1966, generally with a term of 25 years including about 2 years grace at zero interest.[12] German credits have taken the form of debt relief, projects and some program aid. Belgium has given loans for debt relief and new imports at 20 years, including 5 years grace at 3 percent. Announced Italian dollar credits have been at 4 percent with maturities of 10 to 15 years.[13] The United States has postponed principal payments on its AID and related loans (only a small part of dollar amortization has been paid to date) and capitalized some interest payments. Not all other relief terms have been made public.

Conclusion

Under the consortium arrangements, 1963–68, total assistance to Turkey, including IBRD/IDA/IFC, but not the IMF, has amounted to $1.8 billion, of which $1.1 billion was in the form of program loans and debt relief and $717 million in projects[14] (agreements signed basis). How much was actual financing of new imports and how much debt relief is problematic in view of specific donor country arrangements, nor is it entirely clear how much of the debt refunding is net, since some of the credits have been rolled over several times. There is, of course, little difference between a new credit to finance imports equivalent to debt payments to be received and a refunding arrangement except to the extent that the new credit is tied and, of course, it may have preferable "announcement effects." The U. S. share for the 6-year period was $684 million, of which $401 million was in program loans. Germany was the next largest contributor with $232 million in debt relief and program loans and $43 million in projects. The U. K., which was also a large creditor in 1958, has provided $89 million in program and $15 million in project credits. The other creditors have supplied smaller amounts as could be expected in terms of their relative debt claims and smaller economies. Canada, on the other hand, which was not a creditor in 1958, has provided $23 million in project credits. Since the consortium got underway each creditor has refunded its claims directly or indirectly, though U. S. program loans and P. L. 480 helped to cover some of the debt payments made in the earlier period.

12. House of Commons, *Civil Estimates,* 1968–69, sup., p. 65; 1969–70, 2:56.
13. Moody, *Municipal and Government Manual* (1970), p. 3578. In 1970 EEC granted $195 million in financial aid over a 5.5-year period (*IFNS* no. 244, July 31, 1970).
14. Hackett. "The Turkish Consortium," p. 20.

Further refunding was agreed to in 1970. With the devaluation of the lira from 9 to 15 liras to the dollar in August 1970 and the financial program undertaken in conjunction, the IMF provided a standby credit of $90 million, and the OECD provided for credits of $115 million under the European Monetary Agreement. Of this amount, $75 million will refund maturities on the EMA credit as they accrue, with repayments spread over a 5-year period with the bulk falling due in 1974 and 1975. The $40 million in new credits is intended to increase Turkish reserves and is repayable over the years 1971 to 1973. Shortly before this action, the EEC, in connection with the transitional stage in Turkey's entrance, agreed to provide $195 million over a 5-year period in project credits at 2.5 to 4.5 percent and a maximum term of 30 years with grace up to 8 years, i.e., some of the loans may conform to DAC terms and others may be harder. The European Investment Bank may provide a supplement of $25 million under market terms. [15] Part of the Turkish debt problem has been deferred for a few years and individual creditor countries may give additional relief.

The Turkish debt situation continues to be serious. The outstanding public debt including the refunded amounts is more than $2 billion and contractually will require from $100 to $140 million per annum in service. With prospective exports in the range of $500 to $600 million, the debt service will continue to be well above 20 percent of exports. (In 1969 the ratio was 16.7 percent of total receipts.) A trade surplus does not appear to be in prospect, so that regardless of the ratio, there is no prospective *net* payment of debt for some time. The Turkish plan proposes to have the economy externally viable before the end of this decade (1973–75 is a commonly stated date); the gap between plans and realizations may be large. With the prospective decline in U. S. and other consortium aid as now indicated, the debt situation is likely to become more acute rather than less before "viability" is reached. Unfortunately interest payments are likely to go up, but at a lower compound interest rate than the underlying credits, since the refundings have been at concessional rates, whether or not the refunding applies to principal only or interest as well. The creditors will simply have to continue refunding unless they are willing to let the Turkish economy decline. In view of the increase in GNP as the result of assistance, the exchange adjustment of 1970 will help in attaining viability.

15. See OECD, press release A(70) 62 (Oct. 20, 1970); EEC, press release (Tr 26/70) (July 22, 1970). At the end of 1970 total EIB credits to Turkey on behalf of the member governments were $105 million (*European Investment Bank*, 1970–71, Brussels: 1971, p. 20).

For political reasons the creditor-donor countries will have to make an accomodation.[16]

V. INDIA

Setting

The Indian debt question is only one aspect of the long-range development program whose foreign exchange costs for 20 years have been met in good part by loans and grants from donor countries and the International Bank and IDA.[1] There has been no debt crisis in the sense that there has been a sharp increase in contractual debt service due in a short period of 2 or 3 years. Rather it has been a steady increase in annual debt service, resulting from the mounting principal of outstanding debt, even though the terms of this debt have been considerably softened in recent years. India has met payments as they fell due, and possibly could continue to pay, at the price of a drastic curtailment of imports needed for the development program or to maintain consumption even at the pitiful level prevailing (on the average per capita).

Indian debt has to be considered within the framework of multilateral aid to development. The broader ramifications of the Indian development program, its economics, its internal and external political problems, and its sociological aspects, cannot be treated here. Evaluations of policies may readily differ. For the immediate problem the issue is that India is unlikely to produce the surplus in its international accounts that would make possible a *net* payment of debt, at least in the foreseeable future. The Indian national development plans have as a target viability in 10 years, after which the economy could

16. Turkish officials have been quoted as saying that if consortium assistance is not available, Turkey may have to resort to additional supplier credits. They have also threatened to accept Russian aid, and in fact a frame agreement for $200 million has been signed, though apparently not utilized (see *New York Times,* March 10, 1965, Nov. 13, 1965). In fact, however, supplier credits have been drastically reduced and banking credits increased. Governments have provided about $200 million annually.

1. India's imports of goods and services (1965–68) were financed 43.8 percent by official flows from donor-creditor countries and international institutions. About 90 percent of these flows were financed by grants and soft loans (DAC official aid). India received (1965–68) about 17.4 percent of total official flows to all less developed countries, and in 1967–69, when aid to India was somewhat lower, 14.5 percent of all official aid (estimated from DAC, *Review,* 1969, p. 168, 318; 1970, p. 204).

advance without concessional loans or grants. This expectation is, perhaps, too optimistic with the spectre of Malthus continually in the background. Political events of 1971 have postponed viability for a long time.

Relief has been given for 3 years of annual debt payments of about $100 million of the total requirements of about $500 million annually, and it may well be expected that the creditor-donors will give additional relief in the future for a part of the debt burden.[2] The balance of debt service will have to come from assistance. It cannot be met by India from its own resources or earnings without serious contraction of imports or an extraordinary increase in exports. India illustrates the consequences of repetitive borrowing discussed above. The "no net aid" point has not yet been reached because gross aid has increased,[3] but may not continue to increase. Debt relief, therefore, will continue to be an alternative to aid in geometric progression. Indian debt relief cannot be regarded reasonably as a problem of "bunching" or debt service "humps" to be alleviated by some stretching of amortization payment, a halt to inflation or adjustment of exchange rates.[4] It is a long-run problem to be reviewed periodically by the consortium. Debt service to the present has been greatly facilitated by the provision of import credits by the consortium members and IDA and quasi-grants in the form of P. L. 480. In the Indian case, debt relief has been an alternative to additional import financing, as is recognized by the consortium and the Indian government. Debt relief has been given by direct consolidation credits but also by equivalent financing of imports. As of spring 1972 the future of aid to India and additional debt adjustment is completely unpredictable.

2. See House Foreign Affairs Committee, *Hearings*, "Foreign Assistance Act of 1969," pt. 4, p. 797.

3. From 1964 to 1968 inclusive, debt service (after refunding) was $1.6 billion compared with loan and grant receipts of $5.7 million, 27.9 percent. Debt service, 1965–68, was 40.5 percent of total loan utilization (disbursement) in these years.

4. Price rises and an overvalued rupee have been factors in India's poor export performance, though probably not major factors. Wholesale prices September 1971 were 178.3 (1963 = 100). Prices have gone up at about 7.5 percent per annum compounded. Since the end of 1970 prices have risen more sharply than before, 10.6 percent, and there have been reports of rapidly rising prices, especially for food, since September 1971. The rate of increase in prices is less than for some other LDCs.

The devaluation of the rupee from 4.76 to 7.5 to the dollar in 1966 has been followed by an increase in exports from $1.6 billion to $2 billion in 1970 and 1971. Imports fell from $2.8 billion to $2.1 billion in 1970 and to an annual rate of $2.6 billion in the first half of 1971. The import figure reflects changes in aid and increased domestic production of food, as well as the effect of devaluation on "autonomous" imports.

Indian Public Debt

The growth of the external debt since 1956 and the increasing service are shown in Table 23. Data are probably not on an entirely consistent basis, and in recent years have included varying amounts of private debt, particularly exporter credits.[5] While debt service in 1969 was about 6.4 percent of the disbursed outstanding amount, it is about a fifth of commodity exports. The average rate of interest on the debt has fallen from 6.16 in 1961 to 2.75 percent in 1968, reflecting easier terms on more recent borrowings. The rate of amortization has been reduced by the refundings. Debt service in 1970 and 1971 is of the order of $500 million. Future rates will depend on the terms of refunding in the coming years.

It may be noted that there is a large and long lag of disbursement behind signed loans. Projects obviously require time for disbursement. Delays in expenditure under program loans result in part from the attempt to allocate purchases under tied loans (most of the aid is tied) to the cheapest source, and in part from sheer bureaucratic delay in licensing. For a country as dependent on foreign aid as is India, prudence would also indicate maintaining a pipeline since future aid is unpredictable, particularly with the delays in enactment of legislation in the U. S., which supplies about one-half.

The composition of the debt in broad groupings is given in Table 24, and an approximate subgrouping may be inferred from other data of about the same time. Multilateral credits (June 30, 1970) consisted of IDA $1,167.4 million, and IBRD $613.5 million. About three-fourths of the debt was to governments. U. S. dollar repayable credits were $3,310.3 million (June 30, 1970), of which the Ex-Im was $312.9 million (including loans to private firms); CCC, $5.2 million; P.L. 480, $305.2 million; and the balance AID and predecessor agencies. Debt to Germany was about 12.5 percent of the government total, the U.K. about 12.2 percent, and other consortium members about 14.7 percent (Japan, France, Italy, Canada, Belgium, and the Netherlands). Debt to the "rupee area" was estimated in 1969 at about 14.7 percent.[6]

5. The reason for reporting part of the private debt, but not all, is not apparent. These may be obligations which have an implied, but not legally binding, guarantee of government. In 1968, service on supplier credits to government agencies and the included private obligations was $82.6 million of the total of $436.3 million. Supplier credits required service of 18.8 percent of disbursed principal, compared with 7.2 percent on all credits.

6. U.S. Department of State, Bureau of Intelligence and Research, *Communist States and Developing Countries: Aid and Trade in 1970*, pp. 4, 18. Trade figures for 1968 and 1969 indicate an import surplus for India, so that if payment is made through the trade accounts, there appears to have been no net repayment in these years. Military hardware is probably not included in trade figures.

Table 23. India: External Public Debt Outstanding (Repayable in Foreign Currencies) and Debt Payments, 1956–70 (Millions of Dollars).

	Outstanding[a]		Payments		
	Including undisbursed	Disbursed only	Interest	Amortization	Total
1956	529.0	241.7	6.6	3.0	9.6
1957	523.7	271.2	6.9	4.1	11.0
1958	822.5	395.9	8.0	6.4	14.5
1959	1,478.0	775.9	28.6	15.8	44.4
1960	2,094.4	1,069.9	48.0	40.0	88.0
1961	2,411.1	1,357.0	83.6	130.8	214.4
1962	3,003.1	1,693.2	83.8	104.2	188.0
1963	3,779.0	2,003.0	91.8	106.8	198.6
1964	4,279.1	2,610.6	136.1	192.4	328.5
1965	5,491.3	3,848.2	130.4	196.6	327.0
1966	6,268.3	4,711.9	153.0	233.0	386.0
1967	7,358.0	5,365.4	169.4	278.9	448.3
1968	7,678.1	6,071.4	166.8	269.4	436.3
1969	8,485.7	n.a.	n.a.	n.a.	489.9
1970	8,910.5	7,607.5	n.a.	n.a.	n.a.

Source: IBRD, and *Pearson Report*, p. 299.

a. Data for 1965 to 1970 are revisions of earlier estimates for these years. Debt is as of April of the given year and debt service for Indian fiscal years, April 1 to March 31. Some debt of the private sector is included. The increased amount of this debt reported accounts for part of the rise in the later period.

Table 24. India: Outstanding Public Debt, by Creditor Class, 1970 (Millions of Dollars).

Total, including undisbursed	8,910.5
Total, disbursed only	7,607.5
Bilateral official	6,407.0
Multilateral	1,743.0
Suppliers	674.7
Private banks	82.8
Other private creditors	2.9

Source: IBRD, *Annual Report*, 1971, p. 64.

What is euphemistically called the "rupee area" debt consists of obligations to the Soviets and other CMEA countries and to Yugoslavia, which is repayable in rupees available for exports through bilateral accounts. The reported amounts apparently include only obligations for economic purposes. The coverage may not be complete even for these purposes. As of January 1, 1968, the reported committed amount of credits from the East Bloc countries was given as $863.7 million. A U.S. State Department study reports Soviet and other CMEA credits and grants to India of $1,980 million between 1954 and 1970, almost entirely before 1969. How much of this was on a loan basis and how much has been repaid is not reported. The study also reports $1 billion in military aid, mostly since 1963. Since most Soviet aid appears to be on the basis of repayment through trade accounts, it is possible that Indian debt is understated in the IBRD figures by as much as $2 billion. The Indian economy must also service purely private debt, some of which probably is included in the suppliers' credit figures, which probably do not include longer-term obligations arising from investment in industry by foreign creditors. In sum, the Indian economy may have contracted to service debt which may be as high as $11 billion.

Debt has been contracted in several hundred transactions at various times and terms.[7] IDA credits are on the standard terms; recent IBRD credits have somewhat longer maturities and grace periods than the average of World Bank loans. Four-fifths of outstanding U. S. credits are on AID terms as are the P. L. 480 dollar-repayable credits. Ex-Im credits ($495.8 million) have interest rates from 5.25 to 6 percent and maturities between 9 years (jet planes) and 18 years on projects. The Atomic Energy Commission credit ($16 million) is at 4.75 percent. Prior to 1962 U. S. aid to India under the DLF was repayable in rupees ($993.2 million) as were P. L. 480 sales prior to 1967.

Earlier economic assistance to India by some countries was mostly at hard terms comparable to exporter credits, but in the more recent period, new credits, aside from refundings, have been made at relatively easy terms. Germany, the second largest bilateral creditor, has greatly reduced charges over time. Its earliest loan for the Rourkela steel plant in 1958 was reportedly at 6.3 percent with amortization in 3 years. Payments under this credit were refinanced some half-dozen times before the general consolidation, at lower rates and longer terms. Recent balance of payments and some project loans have been at 3 percent and 20 to 25 years. The earlier British loans for projects had rates of interest based on the cost of money to the U.K. government and maturities of 6 to 20 years. The more recent loans have been interest-free with maturities of 25 years including 7 years grace. Canada has given grants and loans for wheat, metals and other Canadian products. Some of these loans are interest-free with maturities up to 49 years.

French aid to India (prior to the refunding) was in the form of supplier credits guaranteed by COFACE with varying interest rates and

7. Economic debt transactions are enumerated in India, Ministry of Finance, *External Assistance, 1965–66* (1968), *1968–69 & 1969–70* (1971). Detail varies considerably so that it is difficult to make exact comparisons. Some transactions are published in India, *Foreign Affairs Record*.

maturities of about 10 years. Japanese credits of varying maturities had interest rates tied to the IBRD rate. Italian credits, denominated in dollars, have had terms up to 12 years and interest of 5 to 6 percent. Other bilateral credits were at, or were comparable to, supplier credit terms. U.S.S.R. credits, repayable in rupees, have generally been at 2.5 percent and 12 years.

These details are given here to illustrate the complex problem which had to be faced when refunding was undertaken. The largest creditors had given some conventional loans, but Germany and the U. K. had refinanced, directly or indirectly, their earlier credits. Canada had given quite easy terms on loans, plus grants. Australia had given only grants. Terms for the other creditors were harder and involved largely guaranteed supplier credits or similar arrangements. The differences in terms of loans reflect the interest of the Commonwealth countries and the U. S. in Indian development, while Japan and the continental countries were supplying goods on their usual terms for exports. In 1961 service was about 15.8 percent of disbursed outstanding debt. U. S. aid at that date was almost wholly on a rupee-repayable basis. With the predominance of concessional terms in later years, debt service was reduced relatively so that in 1969 it was only about 6.4 percent of disbursed principal.

There remains, however, the problem of supplier credits, which have been increasing in amount in recent years, from $429.4 million in 1965 to $674.7 million in 1970.[8] Some of the earlier supplier credits have been refinanced as bilateral governmental loans. As of 1968 they apparently required service of 18.8 percent of disbursed principal, of which 14.2 percent was amortization. These rates are heavy in comparison with the service of governmental loans. In contrast the average for DAC member government loans was 2.45 percent in interest and 4.8 percent of total service on disbursed amounts outstanding. These figures, however, reflect the refunding of government credits. Supplier credits to private firms were generally not part of the refunding for the major creditors. The percent service costs reflect the low interest in the grace period on U. S. loans and the interest-free credits of the Commonwealth countries.

Debt Service, Aid and the Balance of Payments.

At first the foreign exchange costs of the Indian development pro-

8. The reported figures include some of the debt of the private sector. Earlier figures for India showed relatively small amounts of supplier credits. The increase in the figures may not represent a change in the method of finance. It may simply be a matter of reporting.

gram were met largely by a rapid draw-down of war-accumulated sterling reserves, supplemented by project credits.[9] It later became apparent that India could not from its exchange earnings finance its requirements for replacement parts, smaller equipment, and even raw materials as its industry expanded and as debt service became heavier. Hence there was a shift to program or import financing credits, a policy long urged by the IBRD in the consortium.

Total external financing of the Indian economic program from 1951 to March 31, 1970 has been about $17.2 billion, with $11.7 billion in loans, $1.1 billion in grants and $4.4 billion in P.L. 480.[10] (Figures are on a gross disbursed basis.) In addition to P. L. 480, Canada and Australia have given grants for wheat and other raw materials. Grants also included many forms of technical assistance provided by governments and private entities.

About half of this assistance was supplied by the United States. As of June 30, 1970 on a gross commitment basis, AID and predecessor agencies provided $3.1 billion in loans and Ex-Im $509 million. P. L. 480 sales for local currency (less U.S. uses portions) were $3.5 billion and $305 million in dollar-repayable loans, and $528 million in grants.[11] On a net disbursed basis (gross less repayments) total U.S. loans and grants were $8.2 billion. AID loans were $2.2 billion authorized for program assistance (commodities, steel imports, fertilizer, etc.) and $762 million for projects (railways, power, industry). Of the Ex-Im total $210 million represented program imports of capital equipment items.

German assistance to India through March 31, 1970 has been DM4,755 million. Of this amount DM1,117 million has been in the form of "cash assistance" for Indian foreign exchange reserves (1956–61) and DM940 million for commodity imports (1962–70) including one loan of DM100 million for imports of Indo-German firms. In addition Germany has provided some $228.2 million in debt relief of principal and interest, including the refundings of Rourkela. While much of the commodity assistance has been earmarked for specified materials, some has been made available for purchases in any market. Almost half of the equivalent of $1.2 billion has supported the balance

9. Indian exchange holdings, which stood at $1.7 billion after the 1949 sterling devaluation, reached a low of $251 million in 1964. In July 1971 they were $656 million.

10. India, Ministry of Finance, *External Assistance, 1968–69 & 1969–70*, p. 1. Assistance for military purposes is not included.

11. AID, *U.S. Overseas Loans and Grants 1945–70*, p. 15; NAC. *Annual Report*, 1970–71, appendix C, Table B1.

of payments, either by way of direct debt relief, or commodity assistance.

Britain has provided £419 million in loan funds, of which some 70.3 percent was balance of payments assistance in the form of import credits, debt relief and "Kipping loans" (imports for "British oriented industrial activities in India").

Over the last 15 years, then, the major country contributors to the Indian program have supplied the equivalent of about $4 billion in general balance of payments credits on easy terms, plus $4.3 billion in P. L. 480 rupee sales, loans, and grants. Grants from Australia, and grants and loans from Canada also financed commodity imports. Total debt service in this period was about $3 billion.

The Indian goods and services account had an aggregate deficit of $5.8 billion from 1965 to 1970, including a trade deficit of $4.7 billion. Both the trade and current account deficits decreased greatly in 1968, 1969 and 1970, with a sharp reduction in imports and a moderate increase in exports. The trade deficit is, of course, a planned deficit, depending on expectations of the amount of aid to be received, the amount of debt service and the level of exports. With the reduction of aid in these years, import levels were cut, or, conversely, with a somewhat improved trade position, less foreign aid was needed. The deficits have been covered by aid and other capital flows and grants. In the 6-year period, net capital flows were $5.4 billion and net unrequited transfers $1.3 billion. Indian foreign exchange reserves increased by $432 million.

India's imports (c.i.f.) were $15.2 billion and exports $10.5 billion. Total public debt service amounted to about $2.6 billion. It may be regarded as a matter of semantics if the situation be described in terms of the Indian economy financing its debt service and half of its imports, or whether it be said that foreign grant and loan assistance financed debt payments and under half of imports. Certainly the aid was not used directly to pay debt service, except in the 1967–68 consolidation when some countries extended new loans equivalent to debt payments as essentially bookkeeping transactions, though there was a shift from private to public creditors.

Bilateral program credits, with some exceptions, have been tied to procurement in the creditor country and have often specified the commodities to be financed, e.g., wheat or other foodstuffs, steel, railway equipment, fertilizers and types of industrial equipment. Some of the credits, however, have financed the purchase of a wide variety of items, and a few have been completely untied. Since aid in recent years has been predominantly in the form of rather broad import credits available from the main industrial countries, the authorities by careful selection of source for commodity procurement could avoid a good part of the excess costs involved in tying. Commodities which could not be procured under the loans, e.g., petroleum, could be financed from free exchange. Since the credits financed a good part of imports, earned exchange was freed to pay debt service.

It was argued above (chapter 3) that program loans more readily facilitate debt payment than project credits. In the Indian case, as debt service has increased, so have program loans. In U.S. fiscal years 1965–70, AID commodity-financing loans amounted to $1.3 billion. U.S. commodity import loans, however, began in 1958, before the debt burden was large, and have continued almost annually since. P.L. 480, 1965–70, was $1.7 billion, all but $305 million repayable in rupees. German program credits in this period were the equivalent of $217 million and British about $350 million. There were additional credits for debt relief from the U.K. and Germany.[12] That is, in this 6-year period when total debt payments were about $2.6 billion, commodity financing loans from the three major countries were almost $2 billion, plus P.L. 480 of $1.7 billion, aside from direct debt relief and commodity credits from other countries.

IDA has provided $605 million in "industrial imports projects," of which $515 million was in 1965–70. Total IDA credits to India (June 30, 1971) were $1.5 billion, 45 percent of all IDA credits. The cumulative total of IBRD loans committed to India was $1,051.2 million and the outstanding committed amount was $576.5 million (June 30, 1971). Published data do not show the entire amounts repaid on principal or on parts of loans sold. Some of the loans have been completely repaid. Since the undisbursed portion of the loans was on the newer loans, total cumulative principal payments were probably about $475 million. IDA import credits have been larger than the total principal repaid to the IBRD.

In sum then, from 1965 to 1970, total import credits were about $2.5 billion from IDA and the main bilateral suppliers, plus $1.7 billion in P.L. 480 compared with debt service of about $2.6 billion. This comparison is a rough approximation in view of the complexities of the various loans and incomplete reporting. Debt relief was generally

12. *External Assistance, 1968–69 & 1969–70*, pp. 26–30, 49–57. German and British figures are estimated from this source. U.S. sources have been used for American figures.

additional though the same loan transaction often included both items. The rough equivalence of the magnitudes points, however, to the way in which the donor-creditors, by financing imports in amounts about equal to debt service, freed Indian exchange earned from exports for the service of the debt.

Indian Debt Relief 1968–69 and 1969–70

While India has met, and continues to meet debt payments as due, the increasing amount of these payments, in face of the continuing balance of payments deficit, became a matter of increasing concern to India, the consortium countries and the IBRD. To offset these payments by raising the level of import credits would require larger amounts of bilateral and IDA aid than was likely to be forthcoming. The IBRD no doubt had India and others in mind when, as early as 1964, it stressed the need for softer loan terms and possible debt refunding if default was to be avoided or development investment drastically curtailed.[13]

The consortium members were increasingly concerned with the slow progress of Indian development, cumbersome administrative procedures, the rate of inflation and the failure of exports to improve, so that there was little prospect of debt repayment, while importunities for aid were increasing.[14] After long discussions with the IBRD, the IMF, the United States and other consortium members, India adopted internal financial reforms, devalued the rupee (1966) and effected some trade liberalization and some reorganization of the administration of controls of production and trade. To assist in the transition more aid was provided.

The complex debt situation of India made an easy "formula" adjustment (e.g., Argentina, Brazil, Chile) practically impossible when the issue had to be faced squarely in 1968. The consortium countries, as noted, had provided loans at greatly variant terms, from exporter credits to AID and IDA and the British and Canadian long-term interest-free loans. It is probably not unfair to say that the IBRD-IDA, United States, U.K., Canada, Australia and New Zealand, and Germany were concerned with aiding India.[15] They had given grants, concessional loans and a small proportion of "conventional" (i.e. less

13. E.g., IBRD, *Annual Report,* 1963–64, p. 8; 1964–65, pp. 57–59. The references to India (generally along with Pakistan) became more explicit in the last few years.
14. See *Pearson Report,* pp. 282–302.
15. Also to some extent disposing of agricultural surpluses.

subsidized) loans. Other countries had required harder terms since they were primarily concerned with financing exports. Each country, of course, has had its own legal, budgetary and organizational problems. Moreover, certain debts had been refunded previously in various ways by the U.K., Germany, Canada and some others.

In 1967 some $350 million was due to the creditors in principal and interest, and without debt relief the amount would have been of the order of $500 million in the next few years. A reduction by an agreed percentage of the payments due was scarcely equitable. The U.S. as the largest creditor in terms of outstanding principal had small accruals of service because of its liberal terms, with about $60 million due in 1967–68 on a debt of $1.9 billion disbursed and outstanding.[16] Of this amount the Ex-Im had $307.9 million outstanding, with payments during the year of $33 million in principal and $15 million in interest. The balance was due on the 1952 wheat loan and interest on AID loans. On the other hand, almost $300 million was due to the other consortium members, including the IBRD, to which India owed a principal sum of about $3.9 billion.[17] It was argued that the creditors with the harder terms should give a larger percentage of debt relief than those with easier terms, so as to equalize the burden, in part at least, of sustaining the Indian program.

Mr. Guillaume Guindey, the IBRD special consultant on the Indian debt problem, after long negotiations proposed debt relief of $100 million for the Indian fiscal year 1968–69 and equal amounts for the following 2 years. Payments of principal falling due in these years were to be deferred for 10 years. As agreed in the consortium, debt relief was to be regarded as part of the aid pledges for the given year. As finally agreed the U.S. was to provide about $8.7 million in debt relief; the IBRD, $30 million over a 2-year period; and other countries, $75 million.[18]

Total debt relief to March 31, 1970 aggregated $323.8 million: $34.4 million in 1966–67, $63.2 million in 1967–68, $101.3 million in 1968–69, and $125 million in 1969–70. Debt relief formed about 9.5 percent of the total consortium pledges of $3.4 billion for this period.

16. *Foreign credits,* June 30, 1967. (These figures are used in preference to the varied figures used in the negotiations, which were based on Indian data. Only dollar repayable loans are included.)

17. IDA credits of $889 million required service only of 0.75 percent of disbursed outstanding principal. IBRD loans were $671.6 million (June 30, 1967). Bilateral credits were about $2.4 billion.

18. See IBRD, *Annual Report,* 1968, p. 19; House Subcommittee on Appropriations, *Hearings,* "Foreign Assistance and Related Appropriations for 1970," p. 1005; House Foreign Affairs Committee, *Hearings,* "Foreign Assistance Act of 1969," pt. 4, p. 797; NAC, *Report,* 1969, p. 82.

Various methods were used to deal with the problem and specific agreements were made with India.

For the United States, rescheduling of $8.7 million was technically rather simple. Three years before the enactment of P.L. 480, Congress by special legislation in 1951 authorized emergency food aid to India (P.L. 82–48) under loan terms similar to those of the ECA loans, and $189.7 million was disbursed. The original agreement, as did many of the ECA loans, contained a clause for subsequent modification by mutual agreement. It had provided for repayment in 35 years beginning June 30, 1957. In 1958 the term was extended to 45 years, by deferring payments of principal and interest due from June 30, 1958 to June 30, 1967, to June 30, 1986 to December 31, 1995.[19] As part of the consortium arrangements for Indian FY 1967–68, $8.7 million in principal and interest due in 1968 was deferred until 1978, without consolidation interest. Similar action was taken for payments due in 1969. There was no rescheduling of Ex-Im loans, but the Ex-Im, in June 1968, authorized a loan for capital equipment of $20 million. AID loans also were not rescheduled.

The IBRD in 1967 provided relief to India by depositing with the Reserve Bank the equivalent of principal payments falling due in the Indian FY 1967–68. These accounts, denominated in dollars, sterling, DM and yen, were to be drawn down not later than March 31, 1971. As of June 30, 1968 they amounted to $30 million and a year later to $15 million.[20] Subsequently the Bank rescheduled payments of principal equivalent to $30 million accruing to it in Indian FY 1967–68 and 1968–69, so that these deposits were fully drawn. Interest payments have been due according to the original loan terms.

Germany had earlier refunded the entire original Rourkela credit (DM687 million) with new credits at longer term, and gave additional long-term low interest loans for this project. In the debt relief arrangement DM219 million (to 1970) was provided in debt relief, loans and "liquidity" assistance. Principal and interest accruing were consolidated. Part took the form of grants for the reduction of effective interest when contractual rates were maintained. Commodity credits of DM201 million in 1969–70 have been at interest rates of 2.5 or 3 percent with maturities of 25 and 30 years, including 7 and 8 years of grace.[21]

19. See NAC *Report*, Jan.-June 1958, p. 33; AID, *Status of Loan Agreements* (W 224) (June 30, 1969), pp. 78, 185.
20. See IBRD, *Report*, 1968, pp. 68, p. 78, balance sheet and footnote C; 1969, pp. 27, 67, 72.
21. India, *External Assistance, 1968–69 & 1969–70*, pp. 49–63.

British refunding on very generous terms has taken the form of direct debt relief. In 1966 and 1967 the U.K. provided general purpose loans of £25 million of which 20 million were used to refund principal and interest and an additional 15 million was provided in 1969–71 as debt relief. In addition to debt relief the U.K. has provided over £200 million in balance of payments assistance including the "Kipping" loans.[22] Recent (since 1965) loans have been interest free and repayable over 25 years with 7 years grace. The older loans, which have been directly refunded, had rates of interest based on the cost of money to the U.K. Treasury and were of somewhat shorter term.

Canadian aid to India has been over two-thirds in the form of grants for food and a variety of other Canadian products, e.g., metals, asbestos, newsprint and fertilizers. As debt relief, Canada wrote off C$10 million on wheat loans of 1958, and in addition gave some C$3.9 million as cash grants to reduce interest charges on certain exporter-type credits. Recent loans for development, including program loans, have been long term and interest free.[23]

Austria provided credits as debt relief by providing new loans to cover principal and interest at 3 percent with 7 years grace and amortization over 17 years. Belgium provided new program loans, part in cash to meet debt payments at 3 and 2 percent and 25 and 30 years with grace periods of 7 and 10 years respectively. The Netherlands refinancing agreement was at 3 percent. Sweden, which has provided much of its assistance in grants, rescheduled credits so as to allow a 10-year grace period and amortization over 15 years, with interest at 2 percent.

A number of other consortium countries have provided debt relief on rather more onerous terms. French debt relief ($14.6 million) requires repayment in 12 years at 3.5 percent. Italy charged 4 percent with amortization over 12 years including 3 years of grace. Japan rescheduled its loans to allow payment over 10 to 15 years with grace periods of 3 to 5 years. Interest is at 4 and 5.75 percent, only slightly lower than the original contracts.

The U.S.S.R. and other CMEA countries and Yugoslavia have extended credits repayable in rupees to be used for purchases in India. These credits apparently have not been renegotiated.

Tentative Conclusion

Three annual debt relief exercises—the 1970 exercise is not yet com-

22. Ibid., pp. 16–29.
23. Ibid., pp. 32–34.

pleted—have not essentially changed the Indian situation though they have resulted in some softening in the terms of aid, though it is difficult to measure the immediate impact.[24] The burden of part of 3 years' payments has been shifted forward from 10 to 25 years. Debt relief has been largely an alternative to further nonproject credits.

The basic problems remain. About a fourth of the annual debt payments for 3 years has been postponed. Since the Indian balance of payments will probably continue in deficit for the foreseeable future and Indian development will depend on aid, three-fourths of the contractual debt payments will have to be financed indirectly by program loans. Assuming annual debt relief of about $100 million per annum over the next few years the service of public debt will take over 20 percent of exports. The debt ratio is not particularly significant since the payments situation is not likely to reverse. India's capacity to service debt on a net basis will continue at zero, unless imports and development are to be curtailed drastically. Indian exports have been increasing and may improve further as the effect of the devaluation becomes more pronounced and the necessary shifts in production occur. Imports may fall if the recent increase in agricultural production proves permanent. (To the present, however, imports of foodstuffs, largely P.L. 480 and Canadian aid, have not imposed a significant burden on the balance of payments.) There is little prospect for such a shift in the Indian balance of payments as to permit net service of the debt, so that for the immediate future there appears to be likelihood of successive debt refundings and continued indirect support of the debt burden.

Moreover, the prospects for additional aid at the stepped-up pace which might push India over the hump are not great. Aside from a general reluctance on the part of the donors to provide resources, they have a disquieting feeling that too large a part of Indian resources is devoted to financing a military program, which will be repaid eventually through the "rupee area."[25] At a minimum this issue will complicate the successive renegotiations of debt which would seem to be inevitable for the coming years. The hostilities with Pakistan (1971)

24. Despite debt relief, debt service in 1969 was $489.9 million and may now be higher. This figure includes debt service on private debt, not refunded.

25. E.g., House Foreign Affairs Committee, *Hearings*, "Foreign Assistance Act of 1969," pp. 773–77. In the consortium "the U.S. has frequently urged the Government of India to ensure that bilateral trade with Eastern European countries and the U.S.S.R. is carried on with a minimum free foreign exchange cost." It may be noted that while India has an export surplus on commercial account with the "rupee area," this is probably overbalanced by receipts of military hardware not included in the trade figures. Repayment through these accounts will come at a later date.

will no doubt further worsen the Indian economic situation and dim its prospects for a more satisfactory balance of payments.

VI. INDONESIA

Introduction

The successive refundings of Indonesian debt can scarcely be considered apart from their political context. "From its inception in 1945, aid to Indonesia has been primarily designed to help a new and important nation achieve economic viability and prevent or inhibit a Communist takeover."[1] From 1950 to 1964 the United States provided $445.7 million in loans and $334.1 million in grants, in AID grants and credits (repayable mostly in rupiahs), P.L. 480, Ex-Im loans of $162.1 million, and military and surplus property credits. Indonesian military preparation for the attack on West New Guinea caused economic deterioration, and after the settlement of the issue, there was an expectation that development would be resumed, and U.S. aid was stepped up accordingly. In 1963 the IMF took the lead in a stabilization program, assisted by a consortium of Western aid donors. The debt situation was also reviewed by a DAC meeting but no general refunding was arranged. Toward the end of 1963, however, Sukarno proclaimed a hostile "confrontation" with Malaysia, and U.S. and consortium aid were reduced to certain programs already committed, largely technical assistance. Inflation went on apace, the balance of payments worsened, debt difficulties increased. Russian military and economic aid increased as Western aid ceased.

In August 1965 Indonesia withdrew from the Fund. An abortive Communist coup in October 1965 was defeated by the military, and between 1966 and early 1967 Sukarno was effectively ousted and General Suharto succeeded to power. The economy was in a state of collapse. Food and other materials were scarce. Prices rose some 600 percent in 1965 and 1966 and the rupiah depreciated sharply.

The Suharto government sought the advice of the IMF and IBRD on measures of stabilization and rehabilitation. Fund membership was resumed in February 1967, and a program adopted for controlling price expansion, contraction of credit, increased taxation, restoration

1. AID memorandum in Senate Foreign Relations Committee, *Hearings,* "Foreign Assistance Program 1965." p. 574.

of nationalized property and resumption of relations with the Western donors to deal with the emergency. The IMF and IBRD estimated a foreign exchange gap of $200 million in 1967 to keep the economy going.

Since 1967 aid has been resumed by the Western countries with the United States supplying (commitment basis) about half, including P.L. 480. Since 1967 (to June 30, 1970) there has been P.L. 480 assistance of $370 million, $64 million in commodity financing, $58 million in project financing and some additional amounts from AID contingency funds.

The inflationary process has been slowed down, the exchange rate adjusted—the two exchange rates were merged into one in April 1970, except for aid-financed goods until December 1970—and economic recovery started. Presumably aid from the donors will continue for some years, though eventually Indonesia, with its rich resources, should become self-supporting.

The Debt Problem: Refunding

Indonesian debt is now about $3 billion including new debt incurred for economic assistance since the overthrow of Sukarno. The new debt, mostly on concessional terms, has not been an issue in the successive refunding operations, which have applied only to debt incurred before June 30, 1966 (Sukarno debt).

Consolidation 1967, 1968 and 1969

As of mid-1966 Indonesia estimated its long- and short-term debt as $2.2 billion. More than half of the debt was to the U.S.S.R. and other CMEA countries, largely for military hardware. Arrears on payments due were $296 million, of which $193 million was past due on long-term debt and the balance on short-term obligations. In the second half of 1966 a further $180.4 million was due, including $70.6 million on debt of maturities under 2 years. In 1967 payments were estimated at $272.8 million on long-term and $136.8 on short-term debt. In the chaotic situation these obligations could scarcely be met since exchange receipts were expected to be under $500 million in 1967 (exports actually amounted to $665 million). The Indonesian government proposed in September 1966 the suspension of all payments on debt except cash obligations, a spreadout over 4 years of the short-term debt, and a suspension of payment on long-term debt until 1970, pending a refunding operation in conjunction with the stabilization effort.[2]

While the Western countries and Japan were willing to make an adjustment, the attitude of the Russians and other CMEA countries was uncertain, since they had ceased aid with the overthrow of Sukarno and did not participate in the multilateral negotiations. In fact, however, the U.S.S.R. tentatively agreed to a settlement before the Western countries did.

The agreed minute adopted at a subsequent Paris meeting (December 1966) included a refunding of about $249 million due in 1966 and 1967 on credits guaranteed or made by participating countries. No payment was to be made until 1971, when it was to be 5 percent of the amount refunded (rescheduled or refinanced) by each creditor; payments in 1972 to 1974 were to be 10 percent; 1975 to 1977, 15 percent per annum, and the remaining 20 percent in 1978. Moratorium interest was to be between 3 and 4 percent and was to be repaid in 1971–78.[3] The participating countries agreed to consider further refunding in subsequent years. Indonesia was to keep them informed through the IMF of actions taken and also on the progress of the stabilization measures. Indonesia agreed to seek a similar settlement of the claims of nonparticipants (i.e. U.S.S.R. and CMEA countries). In practice the arrangements were substantially the same. Formal bilateral agreements with both Eastern and Western countries took time.

Subsequently similar arrangements were made in 1967 and 1968 to reschedule (or refinance) maturities falling due in 1968 and 1969. These were obviously temporizing measures, in accord with Paris Club practice in earlier cases, and required yearly payments of over $100 million to 1980. Rescheduled debt owed to the West for 1967 to 1969 was about $425 million.

Since Indonesia is expected to have a continuing payments deficit for some years, debt service could be met only by new infusions of aid in such form as to permit Indonesia to service debt from its exchange earnings by supplying part of import requirements through aid. Of course, if exports were to increase sharply a larger share could be met from earnings. The essential stumbling block to a more permanent solution was the question of Russian agreement to a longer deferral of payments. If the U.S.S.R. refused to reschedule further, the effect

2. Statement for General Suharto at the Tokyo debt conference, Sept. 19–20, 1966.
3. Indonesian Aide-Memoire, Oct. 6, 1967. Cf. House Appropriations Committee, *Hearings*, "Foreign Assistance and Related Agencies Appropriation for 1970," p. 811.

would be that the European countries, Japan, Australia and the United States would supply resources on a grant or loan basis and so indirectly facilitate payments of the debt to the nonparticipants.

1970 Consolidation

As a means of reaching an equitable settlement in line with Indonesia's expected capacity to repay, the Paris group commissioned Dr. Hermann Abs, retired chairman of the Deutsche Bank, to work out a scheme. The final outcome of a succession of meetings was the agreed minute of April 24, 1970, submitted ad referendum to the governments.

The main provisions of this minute are:

(1) The refunding applies only to debt incurred before July 1, 1966, as originally contracted or as modified by the refunding arrangements of 1966, 1967 and 1968. These refundings are to be replaced by the new schedule and moratorium interest is to be included in the new principal. Short-term debt (180 days or less) and compensation for nationalized property were excluded.

(2) Payment of principal is to be in 30 equal annual installments beginning January 1, 1970.

(3) Interest accrued on the original contracts or contracted under the prior consolidations is to be paid in 15 equal annual amounts beginning January 1, 1985.

(4) No additional moratorium interest is to be charged.

(5) Indonesian debtors other than the government are to deposit the rupiah equivalent of amounts due on the contracts as originally agreed in a special account with the Central Bank of Indonesia and to be held until payment is made to the creditors in foreign exchange.

(6) The payment schedule may be modified by agreement any time after 1980, on the initiative of any creditor or Indonesia, to accelerate payments or to reduce interest payments.

(7) Indonesia will for 8 years have the right of deferring up to half the installment due in any one year, but not more than an amount equal to 3 installments in the aggregate. (Varying amounts may be postponed in any one year. If 50 percent is taken there could be 6 "bisques." If 8 bisques were taken the amount deferred would be less than 50 percent in some of the years.) Deferred amounts are to be repaid in 8 equal annual installments, beginning 1992. Interest is to be paid annually at 4 percent on amounts so deferred.

(8) Aside from the governments, the rights of creditors, debtors or guarantors are not changed. Indonesia will make bilateral agreements with the creditors for rescheduling or refinancing or both.

(9) The creditors are to take necessary action to enable them to conclude the bilaterals and to make them retroactive in case of delay.

(10) Indonesia agreed to negotiate with creditors not parties to obtain a comparable settlement of their claims.

The 1970 Paris consolidation applied to $607 million of principal and $152 million of accrued interest on debt to the participating countries. The total principal and interest owed to all countries was $2,090.1 million, of which $1,644.6 million is principal and $445.5 million is interest.

Indonesia will repay $54.8 million in principal annually from 1970 to 1999, and in addition $29.7 million on the accrued interest from 1985 to 1999. If Indonesia exercises its bisque privilege to the full extent of $164.4 million, payments of principal will be increased by $20.5 million annually from 1992 to 1999, and the interest on these deferred amounts would be paid annually in addition. That is, annual service on the Sukarno debt will be about $55 million to 1984 and $85 million for the following 15 years. To the extent that the bisques are taken in years 1970 to 1977, annual payments would be decreased by half in any year. Indonesia invoked the bisque clause (50 percent) in 1970, and is expected to do so for the next few years.

In addition to the Sukarno debt Indonesia will have to service about a billion dollars of debt incurred since 1966. Most of this debt is on concessional terms, with long periods of grace. AID dollar-repayable loans have aggregated $121 million and P.L. 480 dollar repayable credits on AID terms, $405 million, requiring service of about $10 million in the immediate years and about $20 million annually from 1977 on. The debt will be increased annually by further AID loans and loans from other countries. If economic assistance from the consortium continues at its current rate of about $350 million a year, total debt by 1980 would be in the neighborhood of $7.5 billion and annual service, as a guess, from $350 to 450 million, depending on the terms of aid. If Indonesian recovery proceeds rapidly, borrowing could be in much smaller amount.

Refunding of Debt to the U.S. Government

As of June 30, 1966, the disbursed and outstanding principal of U.S. agencies dollar-repayable loans to Indonesia was $137.8 million, of

Table 25. Indonesia: Principal and Interest Accrued on Debt Contracted before July 1, 1966 (Millions of Dollars).

United States	214.9
Italy	149.6
Germany	124.0
France	113.7
Japan	93.0
Netherlands	31.2
United Kingdom	32.7
Total Paris Club	759.1
Other Western countries	25.0
Total Western countries	784.1
USSR	870.3
Other Eastern countries	435.7
Total Eastern countries	1,306.0
Total "Sukarno Debt"	2,090.1

Source: Department of Commerce, *International Commerce,* May 25, 1970, p. 32. Data are from Indonesian submission.

which $80.7 million was due Ex-Im, $23 million of ECA and AID loans, $33.3 million in surplus property credits and $781,000 in P.L. 480. (The largest part of the committed amount of $19.4 million had not then been disbursed.) A total of $8.6 million of principal was in arrears and $2.5 million in interest due had not been paid. Half of the arrearage was due to Ex-Im.

In accordance with the 1966–68 agreements Ex-Im consolidated accruals of principal and interest (defer transfers), $30.6 million in 1967, $14 million in 1968 and $12.9 million in 1969, with interest at 3 percent on the deferred amounts. Hence Ex-Im will be required to consolidate $96.9 million of principal and interest under the 1970 arrangement. AID has rescheduled principal of $8 million and capitalized interest of $1.8 million. Payments accruing on P.L. 480 and surplus property were also rescheduled in accordance with the agreement.

The U.S. Attorney General has given an opinion that legislation is not necessary to enable the administration to carry out the terms of the 1970 consolidation agreement. Some adjustment among the agencies will be made because of the provision of the Foreign Assistance Act (Sec. 620(r)—the Dirksen Amendment) which prohibits the forgiveness of interest. By NAC action, the amounts received by the United States will be applied to the AID loans between 1970 and 1980 according to the existing schedule. Thereafter, amounts received on the AID loans will be paid to the other agencies.[4]

Accordingly, a bilateral agreement was signed with Indonesia, March 16, 1971, which provided that payments would be made by Indonesia to the Treasury as agent for the creditor agencies and administrator of the agreement. The principal of $182.9 million (original principal, and capitalized interest in the refunding) will be paid in 60 semiannual payments from April 1971, subject to the bisque privilege. Contractual interest on original agreements accrued to 1969 ($32.7 million) will be paid in 30 semiannual amounts in 1985 and thereafter.[5]

Conclusion

Indonesia has been making appropriate bilateral agreements with the other Western creditors, which also have their internal problems of arrangements between government agencies and private creditors. In August 1970, Indonesia and the U.S.S.R. signed an agreement for refunding on terms comparable to those agreed at Paris.

The 1970 Indonesian consolidation represents the longest stretchout of payments agreed by the creditors for any country in a multilateral consolidation since World War II. Imposing no moratorium or consolidation interest on the amounts deferred from 1970 to 1999 is also more generous treatment than has hitherto been accorded. The "exceptional measures" were taken in view of "circumstances peculiar to Indonesia" and so presumably are not to be regarded as a precedent for other cases which will arise over the coming years. In fact, few countries have gone to ruin as quickly as Indonesia did, particularly in the latter part of the Sukarno regime.

Service on the Sukarno debt will take about $55 million annually to 1985 and $84 million annually from 1985 to 1999. If the bisques are used for the first 6 years, as seems likely, the annual payment to 1985 will be reduced to $27.5 million, and increased to $105 million from 1992 to 1999. Post-Sukarno debt of $800–900 million (1971) will require additional service of $40–50 million for the next few years. Service on present debt will, therefore, be roughly $100 million annually for some years. Indonesia has continued to borrow at various terms to meet requirements. In 1969 alone new borrowings were $471 million, of which $180 million was in AID and P.L. 480. An equal sum was borrowed from the U.S. in 1970. How much Indonesia will bor-

4. NAC, *Special Report on the Indonesian Debt Rescheduling* (March 1971), pp. 8–9.
5. The text of the agreement is given in *TIAS* 7092 (1971).

row depends on the degree of recovery and the size of the balance of payments deficit. The debt service will depend on terms. It could be as high as $400 million annually.

Indonesia exports have increased from $679 million in 1966 to an annual rate of over $900 million in the first half of 1971, but imports (c.i.f.) have gone up sharply. The goods and services account in 1969 showed a deficit of $361 million. With the reconstruction of the economy, including larger petroleum revenues and exports of agricultural goods, the balance of payments should improve. Indonesia could possibly become a rich country in aggregate, if not per capita, terms. For the immediate future it will depend upon aid in one form or other, but the very favorable terms of the refunding should provide a breathing spell so that more of earned exchange can be plowed back into the economy. It is a "wait and see" proposition. The 1970 debt arrangements permit a reconsideration of terms after 1980, on the option of either the debtor or the creditors.

VII. GHANA

Background

Ghana's international debt troubles have resulted largely from the spending spree in the Nkrumah regime and secondarily, from fluctuations in exchange receipts from cacao, which provide about 60 percent of the total.

Since independence (1957) the budget and current account balance of payments have been in deficit annually. The trade balance has improved, and in 1970 was in surplus by $88 million as the result of an increase in export receipts to $433 million compared with $301 million in 1969. The current deficit was reduced from $212 million in 1965 to only $15 million in 1970. The inflation appeared to have been arrested in 1971. From 95 in 1961 (1963 = 100) prices rose to 175 in 1970 but fell to 153 in March 1971. Consumer prices, however, continued their rise to July 1971. The situation deteriorated sharply in the latter part of 1971.

Ghana's foreign exchange receipts depend principally on production and price of cacao. Since Ghana provides roughly a third of world supplies, variations in its output significantly affect world prices, while variations of production in the other producing countries, mainly

Cameroon and Brazil, significantly affect the exchange receipts of Ghana. In 1954, for example, reduced production raised the price to 57.8 cents a pound. Since then, it has fluctuated considerably, but with a generally downward trend except in 1968 and 1969. Debt was incurred at least partly in the expectation that cacao receipts would provide repayment.

During the colonial period exports of cacao had been carefully managed and foreign exchange was used in part to increase official reserves, which were at a high of $532 million equivalent in 1955. These reserves, however, were rapidly dissipated after independence, particularly from 1961 to 1967.[1] At the same time that the Nkrumah regime used up its foreign exchange reserves to pay for imports, largely consumer goods—the gold-plated bedstead area—capital goods were imported and a large number of construction projects were undertaken on the basis of supplier credits.

The Debt of Ghana

To the present, there have been three general refundings of the government's debt, 1966, 1968 and 1970. Unfortunately, such data as are available are not consistent, so that it is impossible to present data on the growth of the debt, the amounts of debt service, or even the precise extent of the debt relief.

The IBRD has estimated the government and government-guaranteed debt, as of December 31, 1969, at $637.9 million, including undisbursed of $73.5 million. Of this total, $303.3 million was in supplier credits, $66.5 million in loans from multilateral institutions and $268 million from governments. Known debt service in 1969 was $38 million, of which $17.7 million was on supplier credits. Data for earlier years are not available on any satisfactory basis.

The multilateral credits consisted of $53 million by IBRD and $24.8 million by IDA (June 30, 1970). (Ghana received $10 million in IDA credits between the end of 1969 and June 30, 1970.) IBRD loans were to the Volta River Authority in 1962 and 1969. U.S. government credits are the largest of the bilateral loans. Credits to the government of Ghana were $108.7 million and to the Volta Aluminum Co., owned 51 percent by the government, $111.4 million. AID dollar repayable loans to the government were $89.9 million and P.L. 480, $18.7 mil-

1. For discussion see IMF, *Annual Report,* 1965, pp. 92–92. Foreign exchange reserves are (Aug. 31, 1971) only $46.3 million.

lion, and Ex-Im $10 million.[2] The Aluminum Company is indebted
to Ex-Im and AID. CMEA credits are about $75 million. Germany
and Britain are large creditors on project, balance of payments and
refunding credits. French official refunding credits were $7.1 million.

These official credits have not been involved in the debt refundings.
The refunding problem has arisen from the shorter-term supplier and
contractor credits. Ghanaian sources report conflicting data. From
one report it would appear that supplier credits increased from $2.5
million equivalent at the end of 1959 to $439.6 million at the end of
1964.[3] A later survey estimates the known supplier credits in 1964 at
$400.8 million and the total debt as $485.5 million. For 1967 supplier
credits were stated as $334.4 million and the total debt as $475.1 million.[4] A 1969 official computation estimated the principal of the outstanding debt on February 23, 1966 (the overthrow of Nkrumah) at
$673.5 million, and unpaid interest of $115.6 million. Supplier credits
were given as $397.8 million. Subsequently, some undisbursed sup-
plier credits of $54 million were cancelled by agreement and an equal
sum has since been repaid.[5] One of the problems in the refundings has
been to determine precisely what and how much was to be refunded.

Refunding, 1966

The refunding of Ghana's debt has been closely related to its drawings from the IMF and the undertakings in connection with standby
arrangements. Fund missions in 1964 and 1965 had made appropriate
recommendations on internal and balance of payments policy, but
there had been no drawings since 1962. The overthrow of Nkrumah in
February 1966 enabled the authorities to work out a new program in
consultation with the Fund, designed to rehabilitate the economy. A

2. *Foreign credits,* Dec. 31, 1969, p. 69. Loans to the Aluminum Company are probably not
included in the IBRD figures. The arrangements among the government, the Volta River Authority (which has borrowed from the IBRD, AID, and Ex-Im) and the Aluminum Company
are quite complex. The smelter uses part of the power generated by the authority, the dam and
power plant would not be economically feasible without the smelter. There are long-term contracts governing power rates, production and taxes. The government revenues from the aluminum complex (profits, royalties, and local costs), will be an important source for eventually
paying off the debt.
3. Ghana, *Economic Survey 1964,* pp. 30–32. Figures have been converted from Ghanaian
pounds, then at par with sterling.
4. *Economic Survey,* 1967, pp. 29–30, cf. Bank of Ghana, *Report of the Board,* June 30, 1967,
p. 48. The 1967 *Survey* makes no attempt to evaluate the pre-1964 supplier credits and recognizes
that the enumeration of credits then outstanding was not complete.
5. Ghana, Commissioner for Economic Affairs, "Note on External Debt," June 27, 1969.
This was a memorandum circulated in Ghana.

standby of $36.4 million in May 1966 was in support of this program.[6] One of the undertakings was that no debt of a maturity of more than one year or less than twelve would be incurred without the consent of the Managing Director.[7]

The Fund participated in the debt meeting of June 1966, called by the U.K., which was the largest creditor on insured supplier credits. Germany was the second claimant. Medium-term debt was between $300 million and $500 million and contractual payments were about the equivalent of $78 million in 1966 and $94 million in 1967.[8]

In view of Ghana's balance of payments situation, with debt service a third of exports, it was clear that the contractual requirements could not be met, and that unless there were an accommodation, default was almost inevitable.

At the close of the meeting Ghana announced that payments of principal and interest would be suspended and new nondiscriminatory arrangements made.

After protracted discussions, the agreement in December 1966 provided that 80 percent of the payments due in principal and interest accruing June 1, 1966 to December 31, 1968 was to be deferred until June 1, 1971 and then repaid in installments over the following 8 years. The rescheduling applied only to credits of more than 1 year and less than 12. The payments covered were about $170 million.[9] Since no new medium-term debt could be incurred without IMF agreement, and in fact only an insignificant amount was incurred, the debt problem was substantially postponed.

Refunding, 1968

In 1968 a second debt conference agreed to a similar postponement of medium-term credit payments falling due from January 1, 1969 to June 30, 1972. In 1969 payment was to be 15 percent of the due amount; in 1970, 20 percent; in 1971 and 1972, 22.5 percent. After 2 years grace the deferred amounts were to be paid in 7.5 years after January 1, 1974. The amount deferred was about $100 million. The multilateral agreement of 1968, like the 1966 arrangement, provided for the negotiation of implementing separate agreements with the creditors.[10]

6. IMF *Annual Report*, 1966, pp. 106–07.

7. Bank of Ghana, *Report*, June 30, 1967, p. 11.

8. *Economic Survey*, 1966, p. 27. This report gives supplier credits as $300 million. The Bank of Ghana, *Report*, 1967, states the figure as £250 million.

9. *Pearson Report*, p. 383.

10. Standard Bank Group, *Annual Economic Review*, September 1966, p. 4.

Separate agreements were made to pay off arrears on current payments over a 2-year period by monthly installments or special arrangements for payment within 2 years in quarterly payments depending on the balance of payments situation.

Perhaps the obligations to the U.S.S.R. and satellite countries were adjusted in a fashion similar to those due to European creditors. They are probably being repaid through the bilateral trade accounts. The 1968 refunding arrangements reduced the payment on supplier credits from $66 million due in 1969 to $17 million. Repayment of the consolidation credits will begin in 1971 and a maximum of $45 million will be due in 1976. Total debt payments in 1969 are estimated at about $29 million and will reach a maximum (on debt outstanding) of $62 million in 1976.[11]

The Ghanaian government was of the view that these payments were too heavy. Exports in 1969 were $301 million, and debt service would be a charge of, say, 15 to 20 percent of export receipts. It suggested that the creditor governments should extend straight consolidation loans on DAC ideal terms, i.e., low interest, long term and extended grace periods. The funds provided to Ghana would then be used to pay off the creditors directly. The consolidation proposed to deal with the refunded and outstanding supplier credits, not the long-term project and concessional import loans.[12] This proposal led to the 1970 debt adjustment.

Refunding, 1970

Neither the data used in the discussions nor the precise terms of the 1970 agreed minute have been released by the Ghanaian government and the creditors, so that the following is approximate. Repayment of the amounts refunded in 1966, with moratorium interest accumulated at the contractual rates, was to begin June 1971, and under the 1968 arrangement in January 1974. Principal and accrued interest of the medium-term credits is about $250 million, of which $212.6 million is owed to IMF member countries and the balance to nonmembers, presumably Eastern-bloc countries. Britain is creditor for about $110 million.[13]

The 1970 refunding applies to payments on these credits falling due

11. Estimated from Ghana, Commissioner for Economic Affairs, "Note on External Debt."
12. Ministry of Finance, *Budget Statement*, 1969–70, pp. 19–22.
13. See *Financial Times* (London) Oct. 20, 1970, p. 24. The article appears to be based on information from Ghanaian sources.

July 1970 to June 1972, amounting to $42 million. Half of this amount is to be refunded for a 10-year period in any of 3 ways at the creditor's option: (1) straight rescheduling to 1980 and later, (2) consolidation or refinancing loans without consolidation interest, or (3) provision of grants or easy-term loans equivalent to the payments.[14] The budget forecasts payments of $15.8 million on the refunded debts for FY 1970–71 and $12.3 million on long-term debt, an amount not much smaller than in 1968 and 1969. In addition, repurchases from the IMF are due for $24 million.

The Ghanaian government is rather unhappy about these results. It had proposed relief from all payments for a 10-year period and cancellation of the accrued interest. The creditors were unwilling to accord such terms, which would have been more favorable than have been given to any country, including Indonesia. The agreed minute provides for further consideration of the debt problem in the future, probably in the context of the aid consortium.

Conclusion

The 1970 refunding will cut payments on the old supplier credits to about half for the next 10 years, and government credits at easy terms will replace the amounts postponed. New supplier credits are restricted as are other private credits.

Payments on the old debts since 1966 have been facilitated by Fund drawings and credits financing imports from governments. Total drawings from the IMF through November 1971 have aggregated $108.4 million, but Ghana has repurchased $69.5 million. The United States has provided (to December 31, 1970) a total of $128 million in import financing, $100 million from AID and $28 million in P.L. 480. (These credits are additional to loans for the Volta River and aluminum project.) The U.K. and Germany and others, in smaller amount, have supplied import credits. The total of these credits, about $180 million in all, covered more in imports than Ghana probably paid on debt.

Ghana has a development program (in addition to the Volta complex) and would like to borrow $50 million annually for projects in agriculture, transport and industry. Additional borrowing, if loans

14. Ministry of Finance and Economic Planning, *Budget Statement for 1970–71*, pp. 32–34, p. 50, Table 3.

are obtainable, will add to debt service unless the loans are quite concessional in terms.

From 1967 to 1970 there was a trade surplus arising from increased cacao exports (73 percent of total export receipts in 1970). The price of Ghanaian and other cacao dropped from 45.6 cents a pound in 1969 to 25–26 cents in October 1971 to January 1972. Ghana's export receipts dropped sharply from an annual rate of $644 million in the second quarter of 1970 to $384 million in the first quarter of 1971. Since then receipts have probably fallen further. On the other hand, imports increased from $411 million in 1970 to an annual rate of $532 million in the first quarter of 1971. Arrearages in import payments mounted in the second half of 1971. Budgetary and administrative reforms are also due. In December 1971, at the time of the currency realignment, Ghana reduced the par value of the new cedi from $0.98 to $0.55, 43.9 percent in terms of current dollars.

In January 1972 there was a military coup. On February 5 the cedi exchange rate was revalued to $0.78, halfway between the old and the devalued pars. The new government also announced that it could not pay according to the 1970 consolidation agreement and that it was unable to accept the arrangements made in 1966, 1969 and 1970. It also cancelled the obligations to four British concerns ($94 million) on the grounds that the original contracts had been fraudulent, but stated that it was willing to arbitrate under the procedures of the International Centre for Settlement of Investment Disputes, affiliated with the IBRD. No further payments on other medium-term debt are being made pending reexamination of contracts made before 1966, and Ghana wishes to have all valid agreements refunded on IDA terms without a "sterile multilateral negotiation." Short-term arrears are to be paid off in time. These actions do not affect the long-term development credits from the IBRD and governmental institutions.[15]

The creditors are not likely readily to accept these terms so that prolonged negotiation seems probable. Acute debt difficulties are in prospect for some years, though eventually with the full operation of the hydro-aluminum complex Ghana should be able to obtain additional budgetary and exchange receipts to enable it to service its debt after readjustment.

15. Ghana, "Statement of the National Redemption Council on Ghana's External Debt Problem, Feb. 5, 1972," *Ghana News,* 4, no. 1 (Feb.-March 1972): 3–5.

VIII. LIBERIA

Background

Liberia is one of the few undeveloped countries which apparently has not appreciably increased its debt obligations in recent years. Moreover, it has not depended upon general balance of payments assistance in the form of program loans to cover debt payments and import requirements. The refundings of 1963 and 1968 have reduced service to levels which probably can be handled. While Fund drawings have helped Liberia over periods of difficulty, most of the credit has been repaid from Liberia's own dollar earnings.

Liberia's debt difficulties[1] have been primarily budgetary. The U.S. dollar is the principal medium of exchange.[2] International transactions are in dollars so that there is no transfer problem. The principal banks are subsidiaries or branches of American commercial banks, one of which, the Bank of Monrovia, holds the government deposits, and with others finances current governmental borrowing. The dollar supply can increase only by increased earnings abroad or foreign grants and credits. Since the government's budgetary debt is a dollar debt, it has been linked with the long-term external debt problem.

While the bulk of the population is in a rather primitive subsistence economy, the monetized sector depends largely on the foreign-owned mining companies and rubber plantations. Iron ore and rubber constitute about 90 percent of exports. The concession agreements vary; some companies pay corporate income tax (45 percent of net profit); others have temporary tax exemptions; the mining companies pay 50 percent of net earnings, either under the concession or through government ownership of stock, supplemented by certain minimum royalties. These payments are generally in lieu of all other taxes and the

1. Liberia's foreign debt troubles go back to 1874 when a sterling bond issue of 1871 defaulted. This issue was secured by customs and excise receipts paid over to the U.S. Minister. The debt was reorganized in 1898–99, secured by rubber revenues paid to the British Consul. A new loan in 1908 was similarly handled. In 1909 the U.S. government intervened and a new loan of $1.7 million in 1912–13 paid off the earlier issues. A receiver of the earmarked revenues was appointed by the U.S. President, and representatives of the U.K., France, Germany and the U.S. supervised administration. This loan was in arrears from 1919 to 1926. A U.S. Treasury loan of $5 million in 1918–20 was proposed as a refunding measure, but was not approved by Congress. In 1927, the National City Bank privately placed a new bond issue of $2.5 million to refund the earlier loans. This loan was readjusted in 1935 with reduced interest rates. The loan had a final maturity of 1966, but was paid off, apparently, in the 1950 period.

2. The Liberian dollar is at par with the U.S. dollar. Liberian coins circulate along with American coins and notes. The proposal for a central bank and an independent currency is in abeyance.

companies may import needed goods free of duty, and remit profits without restriction.

Debt

The Liberian economy boomed in the 1950–60 period with a large inflow of foreign direct investment in iron mines. Public revenues increased, and expectations increased faster on the assumption of large income from mining royalties and taxes. Government buildings and other public works were constructed under "prefinancing contracts," whereby government agencies gave their short-term or medium-term notes to contractors and suppliers at greatly varying rates of interest and maturity[3] and without any centralized control of borrowing. "Prefinancing" debt increased from $0.9 million in 1955 to $30 million in 1961. Current government deficits were financed at short term by the banks. Aside from Ex-Im (15- to 25-year) loans and German government loans (see Table 26), the obligations had maturities of one to five years. Public debt, which was estimated at $13.7 million at the end of 1957 (Moody), increased to $122.6 million in 1963. Contractual interest and amortization in 1963 required $33.6 million, when total government revenues amounted to $36.2 million. At the beginning of 1963 the debt, including short-term, stood at $132.5 million plus $35.9 million in interest. For the 6-year period 1963–68 debt service was estimated at $20 million annually, about half of government revenues.[4]

Liberia joined the IMF in 1962, and almost immediately called for financial and technical assistance to straighten out the financial mess. A staff mission recommended a series of measures, budgetary controls, debt centralization, new taxes and a readjustment of debt to stretch payments over a reasonable period (as long as 15 years) to correspond with expected concession and other earnings. A Fund representative has been resident in Liberia since 1963 as an advisor to the government.

Refunding credits as well as new project credits had increased the principal of the total debt to $178 million in 1968 when a second rescheduling was arranged.

3. One study states that explicit interest and financing charges were about 12 percent, but that hidden interest costs through contract figures on construction and other charges raised the rate to a range of 15 to 30 percent with annual service of from 24 to 40 percent. (Cf. Robert Clower, "Summary Report," *Northwestern University Economic Survey of Liberia*, Evanston, Ill.: Northwestern University Press, 1962, p. 29).

4. Liberia, *Report of the Treasury Department*, 1963–64, p. 15.

Table 26. Liberian National Debt, 1949–70, and Debt Service, 1965–70^a *(Millions of Dollars).*

	Principal	Service
1949	0.6	
1953	2.5	
1955	8.7	
1956	9.3	
1957	12.9	
1958	22.7	
1959	37.6	
1960	46.2	
1961	86.2	
1963	122.6	
1965	175.7	11.6
1966	182.4	9.1
1967	186.0	9.6
1968	173.3	11.5
1969	168.9	12.5
1970	175.6	14.5 (E)

a. Data for 1949 to 1961 were derived from Liberia, Secretary of the Treasury, *Annual Reports.* (George Dalton and Robert Clower, "Notes on Government of Liberia Revenue and Debt," *Northwestern University Economic Survey*, p. 9.) As reported, debt includes short- and long-term. Data for 1965 to 1970, from IBRD sources, include only debt of a maturity of more than one year, as of Jan. 1. Undisbursed amounts are included ($15.7 million in 1970). Short-term debt fluctuates with the budget.

Table 27. Estimated Composition of Liberian Long-Term Public Debt (Including Undisbursed), as of March 31, 1963, and January 1, 1968 and 1970 *(Millions of Dollars).*

	1963	1968	1970
Bank credits	15.5	11.4	9.5
Supplier and other private	59.7	36.9	30.0
Governments	47.4	120.8	128.3
U.S. total	31.1	102.5	106.0
Ex-Im	30.1	30.3	28.6
AID and other	1.0	72.2	77.4
Germany	15.7	16.0	n.a.
Other governments	.6	1.3	n.a.
IBRD	0.0	4.3	7.9
Total	122.6	173.3	175.6

Source: The estimates are based on IBRD data, the U.S. Treasury, *Foreign Credits* and figures used in the debt discussions. Data for 1963 on U.S. government credits did not include the lend-lease credit, which is included in the 1968 and 1970 estimates ($17.9 million). No breakdown by creditor country is available for 1970. The German credits probably were $17 to $20 million, including the refunding credits. Data for Ex-Im and other U.S. credits include only loans to the government. Ex-Im loans to the private companies were $50.5 million outstanding, Jan. 1, 1970.

1963 Refunding

The Liberian government, advised by the IMF staff, proposed a rescheduling of principal repayments on an "equitable" basis. In fact, equal treatment would have been practically impossible considering the variety of terms on which the debt had been contracted. The main difficulty was that the notes issued to contractors and suppliers had been in good part discounted with financial institutions by the original holders or sold to other private parties.

After protracted negotiations with individual creditors, Liberian payments of principal in 1964 were scaled down from the $13.2 million to $4.3 million; in 1965 from $14 million to $3.6 million and so on to 1968 when the figures were to be $8.7 million and $5 million, respectively. The commercial banks agreed to a 4-year moratorium with repayment over 6 years. Ex-Im postponed the principal due 1964 to 1968, $13.2 million, with repayment 1971 to 1978. A variety of arrangements was made with the contractors. Amounts under $1 million were paid as originally scheduled. Unused amounts on two Italian credits were cancelled ($4.8 million). Other private credits were stretched out by agreement. Contractors and suppliers received 25 percent of the principal over the first 6 years, 30 percent over the second 5 years and 40 percent over the final 4 years. "To get all of the principal 23 creditors to agree to the plan was a problem difficult to even describe. It would not have been possible if there was not every assurance of fair and equal treatment to all involved."[5] The Paris office of the First National City Bank was made the paying agent on the various notes. The Fund standby provided part of the cash needed. Interest payments were made on all credits at the original rates and the refunding credits required additional interest.

As a net result total payments of principal and interest were to be reduced to $9–10 million from 1964 to 1968, and $14–16 million the next 3 years. The IMF has importantly supplemented local resources in meeting the revised schedule. With an increase in quota and a succession of purchases and repurchases the Fund has provided $28.5 million in gross drawings, used in part to meet debt payments. The net outstanding has been reduced to $4.4 million (February 1972).

1968 Refunding

With advice from the Fund, Liberia introduced fiscal and administrative reforms, "the austerity program." Expenditures, including

5. Ibid., p. 16.

debt service, in 1968 were held slightly below the revenues of $51.1 million.[6] The receipts from the rubber and iron ore concessions were below anticipations as the result of falling prices and delay in the Lamco project. Some of the concessions were renegotiated.

During fiscal year 1968 debt payments had been $11.8 million, but the contractual amount was scheduled to rise to $17.6 million in 1969, $17.5 million in 1970 and $16.8 million in 1971, an average of $17.3 million for the 3-year period,[7] some 30 percent of expected revenues. Liberia decided to seek some alleviation of the schedule and the Liberian Secretary of the Treasury negotiated arrangements with the U.S. and German governments and financial institutions. The creditors agreed to scale down payments to about $14 million.[8] The Ex-Im has refunded $83.9 million of principal falling due in these years (6 percent) with repayment 1972 to 1974 when Liberian debt service would be lower than in 1969–71 by some $2.5 million.[9] Proportional adjustment in their claims were made by the banks, one of which gave longer terms for repayment of the refunded amounts. Apparently no changes were made in the terms of the debt refunded in 1963 owing to the contractors and suppliers.

Prospects

The net effect of the 1963 and 1968 refundings will be to reduce debt service to about $14.5 million in 1970 and 1971 with payments rising to about $17 million in 1974.[10] This level of payments should be within Liberia's capacity to pay, unless heavy service is required on additional borrowings. German (K.f.W.) and U.S. government credits (AID and P.L. 480) have been on relatively easy terms. Supplier credits have been repaid for the most part and new long-term borrowings have been moderate.

There were budgetary surpluses in 1968 and 1969, and probably in 1970. Since 1964 exports have increased rapidly to a high of $214 million. Imports have varied between $104 million and $126 million.

6. In fiscal year 1968–69 the budgetary surplus increased to $4.7 million (Treasury, *Annual Report*, 1968–69, p. 24).

7. Liberia, Treasury, *Annual Report*, 1967–68, pp. 19, 84, 85. This report states the external debt as $227.6 million including principal and interest (includes short-term debt).

8. Ibid., p. 83.

9. Some of the debt service figures are read from a chart in Treasury, *Annual Report*, 1968–69, p. 85.

10. The *Annual Report*, 1968–69, states the outstanding principal as $184 million. Debt service payments are stated as $18 million (p. 105), but in another place as $12.8 million (pp. 24–27). The difference may be due to the inclusion of short-term in one estimate but not in the other. It may be that the larger figure is gross and the smaller net of refunded amounts.

The trade surplus, which has to provide resources for servicing private as well as public debt, in 1969 and 1970 amounted to about $80 million. Service on Ex-Im loans to the private companies was only $8.4 million, with, perhaps, an equal amount to other creditors. Since the budget also depends on the government's share of the earnings of the companies, the dollar net can be used also to reduce the short-term debt to the banks.

IX. PERU

Background

The current Peruvian debt difficulties are related primarily to the short- and medium-term suppliers[1] and bank credits which constitute about half of the disbursed and outstanding debt. In addition there are short-term (less than one-year maturity) banking and commercial debts, which also have been subject to refunding arrangements. A reduction in the flow of new credits and balance of payments difficulties created a severe debt crisis in 1968. So far there has been only short-term relief.

The Peruvian trade balance depends largely on the price and quantity of exports of metals, cotton, sugar, and more recently, fishmeal. Peru generally has had a favorable trade balance, but the rapid rise of imports from 1965 to 1967 produced trade deficits in 1966 and 1967. Debt service requirements and a net deficit on other invisibles resulted in a current account deficit in all years except 1964 when there was a small surplus and 1970 when the surplus was $110 million. A net inflow of capital, however, permitted an almost steady rise in foreign exchange reserves from 1948 to 1970. The change in the exchange rate of the sol from 26.8 to 38.7 per dollar in mid-1967 was followed by a sharp cut in imports and a considerable increase in exports so that a large trade balance has reappeared.

Inflation had persisted for some years before 1967, with an unbalanced budget and expansion of bank credit, and attempts to deal with the problem were unsuccessful. In 1967 there was "a massive flight of capital from the country"[1] precipitating the devaluation in the middle of the year. In 1968 the government put in effect a series of new measures to curtail expenditures, to increase taxes and to restrict credit, as

1. IMF, press release, Nov. 8, 1968.

well as to secure adjustments of the external debt. To aid in the stabilization effort the Fund entered into a $75 million standby arrangement on November 8, 1968. In connection with the standby Peru undertook not to authorize new public external debt of maturities of from 180 days to 10 years (except for bulk agricultural purchases and certain credits to government banks) and to limit borrowings at 10 to 15 years.[2] Peru met the requirements of the standby, which was renewed in 1969 and 1970. The financial policy of Peru under the standby was directed to rebuilding reserves and attaining a reasonable degree of financial stability. The new program aims at "reactivation of the ecomy" by expanding investment, while at the same time raising additional revenues and limiting government recourse to the banking system. "It would also provide for policies designed to ensure an appropriate foreign debt profile."[3]

The medium- and long-term debt is (January 1, 1970) estimated by the IBRD as $1,117.1 million, of which $858.1 million is disbursed and outstanding. Bond issues and "other private" debt were $167.3 million. The publicly issued bonds represent the refunding of earlier issues in the U.S. and U.K. markets, which were themselves refunding still earlier issues,[4] and also new issues in connection with the refunding. Payments on these bonds have been made according to the revised contracts. Loans from the IBRD and IDB were $184.5 million. Loans from governments were $234.7 million. The U.S. and Germany are the principal bilateral creditors though in both cases a large proportion (almost half) of the commitments remained undisbursed in 1969.

Suppliers' credits stood at $388.4 million. These credits apparently include military equipment from various countries, railway, bridge, highway and irrigation projects, industrial equipment, telephones, refineries, hospitals, educational materials, feasibility studies and minor purposes of the government, its agencies and local authorities. Interest rates are, of course, higher and maturities shorter than on

2. Banco Central de Reserva del Peru, *Economic and Financial Review,* no. 24, (1968), pp. 15–17.

3. IMF, press release, April 17, 1970.

4. The involved history of Peruvian debt, default, refunding, new loans and their relation to to wars, the guano and nitrate concessions, assignment of revenues, fiscal mismanagement, etc., are summarized in Wynne, *State Insolvency,* pp. 109–98. The early loans during the War of Independence (1822–25) defaulted in 1825 and were refunded in 1849. Additional loans and refunding, tied to the guano concession, were issued in 1853, 1862 and 1865. Later loans were in 1872, 1906, and in the 1920s. The general default in the depression and the scandalous operations in the preceding years provided many pages of copy in the Johnson and Pecora investigations. The defaulted debts were negotiated by the Council of Foreign Bondholders in 1938, when the new settlement included the cancellation of interest arrears, the reduction of the rate from 7.5 to 5 percent, and the consolidation of issues.

loans by the international banks or governments. Supplier credits, though mostly denominated in dollars, were extended by Japanese, German, and other non-American companies.[5]

The principal banking creditors are U.S. commercial banks though there are also credits from Canadian and French financial institutions. This debt has increased most rapidly, from $5.1 million at the end of 1964 to $142.2 million at the end of 1969, largely to meet the current balance of payments deficit. These credits were generally renegotiated in 1968.

Refunding

Peruvian total public debt payments in 1966 and 1967 aggregated $88.4 million and $93.8 million respectively. The contractual amounts increased rapidly in the latter half of 1968 and 1969, and in this year and a half about $240 million was to be paid. Peru called on the bank and supplier creditors to readjust the debts. There was no Paris Club type of consolidation, but individual deals were made with some of the creditors and additional funds were borrowed from foreign banks to meet payments on debts not refinanced. For example, the Royal Bank of Canada loaned $5 million to pay amounts due to AID and Ex-Im. The credit was repayable in 8 semiannuals from April 1970 at 2 percent (including commission) above the Euro-dollar rate. Similarly, the Toronto Dominion Bank loaned $5 million to pay amounts due to IBRD, IDB and First National City Bank, (8 semiannuals at 1.75 percent above Euro-dollar rate). The Bank of Nova Scotia loaned $10.5 million (8 semiannuals at 1.75 percent above the New York prime rate) to refund its own prior loan and to finance other payments to IBRD and Ex-Im. The Bank of America rolled over payments due it, $8.4 million (10 semiannuals at 1.75 percent above its prime rate). A consortium of French banks refunded Fr.11.3 million at 2 percent above the Euro-dollar rate, to be repaid in 8 quarterly installments. The Bank of London and South America loaned $2.2 million at 2.25 percent above the 180 day Euro-dollar rate (7 semiannuals). The Franklin National Bank of New York loaned $5 million at 1.5 percent above the New York discount rate (15 quarterly repayments). The K.f.W. provided DM110 million (8 semiannuals at 6.75 percent and 0.5 percent commission) to refinance German credits. The French

5. There is a detailed statement of these debts and payments in Controloria General de la Republica, *Cuenta General,* 1966, pp. 277–330, but it is practically impossible to classify the data in the IBRD format.

government rolled over 75 percent of obligations due it (Fr.23.2 million at 5 percent and 8 semiannuals). The Spanish government loaned $4.8 million at 7.5 percent to refinance 82.5 percent of the amounts due in 1968 and 1969.[6]

The process of individual refundings has continued to the present (1971). In March 1970, short-term debt of about $220 million due to German, French and British creditors was refunded so that three-fourths of the payments would be due in 1976 and 1977 and only a fourth was to be repaid in 1970 and 1971. Interest was at 8.5 and 9 percent. Italian credits were refinanced (8.25 percent) for payment in 1970 to 1973.

Later in 1970 arrangements were made with U.S. banks for refinancing $94 million, to be amortized, 1971–75; Canadian banks, $19.6 million at 1.75 percent above the New York prime rate and amortization in 1970–75; and with a consortium of French banks, for $11 million, to be amortized 1970–72.[7]

In the attempt to secure a better timing of repayment, Peru called a meeting of the creditors in Lima, followed by a second meeting in Brussels in November 1969. The European and Japanese creditors could not agree upon uniform terms and decided Peru would have to continue bilateral settlements. A month later agreements were reached with Belgian, Italian, Japanese and Spanish creditors to defer 75 percent of the amounts due, and a little later with British, French and German creditors.[8] There has been no refunding of the amounts due to IBRD, IDB or the U.S. government.

By these temporizing expedients, amortization payments in 1968 to 1970 were greatly reduced at the cost of higher interest payments on the outstanding amounts. In 1968 effective amortization was reduced from $150.9 milliom to $95 million and in 1969 from $196.9 million to $126.8 million,[9] with the deferred amounts falling due 1970 to 1975.

In 1970 the German government agreed to refinance 75 percent of the obligations to be repaid in 16 years from 1972 with interest at 8.5 percent. The French government refinanced 75 percent of the obligations to French nationals at 9 percent with repayment 1972–76 and the Belgian government refinanced Belgian credits at 9 percent with

6. Terms are summarized from Banco Central, *Boletin*, Nov. 1968, pp. 58–67; Dec. 1968, pp. 75–78; Jan. 1969, pp. 60, 70; June 1969, p. 38; Nov. 1969, p. 65. Cf. K.f.W., *Annual Report*, 1968, p. 105.
7. *Bank of London and South America Review*, March 1970, p. 167; April 1970, p. 230; May 1970, p. 287; July 1970, p. 406.
8. Ibid., Jan. 1970, p. 47; March 1970, p. 167.
9. Banco Central, *Economic and Financial Review*, no. 26 (1969–70), p. 37.

repayment in 1972–75. Spanish credits were privately refinanced at 8 percent with repayment in 1972–76. The Bank of London and South America also refinanced its credits. Other banking credits refinanced accruals of service.[10]

Prospects

The reported debt service in 1968 was $214.6 million and in 1969, $143.6 million, of which principal was $171.8 million and $96.2 million respectively.[11] These amounts include, however, debt payments which were in fact refundings, i.e., the principal of one note was repaid to the banks which provided an equal amount in new loans, plus in some cases, additional amounts to pay interest accrued. Bank credits were $68.5 million January 1, 1967 and were $146.9 million at the end of 1969. Total principal payments on bank credits were $117.7 million and interest, $24.7 million. In 1968, with the complex borrowings and refundings noted, payments to the banks were $103 million, but new bank loans $133.8 million. In 1969, and probably in 1970, the roll over was smaller. In 1968 and 1969 part of the debt was refunded by the issue of securities in the market or privately, and other private borrowings were $131.3 million. Some of the securities replaced banking obligations and supplier credits falling due. Debt to governments increased by $75.1 million, of which $64.2 million was net. That is, governmental debt was rolled over and governments refinanced payments on supplier credits extended earlier by their nationals.

Not all of the details of the ways in which the debt was effectively refinanced and refunded have been reported. The Peruvian Finance Minister[12] stated that no further refunding would be necessary in 1970 and that debt service in 1970 had been reduced by agreement to about 70 percent of the original requirements, a net of $137.4 million. This would be about 13.2 percent of exports. The IBRD shows a drop in the debt service ratio from 22 percent in 1968 to 13.8 percent in 1969.

With supplier credits replaced in part by governmental and banking credits, debt can be rolled over more readily. If exports continue to improve the situation will become more manageable. Peruvian debt will continue to be heavy. It is almost double what it was in 1965. The interest cost on much of the debt is now higher (more than three times

10. Idem., *Boletin*, March 1970, p. 53; April 1970, pp. 49, 56, 60–61.
11. Data from IBRD.
12. Speech of General Morales Bermudez, in Banco Central, *Boletin*, Feb. 1970, pp. 7–8.

the 1965 amount) and will fluctuate with the market, since many of the refunding loans are at floating rates. Political problems have stopped the flow of aid assistance from the industrial countries, particularly the U.S., which has given no AID loans since 1967, and Ex-Im credits have also stopped.

X. URUGUAY

Background

The 1965 refunding was primarily a renegotiation of commercial bank credits to the Bank of the Republic (then the central bank with commercial and investment functions), arising mostly from the refinancing of short-term commercial credits by the bank at an earlier date. The crisis was precipitated by rapid inflation and the maintenance of a greatly overvalued exchange rate.

Between 1963 and 1965 prices had more than doubled (wholesale prices, 1963 = 100) and have risen more rapidly since, to 2440 in December 1970. The peso has been devalued in several steps as successive exchange crises required. In 1964 there were 18.7 pesos to the dollar; in 1965, 59.9; 1966, 76.2; 1967, 200; in 1968, 250; and 370 from December 1971. Uruguay has in recent years had a surplus on trade account, a net of tourist receipts, but deficits on invisibles other than debt payments. In 1965 and 1966 there were relatively large surpluses on current account.

1965 Refunding

In 1965 the outstanding debt was $375.3 million; $133.1 million of the Bank of the Republic, $115.1 million of other public debt including the outstanding bonds, $75.1 million owing by private banks and $52 million by other private obligors, probably for the most part supplier credits.[1] The nonbank public debts presented little problem of payment. The bond issues, included in the miscellaneous item of $42.2 million, required payments of about $5 million per annum.[2] The other long-term obligations were to the IBRD, Ex-Im, AID and Japanese

1. Banco de la Republica Oriental del Uruguay, *Memoria.* 1965. p. 151.
2. Moody summarizes the succession of bond issues in London and after 1915 in New York, with the succession of defaults and refundings and reductions of coupon rates. About $24 million of these issues, including the general consolidation of 1937, is still outstanding.

companies. Payment was not heavy, and these obligations were not refunded.

The Bank of the Republic, however, had obligations of $126.9 million falling due in 1965, including some short-term accounts. Total exchange receipts were estimated at $228 million and import requirements at $205 million.[3] (Actual exports in 1965 were $191 million and net travel $26 million.) The situation was complicated by a flight of capital.

The Bank of the Republic suspended payment on its foreign obligations and renegotiated the outstanding debt. The American banks rolled over credits of $47.7 million of the total of $55.7 million, granted new lines of credit for $21 million and renewed the availability of other credit lines of $25 million. These credits were secured by a pledge of gold. The Bank of Nova Scotia consolidated debt of $7 million and extended an additional line of $3.5 million. The Bank of London consolidated debt of $5.6 million to be repaid in semiannual payments, each of $1 million beginning in June 1966. The Swiss, French and Italian bank consortium extended most of their claims for repayment over 5 years. There was also an agreed deferment of payment on certain supplier credits. Oil companies, British and American, deferred payment ($20 million) until 1966 and 1967. The agricultural machinery credits were to be repaid over a 3-year period.[4] There was an extension of time on the bilateral agreements with the central banks of Argentina and Brazil, and apparently the Uruguayan commerical banks made their own arrangements with their foreign correspondents. The net result of these negotiations was to defer the largest part of the payments due in 1965 to the years 1966 to 1969, though it was expected that some of the banking arrangements would be further extended when they came due, as they were in fact later.

The 1965 refunding was assisted by an IMF standby credit of $5 million in mid-1966. Uruguay undertook to restrain inflation by limiting borrowing. The peso was devalued again.

Sequel

As the result of the 1965 consolidation, debt service was reduced from $24 million in 1964 to $17 million in 1965, but the refunding arrangements and additional borrowing increased the amount to $48.6 million in 1968 and $57 million in 1969. In 1968 the U.S. com-

3. Banco de la Republica Oriental del Uruguay, *Memoria,* 1965, p. 147.
4. Ibid., pp. 148–54.

mercial banks renegotiated the outstanding $51 million debts to them (secured by earmarked gold) with repayment beginning 1970. Supplier credits were relatively small, some $26 million. Credits from the U.S. government did not impose a heavy burden, and the Argentine and Brazilian central bank arrangements have been refunded on a 10-year basis.

The process of rolling over debt has continued, and borrowings from the banks greatly exceeded payments to them. Total debt service to banks was $55.1 million while utilization of bank credits was $133.5 in the 5-year period 1965–69. In this period the outstanding bond issues were reduced by $10.7 million and supplier credits were reduced in 1969, as also apparently, the obligations to the Argentine and Brazilian central banks. Loans from governments and international organizations have increased.

The IMF standby of 1965 was followed by another in 1968. As of February 1972, total drawings on the Fund were $101.2 million of which 67.9 million had been repaid. The United States has provided $30 million in import financing and $23 million in P.L. 480. These forms of assistance have helped deal with the balance of payments problem. The debt situation is no better than it was in 1965.

Prospects

The debt of Uruguay is now about $320 million (January 1, 1970), about 50 percent more than it was in 1965. Debt service in 1969 was $57 million. Total interest cost rose from $5.2 million in 1965 to $14.7 million in 1969. Total public debt service is 22 percent of the disbursed outstanding principal, a ratio somewhat higher than the average world-wide rate on supplier credits. The debt service ratio in 1969 was 18.8 percent. Contractual debt service payment will rise in the immediate future by the terms of the refunding arrangements. To a large extent this ratio is nominal, since the banks in practice will have to roll over most of their claims. The longer-term debt on bilateral account is owed mostly to AID, and amortization will begin on most of it only in 1973. The loans from the IBRD and IDB have higher interest rates and shorter maturities so that their service will be heavier. The main problem will continue to be, for years to come, the periodic refunding by the banks of the outstanding credits, and the compounding of interest costs.

While exports have been increasing in recent periods, so have imports. The prospects for the future are unpredictable. Wool forms about a third of exports. Meat, hides and linseed oil are the other important items, all subject to considerable market fluctuation. The worsening of the internal situation needs little comment; the political unrest has been reported by the press. The inflation resulting from governmental and private borrowing continues.

XI. PHILIPPINES

Financial Situation

The Philippine debt problem arises largely from the financing of a rising trade deficit on government and private account through short- and medium-term borrowing from American (mostly), European and Japanese banks, in a period when governmental deficits increased and prices rose sharply. Longer-term project credits from the International Bank and the Ex-Im have not posed a serious problem.

The trade deficit (f.o.b. basis) increased from $38 million in 1964 to $278 million in 1969, compared with total exports of $855 million. While imports increased by 44.7 percent in this period exports increased by only 15.2 percent. Despite the inflation, an overvalued exchange rate was maintained until 1970, when the rate was freed so that the effective rate for the peso was reduced from 25.4 to 16.3 U.S. cents. The rate has been pegged at about 15.6 cents since the middle of 1970. The trade deficit was reduced to $28 million in 1970, but increased again in the first half of 1971.

The government deficit has been financed by borrowing from the central and commercial banks. From the end of 1964 to the end of June 1970, the claims of the banks on government and official agencies rose from 1.9 billion to 4.7 billion pesos. In 1969, an election year, the increase was P1.2 billion. These claims were reduced slightly by September 1971. Wholesale prices increased from 105 in 1964 to 145 in June 1970 (1963 = 100) and stood at 177 in December 1971. The inflation has so far not been arrested.

Debt Situation

Philippine long-term debt increased from $275.9 million in 1963 to $502.1 million in 1969 (January 1), but these figures exclude some $600 million of private debts guaranteed by public agencies. Service on the reported debt increased from $28.6 million in 1963 to $61.5 million in

1969, but these amounts include considerable rolling-over of debts by commercial banks.

As of December 31, 1969, the IBRD estimated a committed total of $569.2 million and a disbursed total of $443 million. The undisbursed amounts were mainly on U.S. government and international agency loans. The bilateral governmental credits ($171.3 million) had been extended mostly by U.S. agencies, and the international ($201.9 million) by the IBRD with smaller amounts from the ADB. These were primarily project credits at long-term and presented little problem of service. They were not part of the refunding exercise. The debt problem arose largely from the banking credits.

The Central Bank of the Philippines reported the outstanding total debt of the government, governmental corporations and monetary authorities as $890.4 million at the end of 1969 and $1,030 million as of December 31, 1970.[1] This amount included short-term credits which were of the order of $450 million, owed mainly to foreign commercial banks (the groupings of data are not identical). Approximately, long-term government and guaranteed obligations were over a billion dollars, and government short-term obligations about $450 million. There were, of course, private obligations, not guaranteed, of an unreported amount.

Debt Crisis and Refunding, 1969–70

Prior to 1969 apparently the banks frequently rolled over their short- and medium-term credits. By the end of 1969, the situation became more acute. As of June 30, 1969 the Central Bank of the Philippines reported a total of external public debt of $775 million,[2] probably on a disbursed and outstanding basis, but including debt of less than a year maturity of, perhaps, $200 million. Of the total debt $324.3 million was owed to U.S. commercial banks. European and Japanese banks were also creditors.

In 1970, about $325 million was falling due to banks on short- and medium-term credits, and $181.2 million was due for payment in the latter half of the year to American banks alone. A consortium of 33 U.S. commercial banks in June 1970 agreed to "restructure" short and medium debt of $247.4 million, so that only $40 million was payable in 1970, $10 million, $20 million, and $30 million in the following three years, $55 million in 1974, $61.8 million in 1975, and $30.6 mil-

1. Central Bank of the Philippines, *Annual Report*, 1970, pp. 30–32.
2. Idem., *Statistical Bulletin*, Sept. 1969, pp. 260–62.

lion in 1976. Probably, the low payments in 1971–73 on the restructured debt permitted original amortization on the unconsolidated debt. The schedule adopted was said to be based on the central bank's forecast of exchange earnings.

The central bank also began renegotiating the schedule of payments of $27.5 million to European banks and received a one-year line credit of $50 million from a consortium of 15 Japanese banks, at 1.5 percent above the Euro-dollar rate.[3] In this way payment will be stretched for an additional year on these credits unless subsequent arrangements are made. The European banks have refunded their credits for various periods from one year to six. Interest rates were much higher on these credits, to 10.5 and 11.5 percent. American bank credits as refunded were from 5.75 to 8 percent.[4]

The net effect of these debt restructurings will be to reduce the payment hump from 1971–73, so that service on official short- and long-term debt is likely to be nominally from $100 to $150 million a year. The banks may, of course, renew credits again, so that the real burden will be lower. Interest costs have increased greatly. Prior to 1965 most of the debt was at 6 percent or less, but as of 1970 the bulk of the debt had interest rates between 7 and 8.5 percent and some obligations were as high as 12.5 percent.

The Philippine situation was eased by IMF credits, and to a small extent by a P.L. 480 credit of $10 million. The Fund agreed to a standby of $27.5 million in 1970, when the Philippines made the exchange adjustment and undertook to restrain domestic and foreign borrowing. In March 1971, the Fund approved a new standby ($45 million), which explicitly recognized that it would help "meet foreign debt payments."[5]

Prospects

The immediate crisis has been avoided, but debt payment will constitute a heavy burden on the balance of payments for years to come. The consultative group under IBRD chairmanship in April 1971 reviewed the Philippine development program but was greatly concerned about the short- and medium-term debt problem. "It was also recognized that while the Philippines had the capacity to service this debt, it would do so only by foregoing opportunities for growth. The

3. IMF, *International Financial News Survey,* May 22, 1970, p. 166; June 26, 1970, p. 206.
4. Central Bank of the Philippines, *Annual Report,* 1970, pp. 30–32.
5. IMF, press release, Feb. 20, 1970; March 15, 1971.

group was, therefore, of the view that there was need for quick disbursing aid . . . on as liberal terms as practicable."[6] Stated more directly the recommendation was tantamount to asking the governments to provide import finance on easy terms, so as to release Philippine earnings for payment of the debt owed to their banking institutions. In this way, the Philippines could undertake the additional debt to continue its development program.

XII. YUGOSLAVIA

Background[1]

Since 1965 there have been a number of bilateral refundings of Yugoslavian debt, but the amounts and terms of refunding by countries other than the United States apparently have not been published. Other DAC member countries have provided economic resources in loans and grants, and the debt outstanding to them, including undisbursed, was estimated in 1968 as larger than dollar-repayable debt to the United States, though commitments by these countries have not been disbursed as rapidly, since they were not financing current import requirements to the same extent.

By a series of steps between 1961 and 1965, the Yugoslav regime introduced economic and financial reforms. The enterprises (the social sector) were given greater latitude in production and sales, import and export policy. Control was decentralized and greater scope given to the price mechanism. Rapid inflation followed. Consumer prices were 209 in 1968 (1963 = 100) and reached 294 in September 1971. Industrial production also increased rapidly and wages (nominal) more rapidly (index, 504 in July 1971). While exports have increased from $893.1 million in 1964 to $1,678.9 million in 1970, imports increased more rapidly. The trade and current account deficits have increased rather steadily. The deficit has been financed by borrowing on bilateral official and supplier credits. Earnings of Yugoslavian workers abroad have also increased to a sum more than 10 percent of exports.

The dinar was devalued in 1965 and twice in 1971, so that its exchange value in terms of dollars is now less than half the 1964 rate.

6. IBRD, press release, April 23, 1971.

1. Cf. OECD, *Economic Surveys, Yugoslavia,* 1966, 1967 (the *Surveys* do not report the amount and form of debt relief); IMF, *Annual Report,* 1971, pp. 116–17; IMF, *International Financial News Survey,* Feb. 3, 24, 1971, pp. 25, 49.

With the par value change in 1965 and the extension of price controls, the IMF provided a standby credit and after the devaluation of 1971 provided the fourth of a series of such arrangements, with drawing rights of $83.5 million. Total drawings have amounted to $366 million but repurchases have reduced the outstanding net to $111 million in December 1971. In 1965, in conjunction with the other measures Yugoslavia sought and obtained debt relief. It may seek further relief in conjunction with other stabilization measures under the 1971–75 program.

External Public Debt

At the beginning of 1970, the public debt of Yugoslavia was $1.7 billion ($1.2 billion disbursed). Bilateral official credits on a net commitment basis were $963.4 million; multilateral (IBRD), $338.6 million; supplier credits, $247.3 million; bank loans, $140.7 million; and bonds and settlements for nationalized property, $28.3 million. These figures exclude debt of the social sector of $960 million, i.e. the debts of enterprises, mostly on supplier credit terms, and not guaranteed by the government, (since 1966) though there are guarantees by commercial banks. The Yugoslavian economy must, therefore, service a debt of about $2.7 billion, of which about $2 billion has probably been utilized.

The composition of this debt and the terms on which it was contracted have not been published.[2] As of the end of 1970, the outstanding dollar-repayable debt to U.S. agencies was $298.9 million: $66.5 million to Ex-Im, P.L. 480 of $210.8 million, $106 million of CCC credits, and $11 million in AID and other credits. In addition, there were outstanding credits of $287.4 million repayable in dinars.

Other DAC member countries were large creditors, $150 million on a disbursed basis in 1968 (Italy, $94 million; Germany, $30 million; France, $21 million). These credits appear to be in part refinancing credits for supplier credits extended in earlier years. East-bloc governments had credits of $83 million disbursed, with much larger amounts committed but not likely to be used.

The Yugoslavian balance of payments deficit has been financed by incurring debt to suppliers and to governments providing assistance at various terms. From 1956 to 1965 the debt, including undisbursed,

2. The discussion here is based on IBRD and U.S. government data. It is possible that more information has been published by Yugoslavia in Croatian language documents. Any treatment of the Yugoslavian debt is handicapped by the lack of precise data. Data reported in western European languages do not shed much light.

grew from $300–315 million to $1.4 billion ($812 million disbursed).[3] A large part was in supplier credits. A second factor in the growth of the debt payable in foreign exchange was the shift in U.S. policy. Prior to 1961, American assistance to Yugoslavia had been in grants and loans repayable in dinars (as were loans to other countries for development purposes). In 1961, Yugoslavia became ineligible for direct aid without a presidential waiver. There was an Ex-Im loan of $50 million (1961) for various imports. P.L. 480 paid in dinars was tapered off and shifted to long-term credit sales for dollars. When Yugoslavia became ineligible for P.L. 480 (1965), loans were made by CCC, mostly for cotton.

As of June 30, 1965, the outstanding dollar debt of Yugoslavia to U.S. agencies was $202.4 million (Ex-Im, $60.6 million; P.L. 480, $141.8 million). Of the total disbursed (as of January 1, 1965) of $811.9 million, supplier (and contractor) credits were $226.3 million, loans from other DAC members about $120 million, and from CMEA countries $72 million. Total debt service in 1965 was $210.1 million. This sum was 26 percent of the disbursed principal and 19 percent of export receipts. The bulk of the debt service was paid to suppliers ($88.8 million) and DAC countries other than the United States ($55–$60 million), and to CMEA countries ($32.5 million). This was roughly the situation that occasioned the refunding of 1965–66.

Debt Refunding, 1965–69

The situation was rather acute in 1965. Total exports were $1,092 million, with $465 million going to CMEA countries. Debt service to the West was $177 million compared with a trade deficit of about half a billion dollars annually with these countries. Debt service could not have been paid without such a drastic cut in imports as would have defeated the objectives (political as well as economic) of the economic liberalization program at its start.

There was no Paris-Club type of consolidation, and Yugoslavia dealt with the creditors individually. Data on the U.S. portion of the debt relief have been published.[4] There were other adjustments but details are not available. Ex-Im consolidated $3.5 million of principal due on the program loans of 1950 and 1961, to be repaid 1968 to 1971, with consolidation interest of 5.5 percent. The P.L. 480 credits of 1964

3. The data reported to the IBRD do not appear entirely consistent, particularly in the treatment of the debt of the social sector since 1966. Debt service figures are affected most.
4. Cf. *Foreign Credits*, Dec. 31, 1970, p. 37; *TIAS*, 16, pt. 2 (1965): 2064; 19, pt. 6 (1968): 7844.

had principal of $8.9 million due in 1966. By agreement this was reduced to $750,000 in 1966, and the deferred amount was rescheduled for payment in 1968 to 1972. No changes were made in other credits, so that the refunding provided $11.6 million in relief in 1966. In 1968, there was a second agreement to reschedule $15.9 million due in 1968 and 1969 on P.L. 480 credits of 1962, 1964 and 1965. Payment was reduced to $2 million in these years. The rescheduled amounts were added to the principal due 1971 to 1974, increasing these amounts by $2.4 million in 1971 to $6.4 million in 1974.

While precise terms of refunding by other countries are not available, it appears that they refinanced supplier credits or consolidated other payments of principal falling due in various years from 1965 to 1968. The principal outstanding to these countries is roughly the same in 1970 as it was in 1965, since the increase in the bilateral debt is accounted for largely by new obligations to U.S. agencies. Repayment of the consolidation credits and rescheduled principal is due from 1971 on.

The IBRD did not reschedule or consolidate on its then outstanding loans of $134 million. It has, however, given new loans of $223 million to Yugoslavia since 1965. While international competitive bidding applied to these loans, the award of the contracts to Yugoslavian entities provided exchange to cover some amounts of local expenditure. There is inevitably a large local cost in road projects. There has thus been some relief on debt indirectly.

Later Developments

Despite the debt relief given by the creditors in 1965 to 1968, Yugoslavian debt service increased in 1966 to $229 million and reached $255 million in 1968. In 1969, it fell to $213 million, but will presumably rise in 1971 to 1975 when refunded amounts fall due. From 1965 to 1969 total debt service was $1,133.9 million. Disbursements on loan funds in this period were $1,280.5 million, so that utilization of funds was slightly more than service. Payments on suppliers' credits ($467.5 million) were $80 million more than obligations. The total committed amount on these credits has been reduced by about $250 million. This reduction is favorable to the country's position since service on these loans has been annually from a fourth to a third of the principal amounts. The credits from the CMEA have also required heavy service.

For the immediate future the service problem will revolve about the repayment of the governmental credits, largely those from European governments. Debt service in the next few years is likely to be about $250 million a year on the public debt plus, perhaps, $150 million on the relatively shorter-term debts of the social sector.

Total annual payments of $350 to $400 million will be a heavy burden on a country whose exports in 1970 were $1.7 billion with a trade deficit of $1.2 billion. The balance of payments has been helped by U.S. assistance of $1.2 billion (June 30, 1961–June 30, 1970), $625 million in grants and $552 million mostly in soft loans. At present, only CCC and Ex-Im credits are available, but they require relatively heavy service and can cover only a small portion of import requirements.

In the period 1965 to 1969, utilization of loans was only slightly more than debt service. It cannot be expected that Yugoslavia could increase its exports or reduce its imports sufficiently to cover debt service, without increasing new indebtedness. The trading position should be improved somewhat by the devaluations of 1971, and the internal economy somewhat stabilized by the financial measures to check inflation and the wage-cost spiral. Industrial production has increased quite rapidly, and, if it is sustained under less inflationary conditions, the economic level should improve. The prospects for an improvement to the extent that net repayment of debt could begin appear rather dim. Hence for some years it may be expected that debt will have to be refunded as it falls due. The European creditors will probably have to re-refund outstanding amounts.

XIII. TUNISIA

The case of Tunisia is mentioned here because of the relation of program aid to the debt situation of a country with a high debt service ratio. Such refunding of Tunisian debt as has occurred took the form of refinancing of some exporter credits by public agencies. Over time the supplier credits have been replaced by governmental and banking credits, though these changes were effected at various times without any concerted action by the creditors. The debt service ratio of 32 percent of commodity exports (22.4 percent of exchange receipts) in 1968, the highest ratio for any of the countries for which it can be computed, is not particularly significant since the Tunisian economy has depended, and will continue to depend on external aid which covers a large part of the deficit in the balance of payments.[1] In 1967, for example, exports were $147.6 million, the current account deficit, $141.5 million, and net aid from the United States, France and others, $102.3 million.[2] The debt problem arises from continued resort to supplier and bank credits to finance imports not provided under aid programs.

Tunisian outstanding external debt stood at $611.3 million, of which $450.9 million was disbursed, at the end of 1968. Supplier credits were $82.3 million and financial credits $80.8 million. Total debt service was $60.6 million, including $19.1 on supplier credits and $22.2 million on banking credits. Two-thirds of the debt service was required for a third of the debt. The banking and supplier credits appear to have an average maturity between 4 and 5 years. As of the end of 1969 the total public debt, including undisbursed, was $732.6 million, but figures comparable to 1968 are not available. Supplier and banking credits were $193.1 million, an increase of $30 million in a year. The balance of the new debt was in bilateral government and international loans.

The public debt of Tunisia has grown from $225 million (January 1, 1964) to $732.6 million (January 1, 1970), though there has always been a considerable undisbursed amount of about a quarter of the total. Total debt service increased from $19.9 million in 1964 to $60.3 million in 1968. Debt service has fluctuated with the total debt and its composition, as financial credits have replaced supplier credits—the way the supplier credits were in practice refunded. In 1969 and 1970 however, there was a reversal. Financial credits were paid off, but new supplier credits obtained. Private credits had an average 7-year term and 6.5 percent interest. The annual service on the total debt in recent years has been about 15 percent of the disbursed outstanding.[3]

Aside from the financial and supplier credits the debt does not present any short-run problems of service, but in 1970 amortization will begin on some of the governmental credits. For the near future, aid, in the form of grants, program and project credits, and private investment are expected to exceed debt service and to cover almost all of the balance of payments deficit. Foreign exchange holdings have fluctu-

1. Tunisia estimates the ratio as 23.8 percent of exchange receipts in 1970.

2. IMF, *Balance of Payments Yearbook*, vol. 20.

3. Tunisia, Secrétariat d'Etat au Plan, *Rapport sur le Budget Economique*, 1970, pp. 80, 125–30. Tunisian estimates place disbursed principal at $545.5 million in 1969 and $616.8 million in 1970 and annual debt service of $68.6 million for both years. These estimates may include some short-term obligations.

ated considerably but in January 1972, they stood at $138 million, 4.4 times the level of 1968.

From 1961 through 1967 total aid amounted to about $536 million. Grants from the U.S. were $140 million and from others $73 million. The balance was in loans.[4] For the four years 1966–69, total aid was the equivalent of $362 million, of which the U.S. provided $157 million. Grants from all sources were $87 million.[5]

Total U.S. economic assistance to Tunisia to June 1970 has been about $644.1 million, $292.4 in loans and $351.7 in grants. Included were AID loans of $179.9 million and grants of $123.7 million, and P.L. 480 grants of $216.8 million and loans of $112.5 million ($70.9 million local currency repayable). About $98.1 million of AID loans were for commodity imports and $124.5 for projects. Ex-Im loans were small and half have been repaid. The outstanding dollar-repayable debt of Tunisia is $158.4 million (December 31, 1970).

The French government has been the second most important contributer of aid to Tunisia. From 1965 to 1969, total French public aid (net of repayments) was the equivalent of $77.9 million of which $70.6 million was grant aid. French private loans and investments and guaranteed exporter credits aggregated $103 million in this 5-year period. Apparently French private credits have not been refinanced by the government. The bulk of the grant aid has been technical assistance, though a small part provided capital equipment.[6]

The amounts and terms of loans from other countries do not appear to be available. From the movement of aggregates of debt by creditor class, it appears that some earlier supplier credits were refunded by private and governmental financial credits.

Tunisian debt service has been financed indirectly by nonproject aid from various countries, P.L. 480, and to a small extent IMF drawings. In the 5-year period, 1965–69, total debt service was 143 million dinars ($272.4 million), including 105.5 million dinars in amortization. In this period commodity import credits aggregated D62.5 million (U.S., D18.7 million program loans, P.L. 480, Title I, D29.7 million, and other governments D14.1 million), equivalent to $119 million.[7] There were in addition about $50 million in P.L. 480, Title II grants in this period. Gross IMF drawings from 1964 to February 1972 were $54.2

4. IMF, *Balance of Payments Yearbook*, vol. 20. Figures are on a disbursement basis.

5. Tunisia, Secrétariat au Plan et à l'Economie Nationale, *Rapport sur le Budget Economique de l'Année 1969*, p. 91.

6. France, Ministry of Finance, "Mémorandum de la France au Comité d'Aide au Développement," *Statisques et Etudes Financières*, no. 264 (Dec. 1970), p. 53.

7. Tunisia, *Budget Economique*, 1969, pp. 91–95.

million, with a new   .ding of $12 million. Private financial credits increased by $62.1 million. Gross monetary reserves increased slightly to 1968, but rapidly since. They would now cover about six months' imports. These sources provided imports in somewhat larger amounts than debt service and along with project credits financed the payments deficit.

It is clear that there has been no net repayment of debt, and it does not appear that Tunisia could make net payments in the immediate future without a drastic curtailment of its development program or contraction of consumption standards. Alternatively, there could be a debt refunding, which could take the form of further government refinancing of outstanding supplier and financial credits, since the government and IBRD loans are quite long term.

From a long-run point of view the ability of Tunisia to support its relatively heavy debt will depend on the outcome of the development program and the growth of exports. Export receipts have traditionally been derived from phosphates, other minerals and ores, and olive oil. In the last few years petroleum exports have increased sharply ($5.3 million 1970), and if this trend continues prospects will be greatly improved. Since about half of the supplier credits are related to this industry the investment made may prove to be well justified. Receipts from tourism have increased greatly in recent years and have become a significant part of exchange receipts. Tunisia may eventually be in a position to service its debt without reliance on external aid, but for some years the burden will be heavy and credits will have to be refunded indirectly by additional aid or refinancing.

XIV. PAKISTAN

Historical Note

To the present there has been no refunding of Pakistan's external debt except for the rescheduling in 1960 of the 1952 wheat loan. As discussed below, the debt situation indicated the desirability of a refunding operation before the troubles began in East Bengal. The Pakistan government took military measures, beginning March 25, 1971, to suppress the insurrection. The independence of Bangladesh was generally recognized in 1972.

In April and May 1971 Pakistan officials came to Washington to discuss their debt problem with the World Bank, the Fund, and the U.S. government. No debt relief action was taken. On May 1, 1971 the Pakistan government announced that it was requesting a six-month moratorium on debt payments, and also requested a special meeting of the consortium in June to consider refunding.[1] The unilateral moratorium applies only to intergovernmental consortium debts, not to commercial credits, nor to debts to the IBRD and debts contracted outside the consortium, whether to consortium countries or others.

The consortium held an informal meeting in June to discuss the findings of Bank and Fund missions. The Bank, as chairman, did not request the members to indicate the amount of aid they were considering for Pakistan, nor did the members indicate amounts. The governments emphasized that they were willing to provide humanitarian relief in East Pakistan "under the surveillance of the United Nations."[2] Since the Pakistan balance of payments has depended to a considerable degree on external aid, this conclusion could give Pakistan little assurance.

The surrender of the Pakistan army in Bengal to India (December 15, 1971) throws the debt question, along with many other issues, into the political arena. In addition to arranging a refunding plan, it will be necessary to divide debt liabilities between the two areas.

Pakistan Debt

The outstanding public debt of Pakistan (including undisbursed) has grown from about $121.1 million in 1956 to $3.8 billion in 1970, and debt service from $11 million to over $170 million. Data in Table 28 and Table 29 are sufficiently accurate to show the rate of increase. Balance of payments figures indicate rather heavy borrowing by the private sector, probably on supplier credit terms. The reported data also do not presumably include military credits. Hence the Pakistan economy must service debts which amount to more than $4 billion.

The present debt service requirements reflect the terms on which debt has been incurred since 1955. About 21 percent of the loans contracted to June 30, 1967, must be repaid within 10 years; another 8 percent in 10–15 years; 12 percent in 15–20 years; 5 percent in 20–25 years; and 54 percent in more than 25 years, i.e. mostly AID and IDA

1. *New York Times,* May 2, 1971, p. 16.
2. IBRD, press release, June 21, 1971.

Table 28. Pakistan: Outstanding Public Debt and Debt Service, 1956–70 (Millions of Dollars).

	Including undisbursed	Disbursed only	Estimated service
1956	121.1	58.3	11.2
1957	150.3	111.0	31.4
1958	160.1	93.1	19.7
1959	206.5	108.8	16.1
1960	253.2	131.4	25.1
1961	369.6	158.0	27.1
1962	458.0	217.2	34.6
1963	873.2	307.4	70.0
1964	1,224.7	533.6	62.9
1965	1,856.7	825.6	70.3
1966	2,101.5	1,158.1	86.9
1967	2,607.8	1,478.6	115.6
1968	2,970.8	1,906.9	145.8
1969	3,338.0	2,332.4	169.0
1970	3,779.5	2,709.2	n.a.

Source: IBRD data as revised. Principal is as of Jan. 1 and debt service figures are transactions as reported.

Table 29. Compostion of Pakistan Public Debt as of June 30, 1969 (Millions of Dollars).

	Principal outstanding disbursed	Principal including undisbursed
Total	2,539.3	3,637.8
Privately-held debt	192.7	278.9
Suppliers	154.3	230.8
Financial institutions	38.4	48.0
International institutions	512.3	878.8
IBRD	267.4	490.4
IDA	245.0	378.4
ADA		10.0
Governments	1,834.2	2,480.1
United States	1,051.1	1,303.4
Germany	242.4	293.9
Japan	167.5	220.3
U.K.	151.6	178.1
U.S.S.R.	53.9	97.6
China (Mainland)	40.1	107.5
Other CMEA	16.2	51.2
Other Europe	111.4	228.1

Source: IBRD. A full breakdown as of Jan. 1, 1970 is not available. The IBRD *Annual Report,* 1971, p. 65, shows supplier credits of $236.6 million; bank credits of $55.5 million; multilateral institutions, $869.1 million; and bilateral credits of $2,618.3 million (including undisbursed). The moratorium applies to most of the bilateral governmental loans.

credits. Interest rates at 3 percent and under apply to 47 percent of the loans, i.e. AID, IDA and some of the British, German and Canadian credits. About 41 percent of the loans have interest rates over 5 percent. In general the higher interest rates go along with the shorter maturities, so that they probably require service of 17 to 20 percent of principal in any year. While the terms given by the consortium members have softened considerably over time, when AID and IDA money was not available Pakistan borrowed at supplier credit terms from nonconsortium sources, and also in consortium countries, resulting in a rapid increase in debt service since 1967 and in the debt service ratio.

The terms of these loans were quite varied. As of June 30, 1969, U.S. credits disbursed and outstanding, repayable in dollars, were $1,059.9 million (on December 31, 1970, $1,333.8 million). Ex-Im loans were $28.3 million ($73.1 million), CCC credits, $9.5 million ($1.7 million), P.L. 480, $40.2 million ($100.3 million), and AID credits, $981.9 million ($1,158.7 million). All but the Ex-Im and CCC credits are on soft terms. Credits repayable in rupees were the estimated equivalent of $654.1 million in 1969, and $652.9 million in 1970.[3]

German credits were originally largely exporter credits at 10 years and 6 percent, but about two-thirds of the loans now are at concessional interest rates of 3 to 5.5 percent and 25 years including 7 years grace. Earlier credits from the U.K. had an average of 6 percent and 25 years including 7 years grace, but the most recent loans are interest free with the same terms. French, Italian, Japanese and Netherlands firms have supplied exporter credits, but under the consortium arrangements the governments have given somewhat more liberal terms. Canada has given grants and some loans. Some Western nonconsortium members, Australia and New Zealand, have given grants. Sweden has provided funds in conjunction with IDA and at IDA terms. The U.S.S.R., Poland, and Czechoslovakia have provided export credits (10 years) and mainland China has provided interest free loans.[4]

Balance of Payments, AID and Debt

The balance of payments, on trade, and on goods and services account has been in deficit at least since 1956. The trade balance has fluc-

3. *Foreign Credits* data. In 1969 Ex-Im credits as given above included about $10.1 million of loans to private entities and in 1970, $13.7 million. These credits were probably not guaranteed by the government, and so excluded from the IBRD estimate shown in Table 29.

4. Pakistan, Ministry of Finance, *Economy of Pakistan, 1948-68* (1968), pp. 297-333. Data do not include military credits.

tuated with the variation in exports, and net imports have varied with the amount of aid utilized. The current account deficit includes payments of interest but not amortization of loans. The deficits are more or less planned in terms of the amount of aid expected to be received or pledged in the consortium exercise.

From 1963 through 1970 the trade deficit aggregated $3.3 billion and the goods and services account $4.6 billion. These deficits were offset by a net inflow of capital of $2.7 billion and transfers of $1.8 billion, mostly to the government. Grants to the government decreased irregularly from $273 million in 1963 to $38 million in 1970. In 1969 and 1970 private net borrowing increased sharply. On government account more of the borrowing was on supplier terms as aid fell off.[5] There has been only a small net use of reserves. Despite the rise in prices, the par value of the rupee was not changed from 1955 to May, 1972.

Pakistan's exports increased from $417 million in 1963 to $723 million in 1970, but imports have also increased by larger amounts, so that the trade deficit in 1970 was $535 million. Exports fell off in 1971 with the decline in exports of jute and jute manufactures, which form more than 40 percent of the total. The floods, cyclone and tidal wave in August to November 1970 in East Pakistan were followed by the uprising and military incursion in the spring of 1971. The extent of war damage is not yet known. In any event it will take several years before production in East Bengal will be restored, so that there appears to be no reason to expect an improvement in the Pakistan balance of payments for some years.

Total loan and grant aid to Pakistan since 1950 has been over $7 billion, excluding military assistance. Prior to 1955 two-thirds of the assistance was in grants from the United States, Australia, Canada and New Zealand under the Colombo plan. The grant share has steadily diminished. Aid from all countries has greatly exceeded payments on debt. An official estimate placed debt payments at $471.4 million to the end of 1966 compared with loan and grant receipts of $4.7 billion ($3 billion in loans).[6] Since that date debt payments (to the end of 1970) were probably an additional $600 million. Loan utilization was about $1,231 million and grants $511 million. Roughly then, debt service was about $1.1 billion (1950–70) compared with grant receipts of $2.5 million and loan utilization of $4.2 billion.[7]

5. Data aggregated from IMF, *Balance of Payments Yearbook*, vol. 20 (June 1969); vol. 22 (June 1971); *IFS*, Dec. 1971, p. 274.

6. Pakistan, Central Statistical Office, *20 Years of Pakistan, in Statistics* (1968), pp. 322–25.

7. Figures for 1967–70 were derived from IMF and IBRD data and so may not be directly comparable with the 1950–66 Pakistan data. They appear to be approximately consistent.

With the increased cost of debt service and the decline of total annual assistance, the percentage of "net aid" has been decreasing, though it is far from the break-even point.

U.S. assistance to Pakistan since 1950 has been about $3.9 billion, $1.6 billion in grants, $2.2 billion in soft loans, in part repayable in rupees, and small amounts in harder official credits. U.S. aid has been more than half of the total. Of the total of AID loans of $1.6 billion, $984 million was in the form of credits for commodity imports (commitment basis). These credits covered imports of specific commodities, steel, chemicals, fertilizers, pharmaceuticals, vehicles and parts, etc.,[8] a wide range of commodities used for production and consumption. P.L. 480 was $1.3 billion, all but a small part in the form of sales for rupees, which, after receipt, were granted or loaned for development purposes.

Other consortium members, including IBRD and IDA, have mainly financed projects, though IDA has provided $75 million in industrial import programs. There have been smaller program loans from other countries in recent years, with the increased emphasis placed on such loans in the consortium. Under the Colombo plan there have also been grants for commodity imports. Some of the recent program loans may be offsets to debt service on earlier harder-term loans.

It was argued in chapter 3 that commodity import credits facilitate the repayment of loans more readily than project credits. AID commodity loans plus P.L. 480 in the aggregate have been almost double the total debt service paid. It is clear that these loans were not granted with this particular end in mind. Prior to 1966, AID programs were far in excess of debt service; since then they have been smaller. They were intended, rather, to meet the U.S. share of financing the balance of payments deficit, which of course, had debt service as an element. Without these loans, Pakistan in recent years could have maintained debt service but only by a drastic cut in imports. In 1970 for example, Pakistan's imports were $723 million and debt service at least $170 million. Neglecting invisibles, Pakistan while servicing debt could have bought about $550 million in goods, compared with actual imports of $1,151 million. Total debt service to the United States in dollars was under $100 million over a 15-year period and about $18 million in 1970. By providing easy-term loans to cover imports the United States has indirectly helped in the payment of debt service to other

8. AID Mission to Pakistan, *Statistical Fact Book* (1966), Table 9.2 for the break-down.

countries whose terms originally were harder, though most of the harder-term loans have now been paid off.

Conclusion

Prior to the moratorium Pakistan paid debt service by increased borrowing, and receipt of grants or quasi-grants (P.L. 480 local currency sales). There has been no net payment to the present nor is there any likely in the foreseeable future. To make a net payment, either exports would have to increase by several hundred millions, or imports decrease by half.

The situation is rather similar to the Indian position when the consortium countries provided debt refunding as an alternative to additional aid, mainly in the form of import credits, to offset increased debt service. The debt of Pakistan per capita ($33.15) is double that of India ($16.20). GNP figures per capita, for what they are worth, are about the same, $90, though Pakistan's per capita apparently has been growing faster.[9]

The Pakistan national plan, as of 1970, projects a balance of payments deficit of Rs. 20.5 billion ($4.3 billion equivalent) for 1970–75 including debt service of Rs. 5.8 billion. To cover debt service as well as needed imports foreign resources would have to provide $880 million gross per annum. A disbursed debt of $5 billion in 1975 is estimated. If, say, three-fourths of the aid were on concessional terms, Pakistan hoped to be able to service its debt, but a trade deficit was predicted for 1975 and future years. Debt service would continue at about 20 percent of new debt.[10]

The effects of the 1971 war are not clear, though obviously the economy has been worsened, with or without partition. The future of aid is also unpredictable. Without concessional aid, debt service cannot be maintained. In fact, the increase in the amount of supplier credits makes debt service more onerous, and the donor-creditors are not anxious to see their aid used to pay off creditors on harder terms. So far, they have not been willing to give debt relief and have preferred to give additional injections of concessional aid. What the situation will be in 1972 and later years will be a political decision, with debt adjust-

9. Expressed in 1964 dollars. IBRD, *Trends in Developing Countries* (Aug. 1970), Table 2.4. The "Technical Note" in the *World Bank Atlas 1969* (the predecessor publication) stresses the limitations of the data and methodology, limitations which apply a fortiori in this instance, in view of exchange rates and structures.

10. Pakistan Planning Commission, *Outline of the Fourth Five-Year Plan* (1970), pp. 85–90.

ment complicated by the obligations of Pakistan to mainland China and the independence of Bangladesh.

XV. COLOMBIA

Introduction

Colombia, despite its high external debt ($74 per capita), relatively high debt service ratio, and debt service well over half of its utilization of loan funds, has not been in serious debt difficulties[1] since World War II, and is likely to avoid refunding in the future unless expected export receipts do not materialize or U.S. program loans are drastically reduced. The debt service ratio reached a high of 16.5 percent of goods and services receipts in 1966, but fell to 11.2 percent in 1969 as the result of increased exports. The controlled floating exchange rate has moved with the inflation so that in recent years exports have not been discouraged. Control of exchange transactions limits imports to what can be financed from receipts and aid.[2]

Debt

The external public debt (including undisbursed) of Colombia has increased from $725.3 million at the end of 1963 to $1,515.9 million at the end of 1969 (see Table 30). The disbursed amount was $1,079 million. The largest undisbursed amounts were in IBRD loans, supplier and bank credits. Presumably the suppliers' credits and bank loans will be used within, say, a year, as will the AID program loan. The rate of disbursement on the IBRD project loans will be slower.

One factor which has made Colombian debt manageable is the relatively low proportion of supplier credits to the total, 7.4 percent of the disbursed total loans and 9.1 percent including undisbursed. These credits ($141.1 million including undisbursed in 1970) require heavy service, about 26 percent of the amount disbursed and outstanding in 1967–69. Banking credits, which have a high nominal debt service, 55.1 percent of the average disbursed amount (1965–69), appear to be

1. In 1957 bilateral agreements with Belgium, France, Germany, Switzerland, and the U.K. refinanced $36 million of commercial credits, 20 percent of the outstanding, to be repaid in installments over three years (see IDB, *Financiamiento Europeo*, p. 130).

2. The controls with licensing, advance deposits and effective multiple rates are quite complex. Adjustments are made frequently. (See IMF, *Twenty-Second Annual Report on Exchange Restrictions*, 1971, pp. 99–106.)

Table 30. Colombia: External Public Debt and Debt Service Payments, 1963–69 (Millions of Dollars).

	Debt outstanding Jan. 1 including undisbursed	Outstanding disbursed	Debt service
1963	n.a.	n.a.	105.8
1964	725.3	n.a.	103.5
1965	889.3	566.7	101.9
1966	944.6	643.3	109.1
1967	1,015.6	707.7	99.5
1968	1,159.7	800.1	101.4
1969	1,318.1	949.4	99.7
1970	1,515.9	1,079.0	n.a.

Source: IBRD. Moody (1970, p. 3444) gives considerably higher figures for service, presumably as reported by Colombian authorities. In 1967, $151.4 million; 1968, $130.3 million; 1969, $105.4 million; and $396.7 million projected for 1970–73. The Banco de la Republica, *Informe Anual,* 1967, p. 149, stated debt payments in 1967 at $120.9 million. Presumably the figures differ in terms of debt coverage. The larger amounts probably include unguaranteed debt.

rolled over regularly, so that the major effective service is in interest.

The bulk of the debt, $1,294.1 million of the total of $1.5 billion, is owed to governments, mainly the United States, and to the IBRD and IDB. These long-term loans extended under the consultative group arrangements since 1964 require relatively lighter service.

Institutional loans, $634.4 million (January 1, 1970), are project loans for infrastructure, power, railways and roads. IBRD loans were $491.9 million, IDB, $126.9 million, and IDA, $19.5 million. The IDB had also made soft loans for the same or similar projects. Taken as a whole, the dollar repayable multilateral loans required average service of 10.4 percent of disbursed amounts (1967–69).

Bilateral government loans ($659.7 million, January 1, 1970) required annual service of 5.7 percent in these years. Annual service on these loans has sharply decreased from 18.4 percent in 1965 to 4.3 percent in 1969 as harder-term loans have been paid off and the amount of AID loans increased. As of 1970 U.S. government loans, $635.1 million, consisted of $75.1 million of Ex-Im loans, $19.5 million of P.L. 480, and $540.5 million of AID loans. Loans from other countries included hard and soft loans (e.g., the K.f.W. loan of $5.9 million).

Colombia has still outstanding some of the old refunding bonds[3]—

3. The outstanding bonded debt consists mainly of issues, 1940–47, to refund defaulted central government, agency and municipal bonds, now guaranteed by the government. The earliest sterling bonds issued 1822–24, the period of the revolution from Spain, defaulted a few years later. The refunding of 1845 was followed by new defaults, and an arrangement for refunding and providing new resources, made in 1873, resulted in default four years later. Prolonged negotiations were carried on intermittently from 1888 to 1905. The 1905 agreement was

and has borrowed small amounts on the bond market in recent years. The older bonds will be retired in a few years.

Debt Service and Balance of Payments

The Colombian balance of payments has been characterized in recent years by considerable fluctuations in the trade account, deficits in 1962, 1963, 1966, 1968 and 1970, and surpluses in 1964, 1965, 1967 and 1969, related in large part to coffee exports and prices and, to an extent, receipts from petroleum and "minor exports." The overall current account has generally been in deficit with large payments on investments. In addition to debt service there is the remission of earnings on direct investment, while the large errors and omissions in some years probably represent unrecorded capital movements which have been affected by the vagaries of the multiple exchange rate system. It is of course, impossible to predict the future balance of payments. About 60 percent of export receipts consist of coffee sales. Under the concessions of the oil companies a fluctuating portion of the total value of oil produced accrues to the Colombian authorities. "Minor exports" (i.e. excluding coffee and petroleum) have increased rapidly in recent years with the rise in the applicable rate for dollars, $197 million in 1969 and $134 million in 1970 compared with $85 million in 1964. If favorable trends continue Colombia may have receipts which will more readily enable it to meet the service requirements of the mounting debt.

In 1963 service on the public debt took about 24 percent of export earnings and in 1969–70 about 16 percent. Net debt has been incurred in recent years at about $150 million per annum. If this rate continues debt by 1975 would be about $2.3 billion with annual service (at 1969 rates) of about $235 million. In addition there is private debt, which in 1968 required service of $57.5 million on an original principal of $285 million.[4]

The Colombian balance of payments situation has been greatly assisted by foreign aid, which along with private borrowing and direct

abrogated in 1911 and refunding was arranged after World War I, and a later re-refunding followed.

Borrowing in the U.S. began in 1927. The default was general in 1931–33. Some of the outstanding bonds were "repatriated" at a fraction of face value during the default. In 1940–41 new bonds were exchanged for the old with a cut in interest from 6 to 3 percent and the payment of half of the defaulted interest with new bonds. A similar arrangement was made in 1947 for the municipals. Interest payments on the adjusted debt have been met since and the issues gradually retired. (Summarized from Moody; Council of Foreign Bondholders, *Report*, 1938, 1950, 1962; Foreign Bondholders Protective Council, *Report*, 1950.)

4. Banco de la Republica, *Informe Anual*, 1968, pp. 50–55. Some part of this debt may have been guaranteed and its service is included in the figures given in Table 30.

investment have covered the payments deficit. Short-term borrowing and some use of reserves have evened out variations. From 1963 to 1970 debt service has taken about $800 million. In this period AID program loans have aggregated $500 million and P.L. 480, $122 million (FY 1963–70, on a committed basis). AID project loans of $92 million were largely for purposes requiring mainly local currency expenditure. Many of these loans were intended to "generate local currency" for the requirements of the development program. They also helped finance the payments deficit and part of the budgetary deficit. Other consultative group countries, e.g., Germany and Canada, have provided import financing on easy terms. In sum, a good part of debt service has been indirectly assisted by financing imports of a great variety of raw materials and more finished products. Without this type of assistance Colombia would have had to reduce imports of needed goods in order to service debt.

Prospects

The future is uncertain. Colombian exchange earnings depend on coffee, petroleum and minor exports, all subject to fluctuations in price and quantity. If exchange receipts increase fast enough there may be little difficulty in servicing debt, though the development program may not allow much room for improved levels of consumption.

In FY 1970, AID program loans were reduced to $70 million, compared with $85 million in the preceding year. It does not seem likely that this sum will be increased in the near future and the difference will not be made up by other countries. On the other hand, if concessional aid is reduced Colombia may not borrow additionally so that debt service will not mount. If it borrows on conventional terms to a greater degree the debt problem will become more acute. The most onerous debts, however, have been liquidated over recent years. Aside from commercial credits the heaviest service will be due on the conventional credits from the IBRD, the IDB and Ex-Im.

XVI. MEXICO

This brief note on Mexico is included here because Mexico, despite its high debt service ratio and heavy per capita debt ($69 in 1970) has managed its debt problem without the need for multilateral or bilateral refundings. While debt has increased since 1961 to $3.5 billion in 1970, the increase in outstanding debt on a disbursed basis was $2,152 million, $2,380 million on a committed basis, debt service in this period was $3,872 million of which $3,068 million was in principal (see Table 31). Mexico is one of the few countries which has actually paid off part of the principal as well as meeting rather heavy interest requirements. Moreover, this has been done mostly from its own earned income. Its borrowings from the United States have been mainly from the Ex-Im. The IBRD has made conventional loans, and the IDB has provided funds from its special operations in about the same amount as loans from ordinary capital. (Part of the FSO funds, however, have been in pesos.)

A variety of factors account for Mexico's practically unique position among the developing countries. (In fact Mexico is emerging from that status with a per capita GNP of about $575 in 1968.) Inflation has been moderate, roughly equivalent to that of the United States. The peso has been convertible for current and capital transactions, though there are some restrictions on foreign investment. The booming Mexican economy has attracted private investment. Exports have increased by 45 percent, 1963 to 1970. Not least has been political stability since the revolution was "institutionalized" in 1924.

The Mexican goods and services deficit has been approximately equal to its deficit on trade account. Net travel income receipts have about balanced the net outpayments of the investment account, interest on public and private debt and remission of profits. Net travel receipts in 1970 were $709 million, compared with exports of $1,402 million and payments on investment of $687 million. While amounts vary, year by year, this relation has been characteristic of the recent period.

Mexican debt management has been facilitated by the large proportion in the form of bank credits and bond issues (see Table 32). Bank credits can be rolled over more readily than other credits. From 1965 to 1969, Mexico utilized $1.1 billion in bank credits and paid back principal of $1 billion and interest of $153 million. Interest cost in 1969 was an average of 6.4 percent. In the 5-year period net bond issues and other private credits increased by $225 million.[1] The interest cost in

1. Mexico has some bonds outstanding from its earlier refundings. There were several defaults and refundings between 1827 and 1867. The entire debt defaulted from 1914 to 1942 and 1946. As settled in these years, principal and interest were effectively scaled down. Payments have been made as refunded and principal gradually paid off (see IBRD, *The Economic Development of Mexico*, Baltimore: Johns Hopkins Press, 1953, pp. 139–40). Moody in various years

Table 31. Mexican Public Debt and Debt Service, 1956–70 (Millions of Dollars).

	Principal		Debt Service		
	Committed	Disbursed	Amortization	Interest	Total
1956	486.5	419.2	78.0	14.1	92.2
1957	491.1	424.9	64.2	14.9	79.1
1958	557.3	502.8	122.0	17.9	139.9
1959	665.4	598.6	144.6	22.8	167.4
1960	842.0	656.3	182.6	29.9	212.5
1961	1,131.3	812.1	167.4	37.1	204.5
1962	1,172.9	948.5	245.4	51.0	296.5
1963	1,429.3	1,127.2	230.6	55.8	286.4
1964	1,696.2	1,360.8	363.9	72.2	436.1
1965	2,088.8	1,735.6	396.5	88.3	484.8
1966	2,169.1	1,725.2	365.0	91.5	456.3
1967	2,346.4	1,848.9	357.7	113.2	470.9
1968	2,710.3	2,183.6	479.2	144.1	623.3
1969	3,198.1	2,475.7	462.4	151.1	613.5
1970	3,511.3	2,963.5	n.a.	n.a.	n.a.

Source: IBRD.

Table 32. Mexican Public Debt by Creditor Class, Jan. 1, 1970 (Millions of Dollars).

Total committed	3,511.3
Total disbursed	2,963.5
Bilateral official[a]	716.2
Multilateral[b]	889.4
Suppliers	491.0
Banks	711.9
Other (bonds, etc.)	702.9

Source: IBRD, *Annual Report,* 1971, p. 65.

a. U.S. credits as of this date to public entities were $354 million on a commitment basis (Ex-Im $279 million) and $278 million on a disbursed basis. France, Canada, Germany and Japan were also important creditors.

b. *Foreign Credits,* Dec. 31, 1969, shows IBRD credits (including undisbursed) of $729.8 million and IDB, ordinary capital of $208.1. Portions of IBRD and IDB loans sold to private persons are included in "other" in IBRD statistics, but not in *Foreign Credits.*

1969 was 7 percent. By borrowing on the bond market, however, payment of principal could be stretched out. In contrast bilateral government (DAC) and institutional loans cost 5.3 percent in interest in 1969, and had longer maturities. Taking the debt as a whole, payment of interest and amortization 1965–69 was $3.5 billion and utilization of loans $3.8 billion.

gives details of the arrangements. Despite this past history the "new" Mexico has borrowed almost a fourth of the total bonds issued by LDCs in recent years.

The proportion of relatively short-termed debt which has to be refinanced in one way or another, with one form replacing another as opportunity arises, accounts in part for the high debt service ratio, which has been between 21 and 25 percent in recent years. The roll-over makes this ratio nominal, but it points to the difficulties which would be encountered if markets became unusually tight.

From 1966 to mid-1971 Mexico borrowed by public or private sale $443.9 million gross in bonds or notes, issued mostly in Europe. These issues had maturities of from 5 to 15 years. Interest rates on the later issues were from 7 to 7.5 percent. Another private loan was one from the Prudential Insurance Company with a maturity of 18 years including grace of 14.5 years (6.87 percent). The Japanese Export-Import Bank and consortia of German, French and Swiss banks gave loans of from 5 to 15 years with interest rates varying between 4 and 8.25 percent. [2]

Heavy payments on supplier credits, annually more than a third of the disbursed amount outstanding, have been met from the more liquid forms of borrowing, but the proportion of supplier credit to the total is relatively small. Money is fungible and there has over the years been a shifting around of types of debt obligations. But in the period 1965–69, credit utilization ($3,788 million) exceeded debt service ($3,550 million) by a relatively small amount.

In addition to the public debt the Mexican economy must service private debt, which is quite large. In 1969 when interest payments on public debt were $151 million, the total of interest and dividends for the country as a whole was $634 million in the balance of payments. While the total outstanding is not known, and in any case would include debts to American companies owed by subsidiaries, net private capital receipts have in recent years ranged between $300 million and $700 million.

To manage the public external debt with the large relatively short-term component requires dexterity. Most of the public borrowing is by Nacional Financiera, a corporation interlocked with the finance ministry and the central bank. All public borrowing is subject to approval by the Secretary of Finance and Public Credit on the advice of a Special Commission on External Finance. These coordinating devices are intended to limit new borrowing to the amount that can be serviced from available resources.

In summary, then, Mexico has succeeded in handling its heavy debt

2. Mexico, Nacional Financiera, *Informe de Actividades,* 1969, pp. 13–18.

by varying the source of funds. Debt service has been covered in part by new borrowing, but at least part has been covered from current earnings of exchange. In some years borrowing has been more than service, in others less. Mexico has established control mechanisms which should keep the debt problem manageable.

The economy has been growing rapidly and trade earnings have increased. Tourism provides a large element of additional earnings, which depend on conditions in the United States.[3]

The then Finance Minister summed up the situation in 1969: "Mexico has a dynamic future ahead of her, but it is not free of risks. It is imperative to continue complementing judiciously the different elements of economic policy. The stage at which development is irreversible has not been reached yet: the ground that has been won can still be lost with relative facility."[4]

[3]. Imports rise and fall somewhat with the level of tourist receipts. That is if U.S. tourism should decrease the trade deficit would also decrease.

[4]. Antonio Ortiz Mena, "Stablilizing Development" (a paper presented at the IBRD-IMF Annual Meeting, 1969). Mr. Ortiz Mena is now President of the IDB.

5. PROSPECTS

There is no simple answer or generally applicable formula to deal with the problems posed by the accumulation of international debt and the mounting level of service in face of the more slowly rising export earnings and persistent balance of payments deficits of the debtor countries. The preceding theoretical analysis and case studies, it is hoped, will help clarify the issues. Economic analysis, as such, cannot provide normative solutions. It can, however, suggest certain probable consequences of the decisions made by statesmen, politicians or administrators, national or international. Policies are based on value judgments, which are not universally agreed upon. Any recommendations on policy, including those offered here, are debatable.

The long-range questions appear to be of two sorts: (1) how to deal with the existing volume of debt, and (2) assuming the continuance of aid and investment for some time, the terms and conditions of future lending.

Up to the present debt service has been met by some few countries from their own resources; others have financed their payments deficits by incurring more debt in the form of commercial loans, institutional conventional loans, or economic assistance provided on concessional loan terms, and still others reached the point where they were unable, or prospectively unable, to meet requirements so that they had to call upon the creditors for adjustment. The indirect refunding of debt through additional aid has for many countries, at least for a time, postponed debt crises.

DEBT SERVICE

The debt of developing countries as of January 1, 1970, including undisbursed, was estimated by the IBRD at $59.3 billion. On this principal sum, interest and amortization in 1970 were estimated at $5,980 million, and $6,076 million in 1971, for debts whose terms were known. That is, the estimate of service is somewhat low. Debt service on present debt would decrease after 1971 to about $2.8 billion in 1980. This projection necessarily has to be based on the unreal assumption that no additional indebtness is incurred, and that the debtors actually pay off their loans.

Actual debt service in the future will depend on the amount of new debt and its terms. Taking the developing countries as a whole their debt has increased annually since 1955 by amounts which are larger than debt service.[1] On this assumption debt in 1971 probably increased by more than $6 billion. If this process is continued, the total debt would be about $150 billion by 1980 and debt service (10 percent of principal including undisbursed) would be about $15 billion annually. If, on the other hand, the existing debt were replaced entirely by concessional loans, at DAC standards or AID terms, debt service would be reduced to some rate of about 5 percent of principal. By 1980 the total debt would be about $100 billion and service about $5 billion. This latter assumption is quite unrealistic. Not all countries will receive concessional loans; even those countries which receive such loans are likely to borrow additionally from harder sources. The range of $100 billion to $150 billion is merely the measure of the magnitude of debt to be outstanding on the assumption that new loans merely cover the interest and amortization on the present volume of debt. No allowance is made for additional indebtedness, nor does the estimate include service on public debt not reported to the IBRD, such as those military credits which are kept secret. The balances of payments must also service the debt of private entities not included in the figures. Some countries may also be able to reduce their debts, though considering the small number of countries likely to be in that position and the moderate amount of net reduction by them, the effect on the grand total cannot be expected to be great. As a guess it will take about $8 billion in 1980 to service the public debt now outstanding unless in the interim there are far-reaching adjustments.

If there is to be further development in the poor countries, additional net resources will have to be provided by the richer. How much will be, and at what terms, cannot be predicted. One percent of GNP net flow of resources from the advanced countries has been set as a target. This target has not been hit in recent years with the rapid growth of GNP in the industrial countries (in current currencies). Whether it will be, despite various official pronouncements, is another question. Projecting growth rates of 4 to 5 percent from the 1968 level in DAC member countries at 1968 prices, the net flow would be of the order of $27 billion to $30 billion per annum in 1980. If prices rise at 2 percent per annum, the 1980 target figure would be $35–$38 billion. The flow of resources would include grants, private investment and official loans. Under the DAC quality standards, however, the flow

1. Cf. Table 1 above.

would be predominantly in highly concessional loans or grants. Assuming that about half of the net flow is in the form of loans to governments, new net indebtedness would increase by roughly $100 billion by 1980. If this new debt has grace periods of 10 years, service would be an additional $2–3 billion. Subsequently it would rise to about $5 billion a year. On harder terms for economic assistance loans and allowance for nonaid loans, public debt service would be considerably higher.

The Pearson report[2] projected debt service in 1980 of $2.7 billion to $5.2 billion, and from $6.5 billion to $10.8 billion in 1987 on official development assistance on two sets of terms, assuming that assistance was to be 0.7 percent of GNP and half in the form of grants. The higher amounts are roughly at DAC standards, the lower at the Commission's recommended rate which is lower than present AID terms. These figures exclude service on loans from the ordinary operations of the international agencies, other official credits and private debts, sources which would presumably provide the other 0.3 percent of GNP.

Any estimate of the principal of debt and the amount of debt service for a term as long as 10 years necessarily involves arbitrary assumptions. On a smaller amount of aid, debt would increase less. At harder terms, service would be heavier. By 1980 the debt of the LDCs could be as little as $150 billion or as much as $250 billion on the assumption that there is no net repayment and that new debt to be incurred covers service as it accrues as well as some amount of new resources. Debt service could be within a range of $10 to $20 billion, unless refundings to come push off payment of principal to a more distant future.

In 10 years time some countries could attain a position where they could begin a net repayment of principal, or, while rolling over principal, meet the interest costs from their earned resources. Mexico has continued to borrow but repayments of principal have in some recent years exceeded new borrowings. Argentina has done likewise in some years. Brazil may under favorable conditions, halting inflation and devaluing enough, be able to do so in the future. There is less likelihood in the hard-core aid-recipient countries. Some of them might even strike oil.

The crux of the problem of debt service is prospective export receipts. Some countries have indeed rapidly increased their exports. At

2. P. 164. The figures are read from a chart, hence approximate. Implicitly prices are taken as constant.

the extreme are the petroleum producers. Libya's exports in a period of 8 years (1963–70) rose from $336 million to $2,366 million. Ten years ago few would have expected that Libya would move at this rate. There are few Libyas. There are also countries in which valuable mineral resources or manufactures can be developed. Most LDCs, however, depend upon agricultrual exports for which the market does not expand rapidly. Moreover, to the extent that commodity agreements may limit their exports in the hope of sustaining world market prices or stabilizing earnings, their exchange receipts will not necessarily increase. In the absence of such agreements, the development of additional agricultural resources for export may actually decrease exchange receipts in view of the inelasticity of demand. Diversification of production and exports can, of course, be helpful. Several countries have benefited from the expansion of their "minor exports." Some of these newer lines of production may be high cost, for technological reasons, high internal prices, restrictions on production, etc., and they may be priced out of world markets by overvalued exchange rates. These are factors involved in the LDC desire for preferential tariff rates on their exports to advanced economies. The "green revolution" should reduce in some areas the demand for imported foods and feeds, and import substitution as well may benefit their balances of payments. These processes, however, take time and investment. Some countries have been able quickly to increase their exchange receipts by devaluation, an indispensable step if inflation has been long continued.

The IBRD in its 1970 *Annual Report* pointed out that in the last decade, debt principal and annual service have increased at a rate almost double that of export earnings and almost triple the rate of growth of GNP. If this trend continues during the next decade there can be little expectation of net debt reduction for the group as a whole. Calculations made above[3] indicated that the exports of non-petroleum producing LDCs had increased at a compounded rate of almost 7 percent over the 10-year period 1960–70, but that this rate was in fact a projection of the pace of inflation of the last few years. Given the deflated rate of growth of imports, there appears to be little prospect of net balance of payments surpluses.

The Pearson Commission made an interesting calculation on the assumption that borrowing on IBRD terms to meet the projected balance of trade gap would after a 30-year period absorb 101 percent

3. See above p. 59.

of export earnings, if exports increased at a compound rate of 5 percent, and 43 percent at an export growth rate of 8 percent. Borrowing on DAC terms would take 40 or 17 percent of exports on these assumptions.[4] While these calculations were made to illustrate differences in debt service under various loan terms (the Commission recommended terms about half the DAC standards), they pointed to the problem of protracted borrowing to meet deficits.

Actual borrowings by LDCs have been at harder terms than IBRD rates.[5] Merely to roll over the debt by 1980 will take debt service of from $5 billion to $15 billion, depending on terms. Whether or not the donor-creditor countries will supply funds at the rate necessary to cover debt service plus amounts needed for development or balance of payments deficits is of course, unknown. The resource flow would have to increase at some compound rate since constant flows result sooner or later in the situation when debt service absorbs the flow. This point would not be reached in 10 years if the money were provided on AID or DAC terms.[6] In any event most of the LDCs are not likely to be able to reduce their debt by increasing their exports enough.

THE REFUNDING OF DEBT: DIRECT AND INDIRECT

Loans have been directly refunded in the last 10 years for countries which have about a half of the debt outstanding. Some other countries are likely to be in difficulty in the not too distant future. It has been noted that most of the countries whose debt service has for a period of years been 10 percent or more of their exchange receipts have had refunding exercises or, as in the case of Pakistan, a refunding exercise is indicated. Mexico, on the other hand, with its very high debt service, has been able to roll over its debt by capital imports and various refinancing measures in the market without requiring international agreement. While the 10 percent debt service ratio is not a critical value, it seems likely that many countries whose debt service is now below that ratio will reach it not long hence, as they begin to pay amortization after grace periods or incur new debt.

4. *Pearson Report*, pp. 160–63. This calculation made certain arbitrary assumptions about the trade gap. The trade gap is in part determined by the amount of lending and aid.

5. Cf. Tables 8, 9 and 10 above.

6. See chapter 2 and appendix.

If debt must be refunded at least for some countries, the issue presents itself immediately as to how the debt should be refunded, whether directly or indirectly. Secondly, who should be required to refund? And thirdly, that if there is to be a general direct refunding, what form it should take. No unambiguous answer can be given to these debatable, and perhaps even politically sensitive questions.

It has been shown that various devices can be used indirectly to refund debt. The general commodity finance loan is the most obvious form. Commodity loans have postponed debt difficulties in India until recently, and in Pakistan, Tunisia and some other countries. In the recent multilateral refunding exercises the provision of a refunding loan, or a new commodity loan equivalent to the amount of debt service, has been recognized as an alternative to a rescheduling of the maturities of particular loans or the consolidation of the global obligations of the debtor.

There appears to have been a general preference for indirect refunding through additional commodity loans as opposed to direct rescheduling. In part this may represent important institutional factors, particularly where the loans that must be refunded were originally extended by private entities with government guarantee, so that when refunding is necessary some governmental institution must supply the funds to pay off the exporter or commercial bank. Inevitably the refundings fall upon the public treasury with the exception of those cases in which a private creditor, for example a bank, is willing to extend its loan. Indirect refunding by program or commodity loans, or budget support as has been shown, appears preferable to the lending institution since it expands its loan portfolio, and bilateral governmental financing may result in more exports by its own producers.

Unless the offset loan is interest free, there is some compounding of interest cost. The interest-free long term loans given as offsets by some countries do not differ except in form from direct rescheduling or consolidation. Where consolidation interest is charged or new program credits provided, the debt is increased, though a crisis can be postponed if the loan is sufficiently long-term and at low interest. Where borrowing continues over many years there is likely to be difficulty if there is an interruption in the flow of concessional finance.

Indirect refunding may also shift the burden among the creditors. A soft program loan, by freeing earned exchange of the borrower, enables it to pay contractual debt service on supplier credits and conventional loans and project credits, which have higher interest rates and shorter maturities. If all lenders in a particular case extended new loans in proportion to their accruals of debt service, as DAC recommends and at uniform terms, there would be no relative shifting of the burden. In the case of the multilateral consolidation, the creditors ordinarily refund proportionally and on about the same terms. The case of India where for three years' payments the harder-term creditors eventually gave a higher proportion of debt relief than the more concessional lenders, is exceptional. If, on the other hand, the alternative of new program loans is taken, AID and IDA and other soft loans help pay off not only Ex-Im and IBRD, but supplier credits and loans from countries with hard terms as well.

The tacit recognition of this relationship appears in the pleas for more uniform lending terms on the part of DAC, the IBRD, the consortia and consultative groups, and more recently the Pearson and Peterson reports. These bodies have also stressed softer terms in recognition of the limited debt-servicing capacity of countries whose development will require external assistance for long periods. Program aid has been emphasized for reasons other than as an alternative to debt refunding. But if some countries or private lenders provide only project aid and that at somewhat harder terms, or program aid (bank loans) at normal interest, they stand to benefit from the softer contributions of others. As noted, some countries have supplemented their hard loans with concessional credits in the instances where serious debt problems have emerged, and in some other cases. The problem is likely to continue.

The process of refunding debt by the indirect methods can go on as long as the creditors are willing to provide the funds needed. Debt principal and debt service each year become bigger numbers, but if new loans to a given recipient cover service, there is no actual burden on its balance of payments though any loans or aid received progressively add less to net resources for the requirements of a growing population or for improvement in levels of production and income. For the creditors the implication is the provision of more funds at an increasing rate, a process which encounters budgetary and political difficulties. The more concessional donor-creditors may also feel that they are indirectly paying off debts to other creditors. They may also become disillusioned about the lack of (or slow) visible progress on the part of the recipients or their expenditure of scarce resources on military purposes. A reduction of the flow to a recipient with high debt service may precipitate a crisis.

DIRECT REFUNDING

For countries which do not receive much concessional aid, the mere compounding of service may result in the creditors calling a halt in the future, as they have in the past. Hence formal multilateral or bilateral direct debt refunding may be preferred to continued outlays, or may be required by the circumstances of the debtors. Some which have refunded may refund again. New cases will be added in the course of time. How many in the next 10 years cannot be predicted with assurance, in the light of the financial and political uncertainties of the situation.

Some of the issues are: (1) The extent of the refunding—the entire debt or specific parts, or merely the service accruing in one or more years; (2) should interest as well as principal be refunded? (3) the period to be covered by the refunding.

The Extent of Refunding

Refundings to the present have been partial, and with the exception of Indonesia, have included only payments due over a given period on certain specified classes of debt. In bilateral refunding institutional lenders have refunded some of their own loans or refinanced credits originally given by private entities in their country. Multilateral consolidation has applied to supplier credits or accumulated arrearages on short-term obligations, and direct government loans. In Indonesia the largest amounts are payable to the U.S.S.R. and other CMEA countries. Such credits have also figured in the debt problems of Ghana, and to some degree India and Pakistan.

In almost all cases refunding has applied only to the payments (or part) due in a specified period, in the Paris and Hague Club proceedings to an agreed percent of specified types of private credits insured by governments or extended by government agencies. Indian debt relief so far has been for part of the payments due but to secure the needed relief the agreed amounts were applied to a variety of credits, including apparently some credits previously refinanced bilaterally, with each consortium country taken as a unit, whether the credits were official or government-guaranteed. The U.S. refunded the wheat loan, though most of the payments to the U.S. were due to Ex-Im. Other countries supplied their share also by varying institutional arrangements. The IBRD also rescheduled.

Indonesia (1970) is the only case in which the entire debt incurred before the given date was covered by the agreement, rather than merely the payments accruing in a specified period of years. Post-Sukarno debt, however, was excluded from the exercise.

The amount of debt relief given in the past, and which may be given in the future, appears to depend on (a) the severity of the debt crisis and its duration, (b) the composition of the debt, (c) the estimate by the creditors and the debtor of ability to service debt and (d) perhaps most importantly, sheer expediency, including the willingness of the creditors to forego or postpone payment in view of their policies and institutional arrangements.

If a country's debt problem is merely a matter of a hump in debt service for a matter of one or two years it can be handled readily enough by refunding part of the payments due in this period, so that in subsequent time debt payment can fall to its usual level. This is the rationale of the club arrangements dealing with supplier credits or other medium-term obligations. Postponing payment of, say, 70 percent of the amount due in 2 years with repayment over the following 5 (Chile 1965) will be quite satisfactory if earnings in the new repayment period are sufficient. This technique worked for a time in the Chilean case. In the case of Argentina and Brazil, a succession of such short-term refundings were necessary before the situation could be stabilized at least sufficiently to make debt payment possible. Two arrangements for Ghana and three for Turkey (neglecting minor adjustments) may not prove adequate to deal with their problem. Relatively short-term refunding would also seem appropriate if the debtor country has a sudden shortfall in its exchange earnings, e.g. crop failure, collapse of world markets for its exports, or revolution, even though debt service in normal years may not be exceptionally heavy. Fund drawings, even with waivers and compensatory finance, may not be enough.

Medium-term refunding of a series of payments appears less appropriate to cases arising from the long and steady accumulation of debt to finance a development program. It cannot reasonably be expected that India and other countries whose development plans require an annual net inflow of capital will be in a much better position 5 years hence than they are today to have a net balance of payments surplus to enable them to make *net* payments on debt. If their problem is to be dealt with through rescheduling or consolidation it must be recognized that there will be many reschedulings whether at regular or irregular intervals. Postponement of payment for 10 years is better than 5. It pushes off the day of reckoning further, in the hope at least proforma that the reckoning will then be better. The Pearson and Peterson reports favor a longer period for refunding to avoid repetitive consolidation, though this may not be acceptable to the creditors.

In the case of long-run concessional aid recipients—some countries not now in this category aspire to be—the issue is essentially how much aid is to be given in the form of debt relief as opposed to the amount to be given in the form of commodity aid, or other forms of aid. To bring India's debt service ratio down to 20 percent is not particularly meaningful. It is tantamount to concluding that total aid should equal development requirements, a flexible item, plus 20 percent of exchange receipts to cover debt service. Consequently debt principal increases though debt service will decline in proportion to principal the greater the concessionary element in the aid lending. Refunding with low consolidation interest has the same effect. A 10-year period is also long enough to get the credits with the hardest terms off the books, unless new indebtedness is incurred.

In the 1970 Indonesia consolidation a longer range view was taken. Payment is to be spread over 30 years; there is no consolidation interest except when the bisque clause is invoked; payments of the interest accumulated through arrearages and the three preceding short-run consolidations is to be paid in installments only after 15 years. Thirty years is a long time. Indonesia is now stabilizing its economy, exports have been expanding and its resources are ample to provide a prosperous economy in due time. Present expectations which underlie the 30-year term may be too pessimistic, so that the agreed minute provides for a review of the situation in 10 years. The Paris press release stresses the exceptional nature of the Indonesian settlement, which presumably is not to be regarded as a precedent for future settlements for other countries.

The consolidation of payments due in 2 to 5 years with repayment over a subsequent period of 5 to 10 years has certain practical advantages from the creditors' point of view. There is the uncertainty of the future, not only of the debtor's balance of payments, but of the creditors' international accounts. The rapid shifts in the balances of payments of the principal creditor countries in recent years indicate part of their problem. Secondly, such consolidation may deal with the "hump problem." Thirdly, it keeps the debtor on "short tether." Periodic reexamination of the debt situation in the light of domestic policies, the performance of the debtor in the utilization of resources provided, and needs for the future may be more effective than the annual Fund Consultation or the discussions of the consortia and consultative groups. Five years is also a convenient political span. This period is long enough for a change in governments by election or coup d'état, and a change of civil servants and diplomatic officers. The new representatives of creditor and debtor governments can bring a fresh point of view to bear on the problem. At a minimum, mistakes can always be blamed on predecessor governments. The new officials, less bothered by history, may take bolder initiatives and they can more readily believe, or with better grace pretend to believe, in the proposed programs, prospects and the assurances given.

Assuming that there is to be a direct refunding by rescheduling or consolidation of part of a given country's debt, there is some choice among the debts to be selected. Refunding has not generally been applied to short-term (180 days or less) credits, which cover current imports, except where payments have been in arrears or when commercial banks have renewed or extended short-term credits. It has generally been understood that to postpone payments on short-term debt would so impair the credit of a country that new credits to finance current imports would stop and so disrupt normal business. When they have been refunded by central bank operations or arrangements with other governmental institutions, the purpose has been to restore the flow of needed commercial credit.

Payments due to the IMF are technically repurchases by a country of its currency held by the Fund, not debt. While repurchase is normally required 3 to 5 years after the original drawing, the Fund has in some instances postponed repurchases for a short period and in others permitted new drawings under a new standby after a repurchase, so that in effect it refunded the payment for another 3 to 5 year period. By general consensus Fund drawings have been excluded from refunding operations, even though some countries carry them on their books as medium-term debt.

Supplier credits have been the most commonly refinanced item since they usually have the heaviest service requirements. In most cases the refunding has taken the form of substitution of a longer-term and often lower-interest, government-to-government obligation for the original loans due to private exporters or banks. Fund standby arrangements have generally imposed limitations on this type of indebtedness or other medium-term obligations, particularly when drawings have provided the ready cash to meet maturing debts.

The debatable issue is the treatment of loans by the multilateral agencies when general refundings are negotiated. Up to this point the IBRD has rescheduled several years' payments on Indian loans and the IDB has not rescheduled any. Debt to the international organization represents 15.9 percent of total LDC debt (1970). The cost of servicing these loans is high in comparison with bilateral government loans except for Japan and probably Italy, though lower than the cost for supplier and other private credits. The long grace periods on newer IBRD loans, particularly for countries in debt difficulty, have pushed the service problem to the future. Looking forward to 10 or more years hence, the burden of service on IBRD and IDB (ordinary capital) and ADB loans will be quite heavy for the recipients.

Some aspects of international institution lending policies have in practice reduced the burden of service. The IBRD has supplemented its loans with IDA credits (e.g., India). Some of its loans for agricultural and educational projects, while financing highly desirable projects from the long-run point of view, have incidentally provided foreign exchange in the short-run against local expenditures. The 15 percent preference rule for local bidders has the same effect. The IDB supplements its ordinary loans with special funds loans, hitherto almost entirely repayable in national currency,[7] for projects requiring large local expenses. These measures alleviate debt burdens for the recipients, though the relief may be incidental and, perhaps, scarcely intentional. Would direct debt rescheduling be simpler and more to the point?

The Peterson report recommends that "bilateral government and government-guaranteed credits should be rescheduled over a long term. The international lending institutions, however, should not be required to reschedule their outstanding loans. Rescheduling their loans would endanger the ability of international institutions to continue borrowing in capital markets." The Pearson report says in part, "The World Bank and the IMF, as important providers of long-term and short-term finance respectively, must of course participate in rescheduling discussions."[8] They have participated in almost all of the refunding discussions and have prepared much of the data used. The IMF particularly has been used as the channel for reporting on the bilaterals and other related matters. The Pearson report may imply, but certainly does not explicitly recommend, that the IBRD be more will-

7. This rule was changed by the Board of Governors at their 1970 meeting.
8. P. 157.

ing to reschedule in the future than it has in the past. Secretary Kennedy, however, suggested that "creditor nations and institutions (not specifically international) in appropriate cases provide amortization relief."

How important a rescheduling of loans by the IBRD and the IDB would be in effecting their ability to borrow in capital markets is questionable. Their ability to sell their securities in the markets rests probably less on the quality of the underlying portfolio than it does on the contingent liability of the member governments. Morgan, Stanley and Company, The First Boston Corporation, the Deutsche Bank, and their customers probably do not worry too seriously about the quality of the IBRD or IDB loan portfolio. The IBRD as of June 30, 1971 had in its loan portfolio of a total disbursed and outstanding of $6.6 billion, loans to India of $488 million; to Pakistan, $343 million; to Brazil, $289 million; Argentina, $195 million; Chile, $119 million, to mention only the larger countries which have been in debt difficulties. This portfolio in itself would scarcely sustain an AAA rating, if the underwriters and the administrators of trust funds and others who purchase the bank securities did not recognize that the bank's obligations were issued on the basis of the contingent liability of the member governments. This was, in fact, conceded in 1959, when IBRD capital was doubled primarily to increase the U.S. contingent liability.[9] The quality of the IBRD portfolio would probably not be lowered if its loans had had their terms extended to accord with the debtors' real prospects of repayment. Obviously refunding would reduce its cash flow.

The same argument is applicable to the IDB *a fortiori* since in its borrowing agreements it has covenanted not to issue securities in an amount exceeding the U.S. portion of its callable capital.

The essential issue is the extent to which the institutional lenders should refund when the governments do, or whether they should collect according to contract and expect the debtors to be assisted in

9. Cf. Letter of Eugene Black to Secretary Anderson in House Banking and Currency Committee, *Hearings*, "Bretton Woods Agreements Act," March 5–6, 1959, p. 33: "The most significant factor in the willingness of the U.S. investor to buy Bank bonds has been and still is the uncalled portion of the U.S. subscription in the Bank. . . ." Mr. Black noted that the rating services were particularly interested in the ratio of the outstanding bonds and the U.S. contingent liability and the mechanics of implementing this liability. The Executive Directors in their resolution said, "Although the soundness of the Bank's loans and the guarantees of other members have been of great importance, the existence of the U S. guarantee is still in many instances decisive." (NAC, *Special Report on Increases in the Resources of the International Monetary Fund and the International Bank for Reconstruction and Development*, Feb. 1959, p. 34.) Since 1959 the strength of the contingent liabilities of governments has been increased by the convertibility of currencies and the greatly improved position of other creditor countries, which have pro rata liabilities.

making payment by IDA or bilateral (consortial) financing of import requirements plus the incidental relief given by the devices mentioned. Perhaps some of the bilateral creditors might more readily agree to refunding if the IBRD, one of the largest creditors on conventional loans, were more willing to act. The ice was broken with India. Perhaps the World Bank management and its bondholders will become more flexible as new applicants for relief appear.

Bilateral intergovernmental loans have been suggested as appropriate to refunding operations after supplier credits. Some of these loans are conventional with interest charges covering the cost of borrowing and amortization appropriate to the project. Examples are the Ex-Im, the Commonwealth Development Corporation, the Japanese Export-Import Bank and the K.f.W. (own funds). Other government loans are concessional in that they are deliberate aid or refunding of earlier obligations. Refunding can with difficulty make some of these loans much more concessional unless they are forgiven. It is impossible to postpone amortization payments on a loan which still enjoys a 7- or 10-year grace period. When the grace period has expired on some loans, accruing payments may be deferred. Some creditor countries have, however, given harder terms than others. They have more room for maneuver.

In 1968 (using DAC 1969 criteria) the average interest rate on all official credits, including concessional development assistance (two-thirds of the total) official export credits and other official credits was 3.6 percent, the maturity 27 years, including 7 years grace on principal. The grant element in these development loans was 58 percent (the difference between face amount and present values of service payments discounted at 10 percent) and if combined with outright grants, 80 percent. Some of the DAC countries, Austria, France, Germany, Italy, Japan, Netherlands, Portugal, give development loans at less concessional terms than average.[10] France, Germany and Japan are important providers of funds.

To the extent that bilateral credits are to be refunded the obvious candidates are national lending institutions making conventional loans, since they bear more heavily on the balance of payments of the debtor. For example, if refunding is applied to Latin America, as recommended by the Rockefeller report, the burden would fall on the Ex-Im whose cash flow would be reduced, so that if it is to continue to do

10. OECD-DAC, *Development Assistance, 1969 Review*, p. 77. Comparable data for 1969 and 1970 have not been published. It should be noted that France supplies a good part of its assistance in the form of grants to African countries.

business, it would have to borrow more from the Treasury or the market. Similar consequences would follow in other countries.

In actual practice this may not be convenient or expedient. In the Indian case, as noted, though the Ex-Im was the largest claimant, the actual debt relief was given through the wheat loan administered by AID. The U.K., Germany and others have refunded by consolidation credits provided from sources other than the original lender. From the standpoint of the taxpayer it makes little difference whether refunding is by Ex-Im or AID, the K.f.W. or the German budget, or British or Canadian lending corporations or their government budgets. Just as the form of refunding is a matter of institutional arrangements in a given creditor country, the allocation of the burden is a matter of national arrangements in budgeting and accounting.

The situation in each debtor country differs somewhat, as each creditor has its own legal and financial problems. The actual form of debt relief inevitably seems to be on a case by case basis, with some leeway for plain bargaining.

Principal or Interest

It is indifferent to the debtor obtaining relief of payments for a given amount in a year whether it is principal and interest or merely principal, say, $50 million of principal or $35 million of principal and $15 million of interest. The real balance of payments effect is the same, even if the amounts are recorded differently, above or below the line, in formal balance of payments statements. There may be some complications in the internal accounting of the country as between the government or central bank and the private or public entities whose original debt is refunded, with further complications in terms of foreign exchange and domestic currency. In the cases studied these problems do not appear to have been difficult. Changes in legislation or executive decrees may be needed in either case.

What does matter is whether or not there is an additional future interest cost. Consolidation interest must be paid or accrued the next year. Interest accrued and unpaid may be capitalized by the creditor and so compounded, but in the process annual payments may be reduced by the extension of the term of the loan. In the case of the simple rescheduling of amortization there will be additional interest to be paid over the lengthened maturity. If the creditors waive the accrued interest or charge no consolidation interest the costs will be lower, i.e., there is in effect a grant in addition to that implied by the difference between contractual payment and the discounted value of future payments.

To the creditors there may be a significant difference, less in terms of real receipts than in the accounting of the foregone receipts, particularly in the case of corporate lenders. If principal only is refunded there is no direct effect on the balance sheet, and interest receipts continue as usual and so do not affect the profit and loss. If interest as well as principal is refunded, income is reduced with a corresponding effect on profits. The flow of cash to the creditor for a given amount of relief would be reduced the same amount whether the relief is in the form of amortization or amortization and interest. The creditor institution will have to borrow more to maintain its level of activity, and perhaps, pay a higher interest rate than it would have received on the loans refunded. Significant amounts of refunding of interest would, of course, affect the ratio of earnings to interest paid, and so could possibly affect the rating of securities.

Hence giving debt relief in the form of amortization only, i.e. a higher percent of principal would be refunded to get a given amount of relief, is generally preferable for corporate lenders, such as the IBRD and IDB, which have to float securities on the market. Even the Ex-Im and similar agencies of foreign governments like to show a profit. In the actual refunding cases, except Indonesia, principal only has been deferred with contractual interest continuing. In a few cases the creditors have capitalized accrued interest. Generally also—Indonesia excepted—there has been a low consolidation interest charged, though a few countries have given interest free consolidation credits or have made grants equivalent to interest.

Hence, larger amounts of amortization relief are preferable to an equal amount of amortization and interest since the impact of future refunding is likely to bear more heavily on corporate creditors than it has in the past. If the relief can take the form of simple rescheduling it appears preferable to a consolidation loan, if for nothing more than the sake of appearances. A large amount of relief, however, may require rewriting many loan contracts, and so be inconvenient.

General or Particular Refunding

Refundings have been agreed for specific countries in debt crises or as an alternative to additional aid. They are distasteful to both creditors and debtors. Some developing countries are proud of their record of paying their honest debts. Known refunding may well impair a debtor's credit standing and so reduce future borrowing possibilities, though apparently some suppliers are willing to take risks even when institutional lenders are more prudent. Some creditors also feel that "they hired the money" and are reluctant to relinquish what they bargained to get.

Should the parties wait until a crisis is impending or should they forestall it? The Pearson Commission recommends that soft loans be given to "refinance debt payments, in order to reduce the need for full-scale debt negotiations" (p. 167). This has in fact been done on a fairly broad scale. Alternatively, refunding could be undertaken before the problem became too severe and can be more equitable in terms of burden-sharing unless all creditors individually refinanced debt payments by new loans on about the same terms.

It may well be argued that since the developing countries cannot bear the burden of debt as now constituted, it would be more equitable to reduce the burden for all by general refunding, not merely for those approaching the crisis stage. This argument seems cogent when applied to the "hard-core" recipients which cannot reasonably be expected to service their debt on a net basis for, say, the next 20 years. Since refunding in any form is a partial grant, and a succession of refundings on easier terms approaches the grant, as a limit, outright forgiveness or cancellation would be simpler. There are certain practical difficulties with either procedure. The argument appears less applicable to countries emerging from the aid-recipient class, a group that includes some of the largest debtors, which can service conventional debt in the longer run from their exports, or those debtors that for reasons of pride or politics prefer to pay their own way by holding down imports or slowing development.

The practical problems of refinancing à la Pearson, or generally refunding for all willing debtors, are formidable. It has taken long and difficult negotiation to get international agreement in the acute refunding cases. More general agreements would be practically impossible without the establishment of an international debt refunding agency financed *pro rata* by the creditors. Otherwise the refunding countries or those giving equivalent grants or soft loans would pay off the harder creditors. There is little chance that the U.S.S.R. would join an international agreement, though it has been willing to refund in particular cases; the other CMEA countries appear generally to have been more reluctant.

Guarantor governments have refinanced supplier credits though this has in some cases required parliamentary action, legislation, or appropriation. Some unguaranteed loans have been refinanced by governmental agencies, e.g., Ex-Im, others by the lenders' banks or supplying companies when they were large and strong enough. Bilateral intergovernmental credits probably can be more readily refunded. A lending corporation has a general authority to modify its loans.

If refunding were general there could be little assurance that it would be a long-lived solution unless the debtors could be obligated, and the obligation enforced, not to incur future loans other than at some agreed concessional level. They would have to forego, and compel their nationals to forego supplier credits, even though these may be quite useful. The high interest rates on IBRD, IDB, ADB, Ex-Im and parallel entities would preclude them from lending. The reduction in the flow of resources to developing countries would be greatly curtailed unless governments bilaterally or through IDA provided the equivalent in soft loans. Private investment would be stopped except in the form of short-term commercial credits or direct investment, which also puts a burden on the balance of payments of the host country.

In sum, a general refunding for all the aid recipients is not feasible either by consolidation or the Pearson method. From the standpoint of both creditors and debtors refunding should not be carried beyond necessity. Economic development will have to muddle through with a combination of credits, soft loans and grants punctuated by refundings as needed. This does not imply that past mistakes should be repeated or that there may not be possible improvement in the financing of development.

SOME IMPLICATIONS

The DAC *1969 Review of Development Assistance* is an earnest plea to the members to provide more grant and concessional-term loans to the developing countries. After discussing the debt problem and refunding exercises it concludes:

But no wholly satisfactory solution is possible and both harmonization and debt-rescheduling will prove to be temporary and inadequate solutions, unless there are substantial increases over the next few years in the volume of grant funds and of loans at soft terms which donors are prepared to offer to developing countries. This is indispensable to sound growth at acceptable rates. Moreover, it is a prerequisite for the financial situations and the infrastructure of physical and human resources which are required to induce continued high rates of private investment.[11]

The IBRD similarly has pointed out that there are some projects in LDCs "which yield a return on capital at least equal to that earned on projects in developed countries, or more relevantly, to the cost of capital in international markets."[12] Much of the investment, however, must be for purposes which "yield a financial return only after many years." Moreover, many of the recipient countries cannot "transform" local currency earnings into foreign exchange to service debt. When the productivity of capital and the capacity to "transform" are high, conventional or even commercial loans are justified. For others, the "avoidance of debt service problems requires that, on average, foreign capital be available on concessional terms."

These conclusions are as direct as the polite circumlocution necessary to international bodies permits. Some countries have a capacity to service debt in foreign exchange. Most countries, in their present state of development, probably do not, either because they cannot earn exchange or because they lack financially productive projects. Hence if there is to be development[13] it must be on grant terms, or if in the form of loans, the terms must be so concessional as to approximate grants. The former group might well include the more advanced of the developing countries, though as shown in chapter 4 many of these have had to have debt refundings. The oil producers and countries with other mineral deposits that can be worked commercially can service debt. The rest have little prospect.

If "net aid" is provided, even on easy loan terms, principal will continue to mount on a compound interest curve. Debt service will be compounded, though at a lower rate, if DAC or other easy loan terms are employed. Easy terms, as shown above, postpone the date at which service equals new borrowing or aid, in comparison with harder-term loans, as now on the books, and are likely to be part of the total in any event by "blending" provisions on the part of the donor-creditors or the exigencies of the recipient debtors. Eventually some of the poorer countries may attain such current account surpluses that they will be able to pay back. For most this would appear to be in the far distant

11. P. 235.

12. IBRD, *Annual Report*, 1971, p. 53.

13. Any investment of capital, if not wasted, will yield some return in a developing country, often less than the same amount of capital invested in the donor country. An atomic power plant can run along side primitive agriculture. Development, if defined in terms of median per capita real income, may be more difficult in face of the population problem.

future. For many it may never be reached. In the interim the unsatisfactory solution of debt refunding seems inevitable. The donor-creditors may in time realize that their contributions to aid are just that.

Grants versus Loans

It is the policy of the United States and other industrial countries to foster economic development. The reasons for this policy as represented internationally by resolutions in the UN, DAC and UNCTAD, are partly humanitarian and partly political, with humanitarian motives sometimes rationalized as political, and political motives, as humanitarian. It may be taken for granted that economic aid in some form is likely to be a more or less permanent feature of international relations. Myrdal regards it as a moral obligation to redistribute income from the rich to the poor internationally, in a way parallel to domestic tax and welfare policies.[14] The amount and form of this aid will be determined by the decisions of governments, and involves problems broader in scope than this essay. What is relevant here is that the amount will have to be a function of the compound interest formula if it is to cover debt payment as well as physical aid requirements.

Since most of the developing countries are not likely to develop their export industries to the extent that there can be a net payment of debt within prospective periods, the question may well arise, why give aid on loan terms which cannot in all likelihood be met by the recipients according to contract? And even if contract terms were met, the real value of the repayment will be a fractional part of the original sum on long-term loans in view of the probable degrees of inflation.[15] Why not recognize that economic aid is an unrequited transfer of resources from the richer to the poorer countries made for reasons of policy?

The grant versus loan issue has been debated since the Marshall plan, when most of the aid for a period of a few years was on grant terms. The recovery of Europe might not have been as rapid had loan terms been applied. In 1948, however, one of the main considerations was the concern that the U.S. balance of payments could not readily adjust to a repayment of debt in the future. No doubt the rate of recovery was underestimated and the persistence of a U.S. surplus was

14. Myrdal, *The Challenge of World Poverty*, passim.
15. The present value of the final payment on an aid loan, discounted at the DAC rate of 10 percent, is 2.2 percent of the original amount in the case of an AID loan and 0.85 percent on an IDA credit, assuming constant prices. At 2 percent annual inflation of creditor currencies these values would be multiplied by 0.45 and 0.37 percent respectively. Earlier payments would, of course, have higher present values, at either constant or inflated prices. (See chapter 2, pp. 69–70.)

overestimated. Had all of the aid been on the easy loan terms applied to the loan portion, there would have been considerable relief to the U.S. balance of payments in recent years.

It may be argued that the developing countries may also in time be in a position to repay loans. Grants are final. Why give up a claim that may prove useful in the future? There can, however, be little expectation that the current aid programs of the donor-creditor countries and of the international agencies will be of short duration. There will have to be appropriations for a long time whether aid takes the form of grants or easy-term loans. The latter will not produce a reflow in the foreseeable future to constitute a net reduction of the budgetary drain. "Net aid" inevitably results in a piling up of debt. Perhaps grants would be as satisfactory in terms of return to the donor as loans which will not be repaid and will have to be refunded periodically.

This dismal prognosis need not be projected indefinitely, nor for all countries. Some may discover or develop resources that will yield exchange. Some may develop to the point that they do not need external assistance. Population problems will continue for all so that their import requirements are likely to increase, a negative element. Since there is no telling which countries will be favorably situated years hence and which will not, loans, even if refunded from time to time, may produce some return eventually.

Grants, it may be argued, provide less incentive for careful use of the funds provided than if the recipient in good faith expects to repay. The tendency would be for loans to be used on the type of project which is more likely to pay off, at least in local currency, and possibly in foreign exchange, than would a grant which might more readily be used for current purposes which might be less productive in the long run. The cogency of this argument is considerably reduced when loans are used for commodity financing, since the commodities will either be used directly by the government for its purposes or, if sold, the local currency will be used as ordinary governmental receipts. This would apply to either grants or loans for commodity purposes, so that the argument for loan as opposed to grant on this basis is really an argument for having productive projects as opposed to mere maintenance balance of payments assistance.

A loan, however, generally requires an accounting for the loan funds and provision by the borrower for covering costs through the price or tax mechanism. Even if a private borrower pays the government in the national currency with the government in turn paying the lender in foreign exchange, as in the two-step arrangements of AID, the ultimate recipient must cover the amortization of the loan and interest, so that there is greater probability of careful use of the resources than if the funds were made available for a specific purpose without the need of accruing future costs. This discipline may be weakened by loans on easy terms, hence the advantage of the two-step arrangement, which is easy on the balance of payments but involves direct costs to the beneficiary.

It may also be argued that if funds are wasted by the recipient of a grant, the donor has no effective means of checking the abuse. In the case of the loan project, on the other hand, payment is usually by way of reimbursement for expenditures originally made by the recipient, so that if improper expenditures are made reimbursement can be denied. This argument against the grant may be considerably weakened however, if a grant program is repetitive. If the money or goods are used inefficiently or improperly, future grants may be withheld, or reduced by the amount of improper use.

One other argument which may be quite important, however, is that with grants the tendency is to concentrate on direct government operations as the object of the expenditure, while in the loan case the ultimate beneficiary may be a private concern, and for many purposes private enterprise probably is more productive in terms of foreign exchange potential than governmental infrastructure operations. Grant money is not likely to be given to a private enterprise, but governments are willing to borrow and relend, or to give their guarantee to borrowings of a private organization, since the government will have some assurance of repayment.

In recent years there has been relatively little direct grant aid from external sources for economic development except for technical assistance grants and grant-like transactions, in the DAC terminology, such as P.L. 480 sales for local currency. Australia and Canada have also given grants of wheat and other commodities to some of the recipient countries, particularly those in the Colombo Plan. France has given grants to Africa. While it seems likely that there will be little net return of principal of loans made to many of the developing countries, it is apparent that legislatures are not receptive any longer to the grant system. They may feel that loans have some prospect of returning benefits in the future, though they must recognize that at best the return is only partial. The feeling against grants, however, was so great that in the DLF period the United States made loans for both project and program purposes repayable in local currency in the expectation that this would provide an incentive for effective use of the funds provided without imposing a balance of payments burden. In practice then, even if grants in some respects would make the most sense as a means of dealing with the development problems of many countries whose development is at best problematic, political circumstances almost inevitably rule the grant method out except for certain emergency situations, disaster relief, and so on, and technical assistance.

Harmonization and Coordination

The IBRD, in consultative groups and published materials, and the DAC have long advocated a softening of loan terms, but also the provision of assistance by the donor-creditors on more uniform terms. Since the industrial countries provide finance from various internal sources at different terms, and the recipients receive grants or borrow from various sources and in different proportions, reducing aid to a common pattern is a formidable task. While terms have been softened one way or other by the DAC member countries, and there are still considerable differentials in the terms for currently provided assistance, the largest part of debt service accrues from earlier transactions.

DAC has been the organ of the advanced countries attempting to secure more assistance and better terms. It has established quantitative and qualitative targets which the members have not attained. The present DAC recommendations on terms imply a minimum concessional element of about 75 percent of the total official development assistance by each member. This target can be attained by various combinations of grants and soft loans, 2 or 3 percent interest and 25 to 38 years' maturity with grace periods of 7 to 10 years.[16] AID and most P.L. 480 transactions qualify under these definitions, as do recent soft loans by most other DAC members. Ex-Im loans and similar hard loans from other DAC members are excluded from "official development assistance" but form part of the members' performance, which also includes supplier and other private credits in terms of the one percent of GNP, quantitative target, which only France, Germany, Belgium, the Netherlands and Switzerland attained in 1968. In 1969 Denmark, Italy and Portugal were added.[17]

16. The "concessional element" is defined as the difference between face value and the discounted present value at 10 percent of interest and amortization. The calculation can be quite complex with the variety of current loan terms. For precise mathematical formulae and illustrations, see IBRD, *Possible Improvements in Terms of Lending* (an UNCTAD paper, March 20, 1968), pp. 20–50.

17. DAC, *1969 Review*, p. 306; *1970 Review*, p. 180. The figures are partly a numbers game in

The DAC qualitative recommendations provide for a large concessional element in official development assistance, but there is no assurance that donor-creditor countries will offer assistance on these terms to all developing countries, nor that the latter will not borrow on harder terms from other sources. Some will borrow from CMEA countries if only to maintain their stance of nonalignment.

Various industrial countries concentrate their aid loans in areas of political interest to them, their former overseas territories or countries in which their nationals, and sometimes governments, have invested heavily. By giving soft loans or grants to these countries, e.g., the U.K. in India and Pakistan, France in North Africa, the U.S. in Latin America, especially in the form of balance of payments assistance, they indirectly help pay off debts to their own investors and to their official agencies. Some countries apparently give harder terms to the countries where they have no special interest, approximating the terms of supplier credits, or in fact provide only supplier credits or harder project credits, even within the ambit of consortia and consultative groups. At the other extreme, Australia has consistently given only grants, and Canada has given large grants in proportion to its size, as as have Belgium, Norway, Sweden and Switzerland. Germany has softened terms over time and some provision for softening has been made in other instances.

Various reasons can be offered for the terms given. In informed conversations one hears arguments along these lines. "We do not aspire to world political leadership, so we have less political interest than the U.S. in aiding all countries." "We have our own poor areas to worry about." "We are not rich enough to go into the aid business." "We have no aid program or aid agency, so we use the means we have." "That ass ——— (the Finance Minister) says we can't afford aid in our budget." "By tying your aid you give a subsidy to your high cost industries. Ours are competitive." "We have our balance of payments problems, too." "We believe it is better to give hard loans and exporter credits initially, even if we have to refinance them later. The projects are better, the administration simpler and better, than when the loans are on easy terms and so used less productively."[18] In fact one may suspect that some of the hard loans in the past were made in the expectation that official aid would make repayment possible.

terms of exclusions and inclusions. Included, for example, are subscriptions and loans to, and purchases of securities of, international institutions. The last category is a form of investment, alternative to other investments of reserves.

18. These are capsulized paraphrases of discussions. Only one is a direct quotation.

The resulting differences in the "mix" and debt burdens leads to the issue of coordination of loan terms. Essentially, the donor-creditors extending grants or soft loans do not wish indirectly to pay off hard loans given by other countries. Secondly, as has been long emphasized by the IBRD and DAC, most of the developing countries cannot repay loans at relatively hard terms. The IBRD-led consortia and consultative groups have succeeded to a real extent in obtaining softer terms and probably more aid for the countries covered.[19]

The 1969 DAC *Report*[20] summed up the situation:

Even with a clear judgement as to the appropriate terms for a particular developing country, a harmonization problem arises if different donors provide assistance at substantially different terms. From the point of view of recipients the variety of terms provided by particular donors need not be a cause of concern—as long as the overall blend is appropriate. Thus, harmonization is primarily a problem among the different donors and the different financial institutions involved—although in the long run, recipients too are likely to suffer if the problem is not resolved.

For one thing, there is the awkward "bail out" problem. Many donors, providing the softest kinds of assistance, very much wish to avoid situations in which their soft aid flows can be viewed as providing the resources to repay financing by other donors at harder terms. A minimum way of avoiding this problem may be for all donors at hard terms, to remain at least "neutral" during the period (which may last for many years) when a net transfer of resources is required by the particular developing country. That is, donors would agree as a minimum to offset any payments due them with new financing flows. Of course, mere "neutrality" would not contribute to the needed net transfer of resources but it would at least avoid the awkward "bail out" problem.

It follows from this that in cases where particular developing countries already have too much hard debt outstanding from particular donors, it is preferable for the donors responsible to maintain these "floats" of overly hard debt, rather than to use new aid flows from other donors to repay them—though always seeking also for these donors to reduce such debt to more appropriate levels.

The donor-creditors could perhaps prevent the use of their aid to service harder-term obligations by making it conditional upon the recipient agreeing not to borrow on other terms. The creditors, however, cannot give advance assurances that they will supply the "need-

19. It is perhaps significant that these groups mostly cover countries to which the IBRD has made large loans and IDA credits and to which the United States, and in Africa, the U.K., are the largest aid donors. They gave concessional aid while some other countries were providing hard loans.

20. P. 234.

ed" amounts. It would be politically difficult to insist that aid-recipients should not take Soviet credits or supplier credits or even conventional loans.

The Peterson report recommends an international system of development whereby "international agencies would assume primary responsibility for analyzing conditions and policies in developing countries, for establishing close working relations with appropriate officials in these countries, and for determining total capital and technical assistance requirements and the policies necessary for effective use of investment resources." IBRD and IMF in conjunction with the regional bodies would assume responsibility for this general oversight, policy determination, and estimation of requirements. This is a formidable task, if not impossible. Even assuming that planning can work in a developing country under a fair degree of economic freedom, it would require an integration of national plans and a determination by the international group how each country is to develop, what industries should be encouraged, where plants are to be located, how to direct agriculture (note surpluses problem) and prescribe internal policies on savings, taxation, and monetary policy.

All of these things are done to some extent in particular countries under some circumstances. The IMF regularly makes recommendations on monetary and financial policies to its Article XIV members, and may impose rather specific requirements for standby arrangements and drawings. The multilateral banks in giving or refusing loans direct development policy in specific matters, and impose specific conditions to their loans, including local management, price and utility rate policies, or legislation, as appropriate. The institutions are cooperating with each other and with national donor agencies to a far greater extent than formerly.

For more comprehensive direction there would have to be more control than the recipients would relish. It would also require that the donors commit funds for longer periods than they have thus far been willing to do. Either the money would be turned over to the multilateral agencies for administration—there is considerable sentiment in favor of this policy—or national policies of the donors would have to be subject to the supervision of the international group. To the extent that bilateral aid is politically motivated, this would be a severe limitation. In any event the IBRD or the composite control group would inevitably be involved in the politics of both donor and recipient governments to the extent that it might well lose its present advantages of relatively impartial decision. If policy in the developing countries were subject to more direction by the international community it might also arouse sentiments against joint financial imperialism, as long as weighted voting prevails.

Full harmonization of loan terms is a long way off. There is even less prospect in 1972 that the conditions necessary for effective coordination can be fulfilled. For the coming years the prospect is for a continuance of varying policies and institutional arrangements, and for those countries getting into debt difficulties, refunding.

REFUNDING AND THE FUTURE

Refunding in itself cannot prevent the recurrence of adverse conditions. The debtor may promptly contract new supplier credits, especially if institutional or aid-type credits are not available, or will take time, and creditor country agencies are willing to insure. DAC has been concerned about the increasing volume of supplier credits in 1968 in countries such as Argentina, Brazil and India whose debts have been refunded, and countries such as Pakistan and South Korea which have not refunded. The chairman's report is less worried about the oil exporters or countries such as Israel and China (Taiwan) whose exports have expanded rapidly.[21]

The industrial countries will continue to push their exports by direct loans or guarantees of export credits. As noted above, IMF standby arrangements have often imposed limitations on the contraction of additional medium-term credits, and probably in all cases in which Fund drawings were essential to deal with a debt situation as part of a stabilization effort. There is no safeguard when the standby expires.

A similar question arises with regard to international institution loans and conventional-term national lenders such as Ex-Im, K.f.W., the Japanese Export-Import Bank and their analogues in other countries. These loans are generally at longer-term than supplier credits, but under current conditions their interest rates are sometimes higher. Institutional loans bear less heavily on the borrower's balance of payments, but their weight is considerably more than aid-type loans. The multilateral institutions have mitigated the effects by IDA credits, local cost financing, loans from the Fund for Special Operations, and long grace periods. The cost of relatively hard national loans has been

21. *1969 Review*, pp. 15, 16, 57, 135.

offset in part by national soft loans, from budgetary sources in the U.S., Germany, Canada, Japan and other DAC countries. The effect has been rather uneven.

If soft loans, especially commodity credits, which have long been advocated by the IBRD, DAC and others as the proper form of bilateral credits, must eventually pay off the harder credits, would it not be simpler and more direct to restrict institutional loans to the countries that can reasonably be expected to repay from their own resources— as the various charters enjoin—rather than to make more loans, even in limited amounts, to countries that will need aid for a long and indefinite future? The IBRD has made loans to India since the refunding, albeit with a long grace period, and to Pakistan whose debt problem is as severe. There have also been bilateral credits on conventional terms.

The question posed would suggest a more limited role in the financing of development by conventional loans to the poorest countries. If IBRD loans were made only to countries with good prospects, its near future level of lending might be reduced, certainly not expanded at the rate foreseen by Mr. McNamara. IDA could, of course, usefully use as much as the Part I countries are willing to provide. IBRD-IDA would become more of an international aid agency than a bank. The Asian Development Bank and the Inter-American Development Bank, reasonably enough, are well on this road. The latter, as of December 31, 1970, had committed more in FSO loans than in ordinary capital loans. The Ex-Im, if its loans are to help the U.S. balance of payments, would make them to countries which will not need AID assistance to enable them to pay, to developed countries when loans are needed to get the export business, or to the more advanced of the developing countries. Financing development in face of the debt burden and the policies of existing institutions presents a many-horned dilemma. The fairly rigid dichotomy between "aid-recipient" and "credit-worthy" suggested is not easy to apply in practice. The first class would include countries with low per capita incomes with no immediate prospect of self-sustaining "viability"; the second group, those with better export potential and a present low level of debt. If the "credit-worthy" finance their programs by conventional loans or supplier credits they can get in difficulty in not many years if they persistently borrow.

The aid recipients would obtain finance on easy terms, grants or near-grant credits. If they productively use the resources provided and develop their exports in competition with better-off countries, there can be charges of unfair competition. Latin Americans, and some-times North American producers, are not happy about concessional financing of cocoa, sugar, and coffee plantations, oilseed projects, cotton mills or other manufactures which sometimes add to the world supply of products that are already in surplus. If on the other hand they receive mainly maintenance balance of payments assistance there is a trend toward perpetual mendicancy.

In fact some such classification of countries is practically inevitable. Resources for aid are scarce. Not all IDA Part II countries have received credits. The U.S. AID has to limit, now by statute, the number of countries to be aided and the amount to be given them. Theoretically the problem is the reverse of the argument in taxation theory about least sacrifice, equal sacrifice and other variations on the utilitarian theme. As in other cases, when theory cannot provide a precise answer, decisions are made pragmatically by the IBRD staff and management, by Congress and the AID administration, and by legislatures and administrators in other countries. Data on per capita national incomes and debt burdens are far from precise, and export potential is uncertain. They can scarcely provide the basis for a distribution of aid according to formula, and a satisfactory formula, neglecting statistical problems, is more difficult to devise in international matters than it is in domestic grants-in-aid, say, in the United States or the United Kingdom. Decisions are unavoidably political; governments are political by their nature; international organizations are polypolitical.[22] The staunchest advocates of international, as opposed to bilateral aid would scarcely favor aid to mainland China even though its poverty is probably as great as India's or Pakistan's.

In practice IBRD-IDA uses a triple classification. Some countries receive only Bank loans, some only IDA credits, and a fairly large group, a mixture of both. The first class includes the more advanced developing countries, e.g., Argentina, Brazil, Mexico and those with relatively good prospects (e.g., Iran, Israel, Malaysia, Singapore, Thailand). IDA-only countries (as of June 30, 1970) include some of the African states, Bolivia and Indonesia, poor countries and coun-

22. "Under its Articles, the Bank cannot be guided in its decisions by political considerations; they must be based on economic criteria alone." Its staff is a "group of trained professionals recruited on a broad international basis." "However, since a member's voting power is based on the amount of capital it has subscribed to the Bank, a combination of the largest shareholders could together defeat an issue requiring a simple majority of the votes, the normal requirement for decisions." (World Bank, *100 Questions and Answers*, March 1970, pp. 6, 7, 9.) The IDB Articles have similar provisions, but because of its relatively larger subscription, the U.S. has greater weight in ordinary capital loans and a legal veto on the Fund for Special Operations.

tries with heavy debt problems. Most developing countries are in the blending group. The ratio and consequently the resulting cost varies. To some extent this is a matter of projects, with IDA funds going more to educational and agricultural projects which have a slow return, or of credits to countries with serious debt service problems, e.g., India, Pakistan, Indonesia. To an important extent the division has been affected by the availability of IDA resources. If IDA got more from the Part I countries, no doubt the proportion would be higher. In other cases the decision has taken into account the availability of concessional loans from the U.S., the U.K., France and other countries.

Individual creditor-donor countries have also followed the triple policy, and there is some rough correspondence in the pattern, depending on the availability of funds and their political interests. Hence debt service as a ratio to principal will vary with the terms at which a given country borrows. Those that borrow at harder terms will have more difficulty than those which obtain more concessional finance. It cannot reasonably be expected that terms will become uniform, and the "mix" will continue to be somewhat arbitrary in view of the funds available, even if there were any rational way of predicting the ecomic future of the recipients and determining the relative advantages to be given to one country as opposed to others.

CLOSING

The process of economic development will take a long time. How long is impossible to predict with assurance. If India, Pakistan, and Indonesia are to increase their real GNP per capita ($90–100) to the level, say, of Mexico or Chile ($470–490) over time it will take about 27 years with an annual per capita growth rate of 6 percent, and more than 50 years at 3 percent. Their estimated per capita growth rates (1961–67) were, however, 0.9, 2.9 and 0.6 percent respectively.[23] For the African countries (except oil producers) the process will be far longer. It is quite possible that the development process could become one of rapidly increasing returns. Population growth may be slowed over time. Political and administrative reform could speed up the process. To the extent that economic growth is dependent on foreign assistance the indication is that there will be a need for many years.

---

[23]. *World Bank Atlas, 1969.* Too much precision should not be attached to the figures in view of the statistical problems. They do indicate a rough order of magnitude. Per capita means are deceptive in terms of welfare which would be measured by medians, for which data are lacking.

The Pearson Commission[24] guesses that the year 2000 might mark the end of the need for concessional assistance.

Since foreign aid is provided by the donor countries largely on a loan basis, it may be expected that the debt of the developing countries will grow. Their debt service requirements will increase, the rate depending on loan terms. For those countries that will be continued recipients of loan aid, debt service will increase at some compound interest rate of from 3 to 5 percent at AID terms—the higher rate after the expiration of grace—or on other comparable terms conforming to the DAC recommendations; by 8 to 10 percent at the average terms now applied. If less aid is given, debt service will be lighter and growth slower, but the debt situation will be more acute.

The oil producers and some others can service debt even if they do not advance much economically. For the others exports will depend in major part on economic growth and the direction their production takes. If production is concentrated on internal consumption, debt servicing potential does not increase pari passu. This may indeed be what welfare considerations demand. If the economy is export-oriented servicing debt will be easier, but even then the mounting burden will require refunding in many cases. In the nearer future the refunding will be more urgent for existing debt. By 1980 or 1985 it may be necessary to refund concessional debt.

Hitherto, the donor-creditors have preferred indirect refunding by giving new loans, and probably, the recipient-debtors have also. The harder creditors have favored this technique which shifts part of the burden to the easier creditors. The debtors do not like to admit that they cannot pay. There is, however, little likelihood that bilateral or multilateral aid funds will be appropriated in the future at the compounded rates necessary to continue this process.

Accordingly, greater attention has been given to refunding as a "legitimate form of aid." Any refunding has a grant element in it: the present value of a future payment is always less than the amount postponed at any positive rate of interest. It is also the equivalent of untied aid since it releases an equivalent amount of earnings to be spent by the debtor at will. Moreover, it distributes the burden among the creditors, at least in proportion to their debt claims, unless, as in the Indian case, the harder creditors refund a larger portion of their claims, so equalizing the burden to a degree. The indirect methods do not have this safeguard. Finally the creditors may have to accept the inevitable.

24. P. 126.

Debt refundings are not likely to fall into a fixed pattern. The simpler Paris-Hague Club treatments are not as readily adaptable to countries with more complex debt situations arising from prolonged borrowing at different terms. The Indian and Indonesian cases are so far quite exceptional. The creditors probably would prefer a succession of shorter-term refundings to the large commitment involved in the longer-range treatments. Each case will be a separate negotiation. In some cases it will be complicated by debts to the CMEA countries.

Some of the more advanced and export-oriented countries will probably be able to service their outstanding debt, some even without refundings of principal. Others may be in a position to pay interest with rescheduled principal, and eventually pay off principal. This may be as much as the creditors can hope for. For the hard-core aid recipients this is more doubtful within the foreseeable future unless their development is to be curtailed. With the large grant element contained in current concessional loans when made, further increased by rescheduling or refunding, they will closely approximate grants. The donors may for all practical purposes recognize that what they advance as aid will not be repaid for a long time, if ever. They may not be willing to accept as a precept, but be reconciled in fact, to the scriptural injunction ". . . and lend without any hope of return. You will have great reward, and you will be sons of the Most High . . ." (Luke 6:35).

APPENDIX:
REPETITIVE BORROWING (OR LENDING) AND THE PERIOD IN WHICH REPAYMENT EXCEEDS NEW BORROWING (OR RECEIPTS EQUAL NEW LOANS)

Introduction

It has long been known that a country cannot successfully borrow to meet a balance of payments deficit over a long period of years, since after some time a point is reached at which interest and amortization of loans previously contracted will equal (or exceed) the amount of new borrowing. After this point increased borrowing is necessary to cover a deficit of a given amount, a situation which is likely to lead to debt difficulties.

Conversely, a lending agency may increase its volume of loans without correspondingly increasing its own capital or debt since after a point repayments equal new loans made.

These conclusions have generally been illustrated by numeric examples. Following are derivations of general formulae and tabulations of results for varying terms and interest rates. There are two sets of equations. The first applies to straight-line amortization, without and with grace periods on principal payments. These are the usual terms of loans by the Ex-Im, the IDB and ADB, commercial banks, and loans by European lenders, which are usually covered by some form of public agency guarantee. The transactions may be evidenced by serial notes. The second set of relations is given in terms of annual level payments of interest and amortization, with or without grace periods. This is the form usually taken by AID credits and IBRD loans. (In the case of IBRD loans, the level payment is only approximate in that the annual principal payments are rounded.)

The equations and tables are given for annual payments of interest and amortization to simplify computation and illustration. Semiannual installments are more common in practice, though the results differ only fractionally, particularly in the longer periods. For mathematical simplicity it is also assumed that loans are made on January 1 of each year, that interest is payable on the amount outstanding during the year, and that amortization payments are made December 31.

The formulae derived here are general for the assumed terms. In the case of any one country, loans have been secured at varying rates of interest and amortization and other terms, so that an appraisal of its situation requires computation of actual data.

While the equations are general and the illustrative tables were electronically computed from the equations, the limitations of the mathematical construct must be borne in mind in making any application of the results. The tabulations are correct only on the assumption that the amount borrowed each year is the same and that the interest and amortization terms are identical for each loan. If, however, a country borrows more in one year than in another, or a lending agency lends more in successive years, the "break-even" point, at which payments (receipts) equal new borrowings (loans) will be later. If the level of borrowing or lending is reduced, the "break-even" point will be reached sooner. If interest rates rise, the point will be sooner reached, as is evident from a glance at the tables.

IA. *Linear Amortization*

To derive a formula to determine the year in which payments of interest and amortization on a series of annual loans will equal new loans (or receipts by the lender will equal new disbursements) assuming a constant annual loan principal, no grace period on repayment, and amortization in equal annual installments,

Let P = the principal amount of each annual loan,
   i = annual interest on the outstanding balance,
   n = the number of years of amortization by equal annual installments,
   m = the year in which payments (receipts) equal the amount of new loans, and
   R = total receipts to lenders = total payments by borrower in mth year.

Annual amortization on each loan = P/n.

(1) In the mth year, total amortization will be mP/n.
   Cumulative amortization to the end of the mth year will be

(2) $\dfrac{P}{n} + \dfrac{2P}{n} + \cdots + \dfrac{mP}{n} = \dfrac{mP}{n} \dfrac{(m+1)}{2}$; the total outstanding will be

$$mP - \dfrac{mP}{n}\dfrac{(m+1)}{2} = \dfrac{2nmP - m^2P - mP}{2n}.$$

Interest will be payable on the total loaned less the interest on the amounts amortized to the beginning of the mth year, i.e., total receipts in mth year will be

(3) $R = \dfrac{mP}{n} + iPm - iP \dfrac{[m(m-1)]}{2n}$,

(4) $2nR = 2mP + 2imnP - im^2P + imP.$

If the mth year be defined as the one in which $R = P$, then

(5) $2nP = 2mP + 2imnP - im^2P + imP,$

(6) $2n = 2m + 2imn - im^2 + im,$

(7) $im^2 - im - 2imn - 2m + 2n = 0,$

(8) $im^2 - m(i + 2in + 2) + 2n = 0,$

(9) $m = \dfrac{2 + i(2n + 1) \pm \sqrt{[2 + i(2n + 1)]^2 - 8in}}{2i},$

(10) $m = \dfrac{2 + i(2n + 1) \pm \sqrt{4 + 8in + 4i^2 + 4i^2n^2 + 4i^2n + i^2 - 8in}}{2i},$

(11) $m = \dfrac{2 + i(2n + 1) \pm \sqrt{4(1 + i) + i^2(2n + 1)^2}}{2i}.$

Table IA. Cycle of Loans at Annual Amount of P: Years in which Receipts of Interest and Annual Amortization (Equal Annual Payments) of Principal Will Equal New Principal Loaned, with No Grace Period on Principal (Interest Rates Percent per Annum).

n	0.5	1.0	1.5	2.0	2.5	3.0	3.5	4.0
5	4.93	4.85	4.78	4.70	4.63	4.56	4.49	4.42
10	9.73	9.45	9.19	8.92	8.66	8.41	8.16	7.93
15	14.40	13.81	13.24	12.68	12.14	11.62	11.13	10.66
20	18.96	17.93	16.94	16.00	15.11	14.28	13.50	12.79

n	4.5	5.0	5.5	6.0	6.5	7.0	7.5	8.0
5	4.35	4.28	4.21	4.15	4.08	4.02	3.95	3.89
10	7.70	7.47	7.26	7.05	6.85	6.66	6.47	6.30
15	10.22	9.80	9.41	9.04	8.70	8.37	8.06	7.78
20	12.12	11.51	10.95	10.43	9.95	9.51	9.11	8.73

General form: $m = \dfrac{2 + i(2n + 1) \pm \sqrt{4(1 + i) + i^2(2n + 1)^2}}{2i},$

where n = the term of the loan in years, and
$\quad\quad i$ = the annual interest rate.

IB. *Linear Amortization with Grace Period*

Let P = principal amount of each annual loan,
  i = annual interest on outstanding balance,
  n = number of years of amortization by equal annual payments after the grace period,
  g = number of years of grace,
  m = the year in which payments (receipts) equal the amount of new loans,
  m' = the number of loans paying amortization in the mth year, and
  R = total receipts to lenders = total payments by borrower in mth year.

(1) $m = m' + g$.

(2) In the mth year, the receipts of amortization will be $m'(P/n)$, and of interest,

$$iP(m' + g) - iP \frac{[m'(m' - 1)]}{2n}.$$

(3) Total receipts in mth year,

$$R = m'\frac{P}{n} + iP(m' + g) - \frac{iP[m'(m' - 1)]}{2n},$$

(4) $2m' + 2in(m' + g) - im'(m' - 1) = \dfrac{2nR}{P}$.

(5) In the mth year, $R = P$, so that

$$2m' + 2im'n + 2ign - m'^2 i + m'i = 2n,$$

(6) $im'^2 - m'(2in + i + 2) + 2n(1 - ig) = 0$,

(7) $m' = \dfrac{2 + i(2n + 1) \pm \sqrt{4 + 4i(2n + 1) + i^2(2n + 1)^2 - 8in(1 - ig)}}{2i}$,

$$= \dfrac{2 + i(2n + 1) \pm \sqrt{4(1 + i) + i^2[(2n + 1)^2 + 8ng]}}{2i},$$

(8) $m = g + \dfrac{2 + i(2n + 1) \pm \sqrt{4(1 + i) + i^2[(2n + 1)^2 + 8ng]}}{2i}$.

Table IB. Years in which Payments Equal Receipts, with Equal Annual Loans, Linear Amortization with Grace Periods on Principal (Interest Rates Percent per Annum).

$g + n$	2.0	2.5	3.0	3.5	4.0	4.5	5.0
1 + 5	5.61	5.51	5.41	5.32	5.23	5.14	5.05
2 + 10	10.5	10.19	9.85	9.53	9.21	8.91	8.62
3 + 15	14.8	14.11	13.43	12.79	12.19	11.63	11.11
3 + 20	17.91	16.81	15.79	14.85	14.00	13.22	12.51
3 + 25	20.62	19.10	17.73	16.51	15.42	14.44	13.57

$g + n$	5.5	6.0	6.5	7.0	7.5	8.0
1 + 5	4.96	4.87	4.79	4.70	4.62	4.54
2 + 10	8.34	8.08	7.83	7.59	7.36	7.14
3 + 15	10.62	10.17	9.75	9.36	9.00	8.66
3 + 20	11.87	11.28	10.74	10.24	9.79	9.37
3 + 25	12.78	12.08	11.45	10.87	10.35	9.87

General form: $m = g + \dfrac{2 + i(2n + 1) \pm \sqrt{4(1 + i) + i^2[(2n + 1)^2 + 8ng]}}{2i}$

IIA. *Level Payment*

To determine the year in which receipts will equal new loans (or payments equal new loans) with annual level payments of interest and principal, no grace period. The annual installment on each loan (P) is the annuity whose present value at compound interest is $Pa_{\overline{m}}^{-1}$.

(1) In mth year there will be m payments, $mPa_{\overline{m}}^{-1}$.

If payments equal new loans, P,

(2) $P = mPa_{\overline{m}}^{-1}$,

(3) $1 = ma_{\overline{m}}^{-1} = \dfrac{m}{a_{\overline{m}}}$, and

(4) $m = a_{\overline{m}} = \dfrac{(1 + i)^n - 1}{i(1 + i)^n}.$

Table IIA. Years in which Receipts Will Equal New Loans of an Annual Constant Amount, with Annual Level Payments of Principal and Interest, and No Grace Period (Interest Rates Percent per Annum).

n	0.5	1.0	1.5	2.0	2.5	3.0	3.5	4.0
5	4.93	4.85	4.78	4.71	4.65	4.58	4.52	4.45
10	9.73	9.47	9.22	8.98	8.75	8.53	8.32	8.11
15	14.42	13.87	13.34	12.85	12.38	11.94	11.52	11.12
20	18.99	18.05	17.17	16.35	15.59	14.88	14.21	13.59

n	4.5	5.0	5.5	6.0	6.5	7.0	7.5	8.0
5	4.39	4.33	4.27	4.21	4.16	4.10	4.05	3.99
10	7.91	7.72	7.54	7.36	7.19	7.02	6.86	6.71
15	10.74	10.38	10.04	9.71	9.40	9.11	8.83	8.56
20	13.01	12.46	11.95	11.47	11.02	10.59	10.19	9.82

General form: $m = \dfrac{(1 + i)^n - 1}{i(1 + i)^n}$

IIB. *Level Payment with Grace Period*

To determine the year in which receipts will equal new loans (or payments will equal new loans) with annual level payments of interest and principal after a grace period during which only interest is paid (assuming the same rate of interest in grace period as in repayment period). In any mth year, where $m > g$ (years of grace), m' loans will pay amortization and g loans will be paying interest only.

(1) $m' = m - g$.

(2) Total receipts will be $ig P + m'(P/a_{\overline{m}})$. If receipts equal new loans,

(3) $P = giP + \dfrac{m'P}{a_{\overline{m}}}$,

(4) $1 = gi + \dfrac{m'}{a_{\overline{m}}}$,

(5) $a_{\overline{m}} = gia_{\overline{m}} + m'$

(6) $m' = a_{\overline{m}} - gia_{\overline{m}}$,

(7) $m = a_{\overline{m}} + g - gia_{\overline{m}}$,

$\quad = g + (1 - gi)a_{\overline{m}}$,

(8) $m = g + (1 - gi)\dfrac{(1 + i)^n - 1}{i(1 + i)^n}$.

Table IIB. *Years in which Receipts Will Equal New Loans of an Annual Constant Amount, with Annual Level Payments of Principal and Interest, with Grace Period (Interest Rates Percent per Annum).*

$g + n$	0.5	1.0	1.5	2.0	2.5	3.0	3.5	4.0
1 + 5	5.90	5.80	5.71	5.62	5.53	5.44	5.36	5.27
2 + 10	11.63	11.28	10.95	10.62	10.31	10.02	9.73	9.46
3 + 15	17.20	16.45	15.74	15.08	14.45	13.86	13.31	12.78
3 + 20	21.70	20.50	19.40	18.37	17.42	16.54	15.72	14.96
9 + 40	43.54	38.88	34.88	31.43	28.45	25.87	23.63	21.67

$g + n$	4.5	5.0	5.5	6.0	6.5	7.0	7.5	8.0
1 + 5	5.19	5.11	5.04	4.96	4.89	4.81	4.74	4.67
2 + 10	9.20	8.95	8.71	8.48	8.25	8.04	7.83	7.64
3 + 15	12.28	11.82	11.38	10.96	10.57	10.20	9.84	9.51
3 + 20	14.25	13.59	12.98	12.41	11.87	11.37	10.90	10.46
9 + 40	19.95	18.44	17.10	15.92	14.87	13.93	13.09	12.34

General form: $m = g + \dfrac{(1 - gi)\left[(1 + i)^n - 1\right]}{i(1 + i)^n}$

INDEX